Taxation and Representation: The Media, Political Communication and the Poll Tax

For Jo and Jack, with love: DD
For Jen: PG

David Deacon is Lecturer in Communication and Media Studies
Peter Golding is Professor of Sociology and Head of Department,
Department of Social Sciences, Loughborough University

Taxation and Representation: The Media, Political Communication and the Poll Tax

David Deacon and Peter Golding

Department of Social Sciences, Loughborough University

John Libbey
LONDON • PARIS • ROME

British Library Cataloguing in Publication Data

Deacon, David
Taxation and Representation:
The Media, Political Communication and the Poll Tax
Acamedia Research Monograph: 11
I. Title II. Golding, Peter III. Series
336.25

ISBN: 0 86196 390 3
ISSN: 0956-9057

Published by

John Libbey & Company Ltd, 13 Smiths Yard, Summerley Street,
London SW18 4HR, England.
Telephone: +44 (0)81-947 2777: Fax +44 (0)81-947 2664
John Libbey Eurotext Ltd, 127 rue de la République, 92120 Montrouge, France.
John Libbey - C.I.C. s.r.l., via Lazzaro Spallanzani 11, 00161 Rome, Italy

Printed in Great Britain by Whitstable Litho Ltd, Whitstable, Kent, UK

Contents

Acknowledgements

The empirical research that forms the basis of this book was funded by two grants from the Economic and Social Research Council (reference numbers: R000231512 and R000233523). We are grateful to the Council for their support and interest in the research, and to the anonymous referees who constructively commented on the grant submissions and end of project reports.

We would also like to thank Jo Aldridge, Natalie Fenton, Alan Bryman, Karl Ashworth, Andrew Shaw, Julie Johnson and other colleagues at the Department of Social Sciences, Loughborough University for their advice, assistance and support. Our thanks also to Jo Wakefield for her careful transcription of the interviews, Peter Beaman for his technical support, Bob Franklin for his steady supply of poll tax clippings, and Wendy Monk for her meticulous proof reading.

Our further thanks to all the journalists, news editors, politicians, pressure group representatives, trade unionists, business men and women and press and publicity officers, who agreed to be interviewed for the research. Without their co-operation and candour many important elements of this story would have remained hidden from view.

Finally, our thanks to our families, whose forebearance and support during the completion of this manuscript made the creative strain easier to bear.

Preface

'Look! Quick! Wasn't that a policy just now? Too late. It's gone. We threw the proposer out'.
Aristophenes, The Assembly of Women

During the first week of April 1990, the reform of British local government finance was one of the most newsworthy topics on the international news agenda. Newspapers as geographically diverse as Zimbabwe's *Harrare Herald*, The Soviet Union's *Pravda* and *Izvestiya*, France's *Le Monde*, Italy's *La Republicca*, Thailand's *Bangkok Post* and the USA's *Washington Post* ran lead stories on the issue, and in Australia *The Melbourne Age* editorialized 'If a tax could be designed to sow social dissent and earn unpopularity for a government, this is it' (3/4/90: 13). Even media far removed from the international news agency rounds felt compelled to report the political debate it provoked. For example, down in the Falkland Islands, *The Penguin News* ruminated on the political ramifications of 'a good scheme' that had been 'poorly implemented' (7/5/90: 12)

When the British Conservative Government announced in 1986 its intention to replace the existing method of local domestic taxation with a new 'Community Charge' it couldn't have anticipated the controversy it was unleashing. Yet within four years, 'The Poll Tax' – as it became more publicly and pejoratively known – had split the ruling party from top to bottom, precipitated serious breakdowns in public order, compromised the electoral viability and international credibility of the Government, incited a cacophony of derision from a normally quiescent media, and brought down a Prime Minister who merely months before had been considering indefinitely postponing her retirement. In political terms alone, the abolition of the Community Charge ranks as one of the most abject failures in British domestic history.

This book charts the development of this political crisis, and in particular how the issue was reported in domestic media. Our interest in this topic extends beyond the contentious issues raised by the new tax, for its implementation and subsequent abandonment has provided an invaluable opportunity to explore broader principles involved in the communication and formation of public policy. As a major fiscal reform with important constitutional and political implications, the Community Charge was introduced against a background of considerable opposition. The Government energetically promoted the change; and citizens were principally dependent on the media for information about it. How did such promotion occur, and with what effects? What form did public discussions take and with what effect on policy formation? And how far did the media cater for a full public discussion of such a major legislative innovation? In its broadest terms, this case study of political communication seeks to make a more general contribution to our understanding of the significance of the mass media in modern political culture, and the processes by which media agendas are politically generated.

For logistical, rather than ethnocentric reasons, our discussion focuses on the reporting of the Community Charge in England and Wales, rather than in Scotland – which experienced both a different implementative timetable and intensity of media and public debate. The first chapter contextualizes our research within the broader debates currently active within the fields of media sociology, social policy and political science, and outlines several conceptual models that inform our analysis. The second chapter provides a contextual overview of the history of the poll tax, and the main political issues its introduction raised. The third looks at the strategies employed by the British Government, first to promote its flagship policy, and then to ameliorate the political crisis it created. The fourth chapter provides a comparative analysis of how opponents of the tax mobilized publicly. The fifth, provides a detailed comparative analysis of national and local media coverage of the tax, and explores how the terms of reference of media debate shifted as the policy cycle proceeded. The sixth chapter examines the news gathering of journalists and editors in reporting the tax, and the political and strategic factors that shaped their perceptions. The seventh, draws together material from preceding discussions to explain the specific factors that influenced the building of media agendas on the poll tax. It also explores the influence of media discourses over public perceptions of the tax. The concluding chapter considers what broader inferences can be drawn from this case study of political communication.

Chapter 1

Citizenship, Communication, and Politics – The Tarnished Ideal

Democracy in troubled times: on being an informed citizen

This is a book about citizenship. It is concerned with the way in which people are able to take part in the political life of their society. When we talk of citizenship we soon arrive at notions such as participation and involvement, but above all we will inevitably stumble across the phantom of the 'informed citizen'.

Clichés about the 'information society' and the deluge of information to which we are all subject, have become so commonplace that we sometimes lose sight of some simple truths. Democracies, even large scale complex democracies such as ours, in which power is exercised by the few and the remote, assume they are inhabited by informed citizens. Without some knowledge of what the polity is up to, people cannot even begin to exercise any reasoned impact on the system which governs their lives. We therefore foster an ideal, in which people receive a wide range of political information, which they sift, consume and deploy in rational decision making. The outcome may be a vote, a motion at a pressure group committee meeting, a street riot, or a yawn of disinterest and contempt. But the informed citizen exercises choice on the basis of information received.

The tempting metaphor is that of the supermarket, in which the voter saunters among the shelves of ideas and policy options, making shrewd calculations about cost benefit balances and the comparative virtues of the ideological packages on offer. Trolley filled, the citizen strolls to the electoral check-out, vote in hand. The problem, if we extend the metaphor just a little further, is that not everyone can get to the same store. Some can afford bigger and better-filled trolleys. The shelves are far from full, and many goods somehow never make it to the front of the display stands. Some turn out to be very different from the glittering items promised on the packaging. The citizen-shopper is exercising choice within very distinct and effective limits.

This book is an attempt to chart those limits, to find out why the goods are packaged the way they are, and what gets them on to the shelves. For the ideal of the informed citizen is precisely that, an ideal. Analysts have always been aware, of course, of the potential of the modern mass media to interrupt and distort the flow of information from the political arena to voters. It is a long time since we lived in anything approaching the Athenian polis. But in recent years we have been increasingly alive to the limits of our ideal. There are at least two reasons for this.

First, we have been witnessing dramatic changes in the range and control of the media through which political information primarily reaches us. In recent decades the ownership of major national newspapers has continued to fall into the hands of a small number of large corporations, frequently controlled by tycoons with uncompromising and naked political objectives alongside their commercial aspirations (Golding and Murdock, 1991). Several trends have evolved from the increasingly conglomerate character of the media. The political profile of the national press has become steadily less balanced, with a preponderance of Conservative supporting, or at least Labour opposing titles that even the last Royal Commission on the Press recognized as creating a 'gap in political terms which could be filled with advantage' (cited in *ibid.*). The increasingly commercial and competitive character of the press has also fostered what some commentators identify as 'de-politicization', of the popular titles especially (Curran and Seaton, 1981: 123). Politics recedes before a rising tide of human interest, show-biz related stories which transform the press into an appendage of the entertainment industry in both economic and cultural form. Broadcasting, too, reflects this trend; 'Television in Europe thus becomes increasingly an entertainment medium' (De Bens, Kelly and Bakke, 1992: 95). Television, as the major and increasingly prominent alternative to the newspaper as a medium for political communication, has also entered an age in which the high ideals of public service broadcasting are being confronted and displaced by the pressing imperatives of market driven new technologies of distribution (Golding, forthcoming).

Secondly, our ideal informed citizen is further disadvantaged by the growth of the 'public relations state', a phenomenon to which we return shortly. Information designed to persuade is never the same as information passively offered as a service, and while this may naively understate the inevitably ideological character of anything we can sensibly call 'information', it does reflect, as we note below, a sea change in the operation of the modern state.

For many writers within political science the anxieties and critiques implicit in these observations are unfounded. Information flows have increased, electorates have become more sophisticated, and democracy is the richer as a result. Notions of 'cognitive mobilization' suggest that rising levels of education have created better equipped populations. Together with the growth in media provision this nourishes the democratic process (Inglehart, 1977). Thus, as Dalton argues, 'At the same time that the cognitive skills of Western mass publics have improved, so too have the public's resources ... today there is a nearly unlimited supply and variety of political news ... we can [now] be more sanguine about the nature of belief systems in contemporary publics.' (Dalton, 1988: 19, 32).

As will become clear throughout this book our views are far less confident. The changing nature of the communication system is counterbalanced by changes in the expectations of citizenship. Our case study, of the major change in local taxation introduced in Britain in the 1980s, was centrally conceived by its architects as an initiative to change the basis of citizenship. At local level this was designed to be for the better, an argument we examine in the following chapters. The poll tax arrived in the wake of considerable efforts by the ideologues of the new right to seize the moral high ground, and citizenship proved an attractive banner *en route*. As the debate about the tax wound on, this theme became an insistent motif within the political dialogue of the late 1980s. Mrs. Thatcher's speech to the General Assembly of the Church of Scotland in May 1988, insisted that 'most Christians would regard it as their personal Christian duty to help their fellow men and women', from which premise she moved rapidly to the conclusion that 'intervention by the state must never become so great that it effectively removes personal responsibility' (see Raban, 1989). This was paralleled by influential articles by the then Home Secretary, Douglas Hurd, in which he argued that 'the idea of active citizenship is a necessary complement to that of the enterprise culture. Public service may once have been the duty of an élite, but today it is the responsibility of all who have time or money to spare' (Hurd, 1989). The active citizen was someone nurtured by the fruits of free enterprise, and happy to reinvest their well deserved acquisitions into responsible patronage of the less fortunate. It was not altogether surprising that the debate about the poll tax came to adopt this language. As Miller notes, in the battle over the tax 'for parliamentary and public opinion the arguments have had to be put in terms of values which are more broadly shared. These have centred largely on explicit and implicit models of citizenship'. (Miller, 1989: 96).

The citizen found herself constituted in three very different and confused roles. First, and most traditionally, as informed and responsive partner to the state in the management of the polity. Yet here the evidence was less than encouraging, with signs of continuous loss of faith in the body politic, the fragmentation of a civic culture, and pluralist stagnation (see Topf, 1989). Second, the citizen was being urged to become the new, philanthropic active citizen conjured up by the enthusiastic visionaries of volunteer welfare capitalism. The citizen as volunteer received her most authoritative acclamation from the Commission on the subject established by the Speaker of the House of Commons in 1988. In these terms citizenship became a target for schools in encouraging appropriate curricula, and the summary description of community voluntary work (Commission on Citizenship, 1990). Finally, we had the citizen as consumer, exerting civic power through the mechanics of the market, bullishly clamouring for satisfaction in the glass and steel shop fronts of the town hall customer service centre, citizens' charter in hand.

Amidst such confusion the media have a strategic role, enshrining and promoting one or another model, labelling and evaluating the merits and promoters of each. Crucial to such a role is the part played by the state as a dominant source of information and imagery which becomes the raw material for media work. And in that role we cannot ignore the massive expansion of the public relations state.

The rise of the public relations state

All governments like to be well thought of. They promote their own policies and denigrate those of opposing parties as part of the routine business of political life. Even Napoleon invested time and money in making sure the *Moniteur* purveyed the right line. But in recent decades the scale and ferocity of this aspect of public life have escalated substantially. Writing of the United States, Oscar Gandy has drawn attention to the rise of the information professionals within government. 'At every level of government, in every agency, there are information specialists whose responsibility it is to ensure that the nation's public media carry the desired message forward to the general public, other government officials, and key corporate leaders who have a role to play in the formulation and implementation of public policy' (Gandy, 1982: 74).

Gandy goes on to argue that this system works through what he terms 'information subsidies'. These are not bribes or material hand-outs, but measures to reduce the cost to information seekers of obtaining information they need to construct news. By making life easy for the news seekers, information managers can influence and even determine the flow and character of coverage about their activities in the news media. That is, obviously, the basis on which all public relations and publicity work rests.

In the post-war period in Britain it was for long assumed that politics was moving to a steady state of ideological convergence, in which agreement about the nature of the good society was disturbed only by minor squabbles over its administration. This 'consensus' or 'Butskellite' happy state came to a rude end, if it ever really existed, with the return of 'conviction politics' and the launch of the Thatcherite project in the late 1970s. Once more government was in the business of winning hearts and minds.

The state is at the heart of the news machine. Studies of news have perennially plotted the dominance of items about the machinery of government and the routine drama of Westminster life within the broad array of news coverage. Though this has, as we noted above, declined as a proportion of the whole, and indeed its reduction has recently occasioned some distress among politicians (Straw, 1993), the predominant flavour in the daily diet of the news media continues to be the whiff of political grapeshot and the odour of Westminster's hot air. 'News prioritizes the state and its agents, treating even minor state activities as inherently newsworthy, viewing agents of the state as 'reliable' sources and as interesting speakers, and portraying the visible aspects of relations among states' (Knight and Curtis, 1987: 49). Of course this portrayal has its own elisions and evasions (Golding, 1981). But this combination of ideological divergence and the prominence of the state as an object of media attention has created the conditions for a substantial increase in public relations activity by the state.

Many observers have noted the importation of the machinery and practices of the advertising industry into politics. A new branch of this craft appears, in what Nimmo and Combs describe as an 'industry of experience brokers', of 'propartists' consisting of 'professional hypesters with a variety of specialities and skills' (Nimmo and Combs, 1990: 67). That politics is now garlanded by an apparatus of spin doctors, lobbyists, consultants, communication analysts, press officers, and their kin is only too familiar. The political arena is a supremely image-conscious one. After all, as the architect of the *Sun*'s dramatic rise rather innocently puts it, 'it is politicians, rather than newspapermen, who tend to exaggerate the power of the press' (Lamb, 1989: 161).

Government has become a major employer of press and public relations activists, and of advertising. In 1992 HM Government spent £53 million on advertising. Between 1986 and 1991 the increase in its expenditure in real terms was about 16 per cent, and the total expenditure of this kind roughly doubled during the decade. The Government's advertising budget dwarfs that of such mega corporations as Ford, General Motors, and Proctor and Gamble. Moreover the Government's figures no longer include privatized corporations such as British Telecom (£46 million in 1992) or the utilities. Indeed, spending on the promotion of privatization initiatives formed a significant part of this publicity effort. The sell-off of the water industry was supported by campaigns costing £42 million, more than twice that spent on the earlier gas privatization. In May 1990 the then Government Energy Secretary, John Wakeham, was appointed to co-ordinate government publicity and information, and new proposals to give senior ministers PR 'minders' were revealed (*Independent on Sunday*, 17 June 1990). Growing political protests about these developments led to the appointment of a public enquiry by the National Audit Office, which showed the very major programmes of expenditure undertaken by, for example the Department of Trade and Industry on its 'Enterprise Initiative'. Perhaps the two key administrative measures, above all others, which came to symbolize the force of this shift in government promotion were the incorporation of the government statistical service into the supervisory embrace of the Treasury, and the assumption in 1989 by Mrs Thatcher's trenchant Chief Press Secretary, Bernard Ingham, of the role of head of the Government Information Service simultaneously with his other duties (Ingham, 1991: 367–68; Royal Statistical Society, 1990).

The promotion of good news and radical policy initiatives has continued to attract substantial resources. In January 1994 the Secretary of State for Education announced that he was to spend over £2million sending a leaflet into every home in the country giving the Government's views and advice on morality, citizenship, discipline and family values. Between 1989/90 and 1991/92 Department of Health spending on public relations rose from £0.89million to £1.49million (*Hansard*, WA Col. 244, 8 June 1993). A Corporate Affairs Intelligence Unit was established to seek out, and compile for ministerial promotion, stories illustrating the success of the Government's health service reforms. Similarly, in housing, £4.5million was spent on public relations to promote the 'right to buy' policy between 1980 and 1993.

It is in this context that we should understand the promotion of the Community Charge described in this study. While the resources and promotional effort invested in the Charge were exceptional, they were entirely consistent with a trend in the marketing of the state which had been rising for many years (Golding, 1990). But political promotion does not only happen at national level. The local state has not been slow to learn these new tricks. The appointment of public relations officers, publicity units and promotional efforts of varying kinds has become a common feature of the local government scenery. The evolution of municipal newspapers, bringing the good news to every doorstep in the community, is a good indicator of this development, though, as Franklin and Murphy note, they are of such recent origin that they were virtually overlooked in the 1977 Royal Commission on the Press (for detail on this phenomenon see Franklin and Murphy, 1991: Ch. 6; Franklin, 1988).

In all these ways, then, the marketing of government activity has become a central activity of modern statecraft. Inevitably the launch of any major policy initiative will be devised with this apparatus of promotion and information management in mind. The Community Charge became a test case of the limits of this machinery. We need briefly to assess how well equipped students of political communication were to understand this process.

Political communication: the double absence

To understand the process of political communication we need to draw on the insights of both policy analysis and of media and communication research. Unfortunately both have been curiously silent on the interconnection between the two. The detailed intellectual history and disciplinary evolution which explain this are not essential to our concerns here, but we do need briefly to review them.

Political studies frequently pay lip service to the importance of the media and communications. In practice, however, this emerges only in cursory reference to the role of the media, especially as witness to the recurrent and playful clash of pressure groups with the political system. Most policy analysis finds its roots, implicitly if not explicitly, in the kind of systemic model developed, classically, by writers like David Easton (Easton, 1965). In this model the policy process becomes, to use the familiar metaphor, a black box, which produces outputs in the form of decisions and actions. Into the black box go inputs in the form of demands and supports, either as votes, payment of taxes, and obedience, or alternatively as dissent, pressure and articulated claims. While it is not difficult to develop a critique of functionalist models of this kind, even in refined and moderated form they underpin a large number of policy analyses.

Important in such a view is the understanding of policy as a process not a product, and that insight releases the potential of such traditions of policy analysis as implementation theory and incrementalism. Each of them, in practice, however, retains the sense of this process evolving within an 'environment', which contains the economic and social structures of the wider society beyond the polity. Our focus in this book is on the media, and they form a crucial part of this environment. Indeed we are arguing that they are inherently part of the modern policy process, which is inconceivable without the rhetorical and publicity apparatus of political communication. Thus to devolve so much of the essential character of the political process to a residual category of actions in the 'environment' is to miss much of the core of what determines and shapes policy. It is still surprising how minimal an appearance the media and communications make in many policy analyses, and even where they do it is organizational communication rather than media communication which dominates (Nixon, 1980).

At the same time media studies have been concerned, not surprisingly, with the role of journalism and the careful and critical analysis of the symbolic world of media output. Where it has been inclined to address politics it has remained resolutely 'media-centric', rarely drawing on the research and theory available within political sociology or policy analysis.

Perhaps the most powerful concept to be developed in the attempt to understand the determinants of political news is that of 'primary definers'.

The notion of primary definition was formulated by Hall and his colleagues in their analysis of news coverage of 'mugging' (Hall *et al.*, 1978). Dominant forces in society do not dictate directly the terms and vocabulary of news coverage, either conspiratorially or by dictat. They are able, however, through the structures of news production, to ensure that news reflects the interests of the powerful. This reproduction, in the last instance, does not ignore the real autonomy of news producers. But because of the importance of accredited sources with authority to define news salience and form, and the unavoidable exigencies and speed of routine news production, the news process produces 'a systematically structured *over-accessing* to the media of those in powerful and privileged positions. The media thus tend, faithfully and impartially, to reproduce symbolically the existing structure of power in society's institutional order' (*ibid.*: 58). The media thus become secondary definers, dependent on the hegemonic defining power of accredited sources, the representatives of major social institutions.

This model is an insightful and effective one. Not surprisingly, though, it has been regularly criticized within media analysis, not least in a thorough working-over by Schlesinger, who argues that the model forces analysts to ignore both the processes by which sources contest for accreditation, and the strategies they employ to command attention (Schlesinger, 1990). As our discussion of news sources, below, will explain, we would share this reservation about the notion of primary definition, while remaining anxious to retain its essential insight into the relationship which exists between the media and power structures in society.

Primary definition undoubtedly occurs. The media are not the sole sources of vocabularies and rhetorics about policy. Neither are they, however, passive conduits to a torrent of ideology from centres of power. Primary definition is a process, not a characteristic of those who exercise its privilege. The concept, as Schlesinger rightly reminds us, can be too static. However, in rediscovering the dynamics of the definitional process we should not, as Herman puts it, get 'lost in pluralistic conflict' (Herman, 1986: 174). To resolve this dilemma we need to move on beyond primary definition to a more adequate model of the source–media relationship. We tentatively suggest some means for doing this below, and much of this book is an attempt to explore the applicability of a more substantial model of this kind.

The analysis of political communication is, of course, a well developed and extensive area of research and discussion. Yet it remains a curiously unhelpful one in answering the questions posed by this study. There are three reasons for this inadequacy. First, political communication research has been obsessed with the process of electioneering. The natural experiment provided by the spectacle of elections has been just too bewitching to avoid for generations of commentators and researchers, and we readily plead guilty to sharing this fascination (Billig *et al.*, 1992). Yet it should be only too obvious that elections are anything but the normal state of the body politic. The content and volume of public debate, the intensity of political rhetoric, the attentiveness of citizens, and the energy and partisanship of political media are all totally atypical in the periods framed by elections. This does not mean we can learn nothing from the study of elections, but it does suggest we would do well to be wary of generalizing to the political communication process *per se* from the lessons of election research.

Secondly, election research defines the nature of politics and political communication in a very closely framed manner. By politics is meant party politics, and by political communication is meant the competitive appeal of parties to electors. Political communication research has much to gain, but as yet has learned little, from attempts to draw attention to the essentially political character of all communications, the ideological investment in all forms of public communication, whether fiction or non-fiction, whether dealing with the familiar artefacts of policy or the less obviously but equally powerful politics of the domestic, the personal, and the mundane.

Thirdly, political communications research has remained largely obsessed in this country with the metropolitan and national media. This is a mistake for two complementary reasons. First, the continuing saga of central–local state relations has been at the heart of many of the key changes in British politics over the past two decades. We examine these changes later in this study. Such has been the importance of these changes that major debates about the role of the state have been generated by them within political theory. On the one hand it is suggested that we now have a dual state, operating separately at local and national level (Saunders, 1981, 1982). The extent to which this is a genuine separation or a contingent one is important and contentious. On the other hand theorists have suggested that primary social divisions are no longer derived from class positions, but by sectoral divisions determined by people's position as consumers of services, notably those provided by the local state (Dunleavy, 1989).

The other reason why concentration on the national media is a mistake is more obviously rooted in the media system. This country continues to have a vibrant and significant local and regional press. In 1992 there were over 2,000 regional papers, including over 1,000 freesheets, whose numbers had more than doubled in a decade. But even the paid titles have been flourishing. Despite the closure in November 1988 of the *North West Times*, the first new regional daily for 100 years, this is a surprisingly vigorous media sector. Between 1980 and 1992 the number of paid for regional daily titles grew by 12 per cent, and of Sundays by 28 per cent. Nearly 90 per cent of adults read a regional paper.

Behind the bald statistics of survival, however, lies even more impressive evidence of the continued potency of the regional press. The readership and use made of local papers is demonstrated in a wide variety of research which confirms how prominently they feature in people's overall media diet, and most of all, of course, in their consumption of news about local matters.

Despite the high penetration of national newspapers to households in general, national readership is, of course, distributed among a number of titles. Where above 80 per cent of households in a given locality are reading a local paper they are all reading the *same* paper as often as not, since local monopoly is the norm. The power of the local press for local agenda-setting is manifest (Golding, 1989).

Thus both policy analysis and media research have, by operating in splendid isolation, left the field clear to a tradition of political communication research which is itself severely undernourished by virtue of a steady diet of electoral politics. To move beyond this impotence we need to examine a little further the nature of media–polity interaction.

Rewriting the sociology of news sources: a typology of roles

Although the mass media are crucial intermediaries between 'society as audience' and 'society as source' (Elliott, 1972), concerns about the social impact of media representations have always exceeded attention to the processes by which they are themselves socially constructed. Yet to understand the impact of media discourses we must attend to their origins. Oscar Gandy identified it as the need 'to go beyond agenda setting to determine who sets the media agenda, how and for what purposes is it set, and with what impact on the distribution of power and values in society?' (Gandy, *op. cit.*: 7). By exploring the relative influence of institutions and individuals in the formation of media agendas, we are analysing strategic power in our society, which as Silverstone (1990) perceptively points out, is very different from the tactical power of audiences to select and re-appropriate meaning from individual texts.

Unfortunately, primary research into news sources remains scant and intermittent (Gandy, *op. cit.*; Ericson *et al.*, 1989), with most of our understanding derived from 'internalist' analyses of journalists at work (Schlesinger, *op. cit.*). Nevertheless, several important conceptual principles are already available which provide an invaluable foundation for this book.

The first is that journalists and their sources exist in an exchange relationship, where information is bartered for publicity (Tunstall, 1970). However, in this market place of ideas, certain vendors sell their messages with greater ease and in far greater volume. Gans (1979) identifies four major factors that influence the performance of news sources in shaping media agendas, that encapsulate a range of current debates around news sources and their influence.

The first factor is the *incentive* a source has to seek publicity through the media. Gans concentrates on the endemic disposition of institutions and individuals towards the news media – contrasting the 'eager' sources who would suffocate without the oxygen of publicity (such as pressure groups and politicians), with 'recalcitrant' sources, who are habitually more indifferent or fearful of media scrutiny. However, it is also important to appreciate that the degree of incentive a news source has is contextual. Even the keenest news sources will have certain issues they would prefer to keep private, not just because they may have something to hide, but also because every human being and organization requires private space behind their public face – a 'private culture' within which decisions can be made and confidences respected (Ericson *et al.*, *op. cit.*). Conversely, even the most reluctant source can experience difficulties if it fails to respond appropriately to media scrutiny, not least in risking further dangerous intrusions into its private affairs. It may also, of course, use the media to further its own political ends (Miller, 1993).

Gans' second factor is the *power* of a source. His point, that the recruitment and access of news sources reflects broader social and political hierarchies, is also prominently emphasized – albeit to different degrees – in other analyses of journalists and their sources (Sigal, 1986; Ericson *et al., op. cit.*; Gandy, *op. cit.*; Herman and Chomsky, 1988; Seymour-Ure, 1987, Hall *et al., op. cit.*). Schlesinger characterizes this as the 'cultural capital' of a news source – i.e. its perceived legitimacy, authoritativeness and respectability, which is derived 'from the location a source has in the institutional field ... Official sources may not always have to be believed, but they do have to be taken seriously' (*op. cit.*: 81). Those with a high cultural capital will receive coverage as of right, whereas other sources have to compete for media attention by developing media strategies.

The third factor is the *ability* of a source to provide information in a form, and with the regularity, demanded by the news media. The ability to be newsworthy requires resources and skill, which go hand in hand with economic power. This point is pivotal to Gandy's notion of 'information subsidies' introduced earlier. Gans' fourth factor is the *geographic and social proximity* of a news source to journalists. This relates both to the physical closeness of sources to the media news net, and their social and cultural affinity with news professionals. Effective agenda-building involves establishing relationships with journalists. There are certain individuals and institutions who will more readily relate to news professionals and whose social status, in turn, is more immediately recognized by journalists.

From this work, it is possible to discern several general themes about the power of institutions and individuals to shape media discourses that are salient to our discussion. First, as not all publicity is good publicity, the power of news sources is not just located in their ability to attract media attention, but also to manage the nature of that coverage, and where necessary to suppress or divert media attention. As Tuchman (1978) points out, the power to keep an occurrence out of the news is an important aspect of agenda-building power. This is the significance of our earlier observation about the new management regime of official statistics.

Second, powers of 'enclosure' and 'disclosure' (Ericson *et al., op. cit.*) are differentially available, and are closely linked to broader configurations of political and economic power. This is most evident in the power of sources to censor media debate, such as in the ability of the state to impose a range of unique sanctions on the media, and of the rich to employ the legal system to threaten or punish journalistic transgressions. However, these sanctions are used intermittently. More significant is the ability to enclose discussion by disclosing information – misinforming or diverting media debate by employing defensive strategies of 'deception', or offensive strategies of 'selection', where media attention is drawn towards less threatening, or more expedient, matters (Ericson *et al.*, *op. cit.*). As Downing points out, 'Secrecy is not used as an impermeable shield blotting out all communication, but as a device to allow the pinnacle of the power structure to communicate how and when it prefers' (Downing, 1986: 157). In this publicity game – and the field of public relations more generally – economic power counts for a lot, whether in recruiting trained public relations personnel or covering the costs of producing and distributing information subsidies. However, political and cultural power also exerts a significant influence. Those news sources who can disseminate information privately as well as publicly to journalists (Ericson *et al.*, *op. cit.*), have a very significant advantage over those sources who have to lobby loud and hard in the public arena. As Gandy points out:

> 'Often the value of an information subsidy for any source is increased to the extent that the source can disguise the promotional, partisan, self-interested quality of the information. This is often accomplished when news stories convey the desired information without identifying its source. Information that would be accepted only with caution if its source were identified as a partisan in a debate is much more powerful if it is a received objective fact, reported by an uninterested journalist' (*op. cit.*: 14).

These covert mechanisms of disclosure are going to be more routinely available to those sources with the greatest 'cultural capital', who automatically receive the attention of the media, and can trade off partial journalistic access for confidentiality and non-attribution.

These points provide an important context for our analysis of the interaction between news sources and journalists in the construction of media discourses over the Community Charge. However, before starting our substantive analysis, we need to introduce a further conceptual distinction that is fundamentally important to our discussion. This is between 'advocates' and 'arbiters'.

In the 1950s, Westley and MacLean (1957) suggested we should conceive of the media as information brokers between an information seeking public and so-called 'advocates' in society – institutions or individuals who have something to say (or something to sell). The notion of advocacy seems to us to be a useful way of partially conceptualizing news sources. In our analysis 'advocates' are the sources that journalists recognize as having explicit, vested political or professional interests which frame and inform their contributions. As such, they provide the raw material of media coverage: the conflict upon which news depends. In the exchange with advocates, journalists are not just seeking information, but also opinions and assertions.

However, the news media are expected to comment quickly and authoritatively about an uncertain world, plagued with complex issues and moral dilemmas. If journalists spend a large proportion of time reporting a froth of opinion, conflict and conjecture, they never lose the impulse to establish a bed-rock of 'facts', on which to ground their reports. Indeed, journalism remains one of the last bastions of empiricism: searching for the unvarnished truth behind the best possible gloss, clinging to the belief that 'facts' can be rescued from hyperbole. In this search journalists often elect sources who, because of their perceived expertise, willingness and ability to communicate with journalists, are used to evaluate assertions and interpretations made by advocates in a political debate. As one local government correspondent explained in an interview with the authors:

> 'A journalist is always looking for someone who can tell them that they're not being mislead or led by the nose. And [the poll tax] isn't merely just a soft sell, but is in such a complex area.'

We refer to these sources as the 'arbiters' of a particular field of discourse.

Arbiters appear far less frequently than advocates – indeed, their comments may not even be cited even when contact has been made – but their perceived expertise is highly valued by journalists. Because of journalists' reliance on their expertise, the evaluations of arbiters resonate beyond the specific moment of contact, and far exceed the regularity of their appearance. Tuchman (*op. cit.*: 84) asserts that journalists view all sources as 'questionable'. Our research suggests an important qualification to this generalization. Although claims and assertions by advocates are ritually approached with a degree of suspicion, this scepticism applies far less to arbiters. This is mainly because of the nature of the exchange relationship between arbiters and journalists. Firstly, arbiters don't pursue journalists: they are elected by journalists. Therefore, their selection is inextricably linked to a journalist's sense of her own political and professional judgement. By trusting an arbiter, the journalist is, by extension, trusting her own initial judgement. Second, arbiters are most highly valued where issues are new, complex or uncertain. This inevitably places journalists in a far more vulnerable and dependent position.

The arbiter role here is comparable to that of the intellectual, in particular to what Bauman has identified as the 'legislator' function. This is 'making authoritative statements which arbitrate in controversies of opinions and which select those opinions which, having been selected, become correct and binding' (Bauman, 1987: 4). The perceived 'professionalism' of an arbiter is crucial to their selection, and mirrors how the reification of journalistic professionalism enables journalists to construct their own 'objectivity'. The professional status of arbiters is seen to remove them from the vested partiality of party political debate, and allow them to comment dispassionately, intelligently and 'objectively' about complex and controversial matters. Beyond this, the selection of arbiters is also governed by their 'media friendliness'; assessed, on the one hand, in their co-operativeness, and, on the other, in an ability to render complex issues intelligible to journalists and their audiences.

However, if the perceived expertise of these sources gives their views a particular power and authority, it is necessary to question the nature of their 'objectivity'. There are two dimensions to this issue. The first is whether these sources are as politically detached from the matters upon which they are commenting, as journalists assume – indeed, whether they may themselves be covert advocates. For example, several commentators have recently challenged the widespread use of financial analysts from the money markets by the media to adjudicate on broader matters of fiscal and political policy (Billig *et al.*, *op. cit.*; Gavin, 1992). In the case of the poll tax, as we discuss in Chapter 6, some of the most influential arbiters in coverage were the local government finance officers responsible for administering the system. However, when we interviewed several of these professionals it became clear they were far more actively engaged in the political debate than many journalists assumed. For example, they harboured serious professional grievances against the tax – because it made their work more problematic and seriously compromised the financial viability of their authorities – and often communicated their antipathy to journalists (albeit privately). Furthermore, in some cases, they were highly selective in the information they gave journalists. For example, one finance officer deliberately suppressed information about the level of non-payment in his area to avoid giving succour to local anti poll tax campaigners. (As he put it, 'I always turned their question round into what I wanted to tell them'.)

The second dimension to this issue is epistemological. It is not necessary to accuse every arbiter of pursuing a hidden agenda to question their objectivity. Clearly, many arbiters seek to be as accurate, dispassionate and impartial as possible in the evaluations they provide. Nevertheless, their contributions are not, and can never be, completely value free. Arbiters' verdicts are professional judgements derived from institutional vantage points and personal experiences. As such they are always potentially contestable. To the social researcher the impossibility of absolute value freedom and objectivity is not an alien concept and, indeed, is why the philosophical culture of the social sciences is so finely attuned to questions about the conditions and production of knowledge. However, such notions are inimical to some of the most cherished notions of journalistic professionalism (Haslam and Bryman, 1994) and, as a consequence, can be seen as hostile to the practice and integrity of journalism as a craft, rather than as a description of the inextricable structural conditions of its practice (Golding and Elliott, 1979: 12–16).

Throughout this study we explore the nature of media–source relationships, bearing in mind the distinction drawn here between the roles of advocate and arbiter. However to take our model forward a little further we need to examine two additional vectors in our analysis, the dynamics of the policy process and the nature of media coverage.

The natural history of political communications

It remains for us to set out briefly two conceptual devices which will form important props in the analysis which follows. The first relates to the policy process itself. We have argued earlier that the models of that process commonly on offer in policy studies take inadequate account of the 'environment' in which policy evolves. The triangular relationship between politics, public opinion and the media is a particularly crucial aspect of this environment, and is certainly the focus of our discussion in this book. Our model here is distinct from that developed by symbolic interactionist researchers who seek a description of 'social problems as products of a process of collective definition' (Hilgartner and Bosk, 1988: 53). The emphasis on social problems as entirely 'a putative condition or situation that is labelled a problem in the arenas of public discourse or action' (*ibid.*: 55) rather detracts from the necessary analysis of the material conditions which give rise to those problems, and which are also the backdrop for the contest required to force them to public attention. Equally the emphasis on the media as one among many potential 'carriers' elides the potent centrality of the media in the policy process. Nonetheless the perspective, while inadequate to the analysis of the deliberate mobilization of symbols on which politics subsists, usefully reminds us of the cultural component to the manufacture of politics.

The Community Charge is an unusual example of a policy which has a detectable birth and an even more pronounced ending. But, exceptional though this may be, we wish to suggest that any policy initiative goes through a sequence of phases. These are primarily defined in terms of the legislative process, but are designed to invite an assessment of the links between the three points of the policy triangle mentioned above.

The first phase we have called *inception*. This is the varying and indeterminate period in which perceptions of the need for change are fostered and crystallized. This can be a lengthy phase in which long seated problems are ignored, masked or unarticulated, or a brief and dramatic heightening of awareness precipitating urgent action (as in 'moral panics'). The second phase is *presentation*, and is the point at which the government 'goes public' with plans or aspirations, either through kite flying or more formally. This merges almost immediately into the third period, of *consultation*, when interested parties react to the proposals, and a dialogue, often unequal, and frequently marshalled within the media, addresses and sometimes contests definitions of the newly announced initiative. The fourth period is that of *formulation*, wherein the Government refines or redesigns it proposals on the basis of the conclusions of the consultative process. However, as we show later, this formulative stage was of negligible importance to the introduction of the Community Charge, which was imposed in spite of the conclusions of the consultative process. Therefore, our description of the media's coverage of this particular policy combines this stage with the consultation period. The fifth phase is *legislation*, in which the full cycle of parliamentary scrutiny takes place with a varying amount of public attention. The sixth phase is *preparation*, during which administrative arrangements are organized for its implementation. The seventh phase is *introduction*, when a new piece of legislation finally comes into force. This stage may of course be staggered, as a new policy is phased in. The eighth stage is that of *evaluation*. Although polices are continually evaluated throughout the policy cycle, it is during this phase that claims for the policy in principle are assessed against its performance in practice, and the doom-mongers are congratulated for their prescience or ridiculed for their pessimism. However this stage remains an ideological as well as empirical phase, often characterized by vehement disputes over the validity and relevance of evidence presented. The outcome of this stage determines the final stage of the policy cycle, namely *assimilation*. In this phase the policy becomes invisible, part of the political rote, literally unproblematic. If this is not achieved then the policy is forced back into a continuing evaluation phase, and an alternative outcome of *abolition* may result.

This model is no more than an abstract description of the necessary phases of the natural history of a policy process. It does draw attention to the presence at every phase of a dialectic relationship with a communicative and publicity environment. In this sense it is not a single linear sequence surrounded by an environment, with feedback restrained until the final phase. Rather feedback, if that is the right term, is continuously impacting on each phase of the sequence, and determines the timing and nature of each successive phase. The real environment for this process is the distribution of power and resources which enables access to those feedback flows.

The second conceptual tool we shall employ is the distinction between the *evaluative* and the *interpretative* dimensions of media coverage (Golding, 1990). In conventional terms the adequacy of a media report is judged by its fairness, objectivity and impartiality as an account of some event or person. Is the report pro or anti some policy, party, or initiative? This is the *evaluative* dimension, but it is only one vector. We need also to examine the question of what aspects of the policy are rendered visible, named and promoted. This is the *interpretative* dimension and asks the simple question, what is this issue about? In this study we shall be assessing both dimensions in relation to the coverage of the poll tax, and indeed arguing that the process of 'primary definition' can only be understood in relation to this distinction if we are to make sense of the history of the poll tax. We shall also be assessing the evaluative and interpretative capacity of news sources, and suggesting that the power of arbiters, for example, is far more limited in defining the interpretative dimension of policy than it is in relation to evaluation.

We begin the analysis by assessing the genesis and background of the Community Charge.

Chapter 2

A Brief History of The Poll Tax

The introduction of the Community Charge raised issues that extended well beyond the specifics of local government finance. Indeed, arguments about its technical and financial adequacy masked 'a deeper constitutional and political argument about what form of local government is needed in the UK' (Quirk, 1986: 4). In this chapter we set out the key aspects of this broader debate, as an essential context to our general appraisal of the media's performance and influence in reporting the poll tax.

British local and central government relations (pre-1970)

As with so many British political arrangements, the role and responsibilities of local government have never been constitutionally inscribed. Rather, its powers and obligations have been shaped politically and historically, and remain contested. At the centre of this dispute has been the appropriate relationship that should exist between central and local government, and in particular the degree of autonomy the latter should be permitted.

Some analyses, whilst acknowledging the value of the devolved administration of local services, ultimately insist that local government should act as the agent of central government: the conduit rather than progenitor of policy (Ridley, 1988). In contrast, others portray the devolution of political power as an essential precondition for healthy democracy (Blunkett and Jackson, 1987; Hillyard and Percy-Smith, 1988). The introduction of the Community Charge was seen by both sides as representing a crucial moment in this evolving constitutional debate, whether as heralding a new era of local accountability or driving the final nails into the coffin of local democracy.

In pre-nineteenth century Britain, local government experienced little political intervention from national government. The two tiers were essentially discrete political universes, with national government concerned with matters of national security and foreign policy, and the many and varied local authorities responsible for the distribution of alms and the maintenance of local amenities in any manner they saw fit (DoE, 1986a). Inevitably, this *laissez-faire* system of local governance produced 'a chaos of institutions, areas and rates' (Richards, 1980: 15).

The nineteenth century has been described as the 'golden age' of local government reform in Britain, with many of the changes wrought during this period establishing the foundations for the modern system (Smellie, 1968; Goldsmith, 1979). The main impetus for reform came from the first industrial revolution which transformed the demography of the nation. As densely populated urban areas mushroomed, problems of social deprivation worsened which placed growing pressures upon the limited civic amenities and welfare provision. By 1830, it was clear that there was an urgent need for a strategic response to the problems of poor relief, housing, sanitation, policing and public health. A restructured system of local government provided the principal means by which these pressing issues were tackled.

From the early nineteenth century through to the mid-1970s, three patterns in the development of local government in the United Kingdom are evident. First, levels of local government capital and revenue expenditure increased; slowly at first, but then with a growing impetus. Second, central government influence over local government activities correspondingly increased; whether in ensuring uniform, minimum standards of service provision, or in removing certain services wholly or partially from the jurisdiction of local authorities. Third, and largely as a result of this increased intervention, central government became an ever more significant source of revenue for local government.

In the thirty years from 1945, these trends accelerated dramatically. In real terms there was a 300 per cent increase in local government revenue expenditure between 1950 and 1970, and a 250 per cent increase in capital expenditure (Keith-Lucas and Richards, 1978: 130). Control of many services such as poor relief and public health, along with public utilities such as water, shifted to the centre. And by 1974/75, 66 per cent of local revenue was provided by central subventions.

The principal reason for this change was the establishment of the 'welfare state' in Britain after the 2nd World War. The Labour Government's manifesto of 1945 marked the first explicitly national view of local government, in which local authorities were deemed as *instruments* of central government, rather than semi-autonomous agents. This diminishing of local autonomy and change in the texture of local/central relations was accepted or ignored as the standards of public services increased (Alexander, 1990; Golding and Middleton, 1982).

The immediate post-war years also saw a qualitative transformation in the party politicization of local government (Goldsmith, *op. cit.*: 18). Although party politics had assumed a growing significance in local government over the preceding century, it was during this period that we see a 'nationalization' of party affiliations in local government with 'repeated attempts to bring local and national politicians of each party to march in step' (Gyford, 1985: 86). This injection of party politics into local government introduced a significant potential source of tension between central and local government, the full extent of which was only fully realized in the 1980s, when a resurgent municipal socialism ran full tilt into a national government passionately committed to the free-market and swingeing cuts in public expenditure.

Until the early 1970s, these incipient tensions remained largely hidden, and the exponential increase in local government expenditure and central government subventions continued. However, from then onwards, the period of expansion in British local government, that could be traced back more than a hundred and forty years, was thrown into reverse.

Local government in the 1970s: 'the party's over'

The unexpected victory of a Conservative Government in the 1970 general election opened the first major fault lines in the local/central relationship. Although the political energies of the Heath administration were principally concentrated on their dealings with the trades union movement, it also implemented policies which held major implications for the future form and finance of British local government. The most significant was the

1972 Local Government Finance Act, which introduced a new two-tier system of local governance.

At the same time, the issue of the equity and adequacy of the existing system of local domestic taxation was also propelled on to the political agenda. The rating system (or 'the Rates', as it was widely known) was a property-based domestic tax that had remained unchanged in principle since the introduction of the Elizabethan Poor Law in 1601. Local rates were set and levied according to two component calculations. The first was the 'rateable value' of a property, which was determined by its estimated rentable value. The second was the rate poundage, which was set by the levying authority according to the gap between its total spending and its income from all sources, in particular central government subventions, and local business taxes (which were set and calculated by the levying local authorities in a similar manner to domestic rates). The levying authorities were 'second tier' authorities (i.e city, district or borough councils), who raised revenue on behalf of themselves and overarching county-wide authorities and smaller parish councils.

This property-based system of local taxation required periodic 'revaluations' of the properties to be undertaken, to maintain the buoyancy of the local tax base, and it was the last revaluation held in England and Wales in 1973 that shifted the issue of local government finance reform to the centre of the political agenda. The resulting redistribution in the local tax burden it produced, which was exacerbated by the cost of local government reorganization and high inflation, caused considerable public controversy and media comment (Gyford *et al.*, 1989). Various 'rates strikes' were organized by residents in the hardest hit areas, and the furore prompted a manifesto commitment from the Conservative Party, which Margaret Thatcher personally championed, that there would be a fundamental reform of the rates in the event of its re-election. Its subsequent defeat, however, prevented the Party from acting upon that promise.

The immediate response of the new Labour administration to this political controversy was 'to spend money and buy time' (Boyne, 1986: 428). In 1974/75 an *ad hoc* subsidy of £150million was provided to hold down domestic rates, and the Layfield Committee of Enquiry was established to report on the financing of local government. The Committee's deliberations (Layfield, 1976) concluded that a local income tax should be levied by local authorities to supplement the existing rates. Crucially, the Layfield report's support for a local income tax 'was specifically associated with the wider question of relations between central and local government' (Richards, *op. cit.*: 109), and in particular that greater powers of decision should be given to local authorities. The additional revenue needed for such a major transformation would be provided by this additional income tax.

The Labour Government rejected the conclusions of the Layfield report, and sought instead to exert greater control over local expenditure. As Richards observes, Layfield's 'localist' vision was 'throttled by the requirements of macro-economic planning' (*ibid.*: 163). Throughout the 1970s, extensive difficulties with the country's economy, exacerbated by the international oil crisis, had forced the Chancellor to seek external assistance from the International Monetary Fund, which had placed great pressures upon Government spending. One of the major conditions of IMF support was that public expenditure would be reined in. In 1976, the Secretary of State for the Environment warned local government that 'the party's over', and in the Labour administration's final years significant reductions were achieved in aggregate local expenditure. By 1978/79, the percentage of local government expenditure covered by central government grants fell more than 5 per cent to 61 per cent.

Although these harsh financial realities hit local authorities heavily, the cutbacks were generally achieved in a spirit of grudging co-operation. However, the Conservatives' victory in the 1979 General Election marked the beginning of a period where the latent tensions between central and local government exploded into a political conflict that tore their long established relationship to shreds, and called the whole structure of local governance in Britain into question.

Thatcherism and local government (1979–90): 'Where there is discord may we bring harmony'

Although the passage of the1970s exposed a growing conviction in central government that local government spending was out of control, often wasteful and inflationary, and undermined central government's powers to control the macro economy (Hillyard and Percy-Smith, *op. cit.*), it was only with the accession of Margaret Thatcher that central government moved in a systematically coercive way to curb local expenditure. The new government's ideological commitment towards 'rolling back the frontiers of the state', coupled with their antipathy towards high taxation and public expenditure, brought many of the founding precepts of the welfare state into question. As the cause of nearly a quarter of public expenditure, and in the context of a public sector borrowing crisis, it was inevitable that local government would be a prime target for Government cuts.

Loughlin (1990) describes one of the defining features of the Thatcher period as being the *juridification* of local and central government relations. Previously this relationship was governed by conventions of consultation; with both tiers of government broadly interacting within a framework of consensus. However, throughout the 1980s, central government took precipitative, unilateral action to control the activities and expenditure of local authorities by legislating sweeping powers. Nowhere was this process of *juridification* more evident than in the realm of local finance.

The first significant measures taken to control local expenditure were included in the 1980 Planning and Land Act. Alongside new restrictions upon capital expenditure, the Act added a new 'Block Grant' component to the existing Rate Support Grant system. Councils' expenditure was linked to a central Grant Related Expenditure Assessment (GREA) to discourage high spending. Any expenditure in excess of this GREA led to a decrease in the grant paid to an authority and the greater the overshoot, the more punitive the penalties became (Sills, Taylor and Golding, 1988).

This major change was immediately strengthened by an additional set of expenditure targets based on *actual* levels of expenditure rather than *assessed* expenditure needs, as it was feared that those authorities whose expenditure were below their GREAs might take the opportunity to 'spend up' to this assessment. To the Government's view, these targets offered the basis for attainable expenditure reductions, and between 1981 and 1986 the grant penalties for spending in excess of these estimates became progressively harsher. This method was finally abandoned in 1986/87, when the underlying Block Grant arrangements were altered so that authorities automatically lost grant when they increased spending (instead of only losing grant when expenditure exceeded the designated targets).

The 1982 Local Government Finance Act provided greater governmental leverage on local authority finance by removing the right of councils to levy supplementary rates throughout a financial year to cover any shortfall. This represented a significant step in local/central relations as it was the first time a limit had been placed on authorities' freedom of access to the rates as an independent source of taxation (Blair, 1989). The Act also removed the right of local authorities to appoint their own auditors, appointing in their stead one centralized body: the Audit Commission. Although the Commission's remit has been to encourage good practice, assess the impact of new local government legislation and improve the value for money of local services, their principal *raison d'être* is to achieve significant cost cutting (Hillyard and Percy-Smith, *op. cit.*).

After the Conservative Party's victory in the 1983 General Election, Government legislation against local authorities gained momentum. Its commitment was bolstered by increasingly acrimonious confrontations with several Labour authorities, who not only sought to frustrate the Government's economic strategies but also foster 'some sort of socialist alternative' at a local level (Boddy and Fudge, 1984: 14).

The 1984 Rates Act introduced two further major controls of local authority finance. The first was a statutory requirement for local authorities to consult with businesses and other non-domestic rate payers before setting their business levy, thereby increasing the accountability of local authorities to their non-domestic payers. The second was the introduction of 'rate limitation', widely known as 'rate-capping'. This involved the Department of Environment setting optimum levels for domestic rates which local authorities were not permitted to exceed. The Act provided the Government with the option of capping the rates of specified authorities or all councils; but after widespread opposition from Conservative ranks, the Government only exercised the selective option. In 1985/86, eighteen highest spending authorities were rate-capped, sixteen of which were Labour controlled. In response several capped authorities set illegal budgets which flouted the new restrictions, but this defiance was short lived. As these authorities teetered on the brink of bankruptcy, errant councillors capitulated when threatened with personal liability for all excessive expenditure.

As the political tensions between central and local government increased, and the financial controls on local authorities tightened, the issue of reforming the whole system of local finance, which had laid dormant since the report of the Layfield Commission, returned to the political agenda. During his first period of tenure as Secretary of State for the Environment, Michael Heseltine published a Green Paper on rate reform in 1981 which explored the reform options. This Paper (DoE, 1981) outlined several reform options, including a local income tax, a sales tax, a poll tax, a system of centrally assigned revenues, and a reformed rating system. However the consultation process produced no consensus on a preferable alternative, and in the subsequent White Paper, it was concluded that the rating system 'should remain for the foreseeable future' (DoE, 1983: 14). Moreover, the problems with the poll tax option were explicitly stated:

> 'The tax would be hard to enforce. If the electoral register were used as the basis for liability it could be seen as a tax on the right to vote. A new register would therefore probably be needed. But this would make the tax expensive to run and complicated, particularly if it incorporated a rebate scheme. Without a rebate scheme a poll tax would bear harshly on people with low incomes ... The Government agrees with the Environment Committee that this option should be rejected' (*ibid.*, 1983: 12).

As a statement of political intent, the Paper could not have been more categorical. Yet within a matter of months the Government chose to renege on both its general resolution to keep the existing system in place, and its adamant rejection of the poll tax option.

The return of the poll tax

The main reason for the Government's sudden rethink was its increasing frustration at the failure of its fiscal controls to secure dramatic reductions in local expenditure. In its view, there had been limited successes: the annual rate of growth in local revenue expenditure had been restricted to under 1 per cent (compared with levels in excess of 3 per cent during the 1960s and 1970s); there had been major reductions in local government employment levels; and the proportional contribution of exchequer grant to local expenditure had fallen from 61 per cent to 47 per cent (Dunleavy and Rhodes, 1988; DoE, 1986a). However, these limited victories paled alongside the 18 per cent increase in local authority current expenditure for the same period (Ridley, 1988; DoE, 1986a).

The failure of their incremental measures was linked to the defensive responses of local authorities. Before rate-capping, many authorities compensated for penalized losses in central grant by increasing their levies on local ratepayers. Other local authorities chose to consistently 'spend up' because they rightly recognized that compliance with the Government's expenditure targets would simply lead to further decreases in subsequent expenditure targets. Furthermore, many authorities exploited the complexities of the finance system to minimize the effects of grant penalties (and, latterly, rate-capping) by employing an increasingly sophisticated range of creative accountancy techniques. In 1984, an Audit Commission report suggested that the complexities of the Block Grant system were inflating rather than reducing the amounts raised locally through the rates.

It was this frustration at the thwarting of macro-economic objectives, coupled with a series of increasingly acrimonious confrontations with several Labour councils, that encouraged the Government to reconsider the reform option. At the Conservative Party conference in October 1984, the Secretary of State for the Environment announced that rates reform was back on the agenda and a new review of the reform options would take place.

The key decision-making concerning this review was made at the highest level of Government, and involved secretive consultations between senior government ministers and their policy advisors. The task of reviewing possible reform options was delegated to two junior environment ministers and then onwards to a secretive 'task force' convened by Lord Rothschild, former head of Edward Heath's Policy Review Staff.

However, even at this stage, the review might have come to nothing had it not been for the political impact of the 1985 rating revaluation in Scotland. In Scotland rating revaluations had to be carried out every five years, and the effects of the 1985 revaluation proved particularly harsh, with a substantial percentage of the burden for local taxation shifting from non-domestic to domestic properties. The resulting public outcry created consternation among Scottish Conservatives, and stirred paranoic projections about the likely political effects of a similar revaluation in England and Wales (which was well overdue). Against such a prospect, abolition seemed a far preferable option to revision.

The rehabilitation of the poll tax as a reform option was crucially aided by a paper published by the influential Adam Smith Institute during the review period. In it the author chafed against the 'pointless pursuit of perfection' in previous reviews and concluded, 'It is clear that a *per capita* tax more nearly matches the requirements than any other possibility' (Mason, 1985: 23). The forcefully argued case for the poll tax proved very influential on the deliberations of the policy think tank (MacGregor, 1988).

Despite internal disagreements between members of the secretive task force, the report finally submitted to the Department of the Environment advocating the poll tax option, was enthusiastically received, and the supporting ministers proposed to seek its adoption as Government policy. In cabinet discussions the proposals had to weather further opposition, particularly from the Treasury and the Chancellor of the Exchequer (Lawson, 1992). However, by mid-1985 the policy was officially accepted, and in January 1986 a Green Paper entitled 'Paying for Local Government' was released, which stated the Government's intention to replace the rates with a poll tax – or as it had been renamed: the Community Charge.

'The way forward': the case for the Community Charge

Whatever subsequent judgements may have been made about the claims made by the 1986 Green Paper, it still remains the most comprehensive and categorical exposition of the Government's rationale for replacing the rates with a poll tax.

At the heart of the document rested the proposition that there was a malaise in local democracy, the roots of which could be directly traced back to the inequities and inefficiency of the rating system. This was termed a crisis of 'accountability', and revealed several dimensions. First, in an inversion of the historical evil of taxation without representation, it was claimed that too many people could vote for higher local rates without having to pay for them. As a consequence of this, profligate authorities could continue their excessive expenditure secure in the knowledge that the local tax burden would be borne unevenly, and that many local electors benefitted from services they didn't have to pay for. Second, non-domestic rate payers were subjected to punitive increases in their local tax bill, whilst having no opportunity of redress at the ballot box. Third, the complexities of the extant grant system were so great that they helped obscure the consequences of local expenditure decisions. Fourth, these factors were compromising the power of central government to pursue important macro-economic objectives in controlling public spending.

To rectify this crisis, four main changes were proposed. First, the domestic rates would be replaced with a flat rate tax on all adults over the age of 18, levied by each local authority according to its expenditure level relative to income from other sources. People with low income could be eligible, through a means test, for rebates of up to 80 per cent on their tax. Second, local control of non-domestic rates would be removed. Although councils would still collect this revenue, the amount levied would be set nationally and any further increases would be index-linked. The resulting revenue would be pooled centrally and then re-distributed back to local authorities according to the size of their population. Third, there would be dramatic revisions to the local government grant system, with a simplified system of spending assessments (later dubbed Standardized Spending Assessments) determining the allocation of the new Revenue Support Grant. Fourth, two transitional mechanisms would operate to ameliorate temporarily the major redistribution in grant allocations and individual tax burdens that would occur under the new system. The first was a period of 'dual running', where the poll tax would run alongside the rating system for a ten-year period, and only accretively take over from the old system. The second was for a system of 'safety nets', where those local authorities who gained income through the changes would temporarily have these benefits redistributed to authorities who lost out.

As part of the process of increasing the accountability of local government, the Paper asserted that people needed to redefine how they thought about local domestic taxation. Rather than measuring the fairness of a local tax according to the 'redistributive' principle (i.e its relation to the ability to pay), it should be tested against the 'benefit' principle (i.e the extent to which people who benefitted from services contributed to their cost). In this respect, the semantics of the Government's decision to refer to the impost as a 'charge' rather than a 'tax' were very significant. By conceiving of local taxation as a charge for services, it was claimed that the new levy was far fairer than the rates, as everybody was required to contribute something to the public services they benefitted from. Furthermore, this would give them a financial stake in local government and a vested interest in monitoring local expenditure decisions.

It was claimed the removal of local control of non-domestic taxes from local government and the simplifying of the grant allocation process would further enhance the financial accountability of councils, as any expenditure above Government spending assessments would have to be met by increases in Charge levels. Local authorities would no longer be able to use the complexities of the Block Grant system, or punitive rises in non-domestic rates, to hide their overspending. This would mean that local electors would, for the first time, have a straightforward measure of the relative efficiency and expenditure of their local authority.

Criticisms of the Green Paper

From the outset it was clear the Government had taken on a major task in promoting such an ambitious policy. Although the Green Paper initially received a positive response from Conservative MPs, the proposals were widely and intensively criticized from other sources. In Chapter 4 we identify the main sources of this opposition and describe how they politically mobilized to challenge the Government's reform programme. In this section we concentrate on the main aspects of their objections. These criticisms centred around the equity and redistributive implications of the new system; its efficiency; its implications for personal privacy; its impact on the franchise; and its constitutional impact on local and central government relations.

Equity: 'winners and losers'

As with any major tax reform, considerable attention focused on the redistributive implications of the new system. The criticisms made on this issue related both to specific components of the reform package, and to its overall operation.

The main criticisms of the Community Charge concerned its manifest regressiveness. Although the Green Paper projected that 'winners and losers' under the new system would be roughly equivalent (DoE, 1986a: 41), critics argued that these figures were calculated in a way that best supported the Government's case* and masked the structural inequities of the new system.

These inequities had several intersecting dimensions. At a most basic level, the flat rate levy would hit lower income groupings severely, particularly the 'nearly poor' – those individuals whose modest incomes prevented them from qualifying for rebates. As a consequence of this, it would dis-

* That is, by quantifying winners and losers by household rather than on an individual basis.

criminate against many disadvantaged social groups. Many ethnic minority communities would be heavily hit by the tax, as they tend to live in larger adult households (Brown, 1984); are more likely to be based in inner city areas where it was projected the poll tax would be highest (ALA, 1988); and are more likely to experience economic deprivation (Oppenheim, 1987). Similarly, the policy was seen as sexually discriminative, as women are more at risk from poverty due to lower levels of pay; are more reliant upon income support; are more likely to be unemployed; and were specifically disadvantaged by the rules on partners' 'joint and several liability' for each others charges (CIPFA, 1987). The tax also penalized young people for similar reasons, and because a disproportionate number of the new additions to the local tax base would be adults under 24 years of age (Low Pay Unit, 1987).

Critics also recognized the party political dimension to the winners and losers issue. The Government made no apologies for the fact that it anticipated poll tax levels to be very high in areas run by 'high spending' Labour authorities. In a BBC interview, a junior environment minister anticipated the system would 'run a coach and horses through the control that [Labour authorities] have got in many areas where, at the moment, not enough people are making a contribution towards the cost, and don't understand, as a result, the high price that Labour councils impose' (Christopher Chope, *On the Record*, BBC1, 17/9/89). Opponents argued that this amounted to a crude exercise in political gerrymandering, creating a situation where individuals could not afford to vote for adequate service provision. One commentator described this as an abuse of the concept of political accountability, which not only concerns fiscal decisions, 'but also the relationship between the substance of local policies and local preferences ... When the humbug about accountability is stripped away from the Green Paper, the proposed reforms emerge as an attempt to restrain rate revenue' (Boyne, 1986: 431).

Apart from criticizing the Community Charge in redistributive terms, critics also attacked its fairness in relation to the 'benefit principle'. For, unlike charges for other services, individuals could not opt-out of paying the Charge by declining the services it provided, and this compulsion to pay prevented it from qualifying as a charge. Furthermore, the untested assumption in the Green Paper that those who paid the least for local services benefitted from them the most was challenged as ill founded, with evidence provided that those who paid the most under the rates also tended to have greatest benefit from local services and amenities (Bramley *et al.*, 1989).

It was also claimed that the particularly regressive aspects of the *domestic* taxation changes, would be exacerbated by the new methods for grant allocation and non domestic taxation. This was because these accompanying reforms would shift revenue away from poorer, industrialized inner city authorities, towards more affluent suburban and rural regions (LGIU, 1989; Esam and Oppenheim, 1989). For businesses, the rating burden would shift from North to South, from the manufacturing to retail sector, and from big to small business.*

Efficiency

The efficiency of the new system was also questioned. By taxing people rather than property, and thereby nearly doubling the local tax base, the administrative logistics and costs of local taxation were substantially increased, with the prospect of widespread evasion of the tax. The fact that these additional adminstrative costs, and any shortfall in revenue due to non payment, would have to be paid by the charge payers themselves, added a further piquancy to these objections.

Privacy implications

A further concern raised by the increased administrative demands of the system, was that it might encourage greater intrusiveness by councils in people's private affairs in their efforts to enforce the tax. In 1988, the National Council for Civil Liberties commented:

> 'The Government's plans to replace the domestic rates based on property with a flat rate tax is not in itself a civil liberty issue. But the way in which the new tax will be administered and enforced will pose serious threats to the privacy of the entire adult population, and create the potential for greater control by central and local government over the individual' (NCCL, 1988: 1).

The concerns of the influential pressure group were fivefold. First, that there was no safeguard in either the legislation or the Data Protection Act to prevent local authorities from gathering unnecessary information. Sec-

* In addition, it was feared that centralizing business rate control would undermine the partnership between local authorities and their business sectors.

ond, that councils might hold secret files behind their public register, '... recording the notes, anecdotes and suspicions the authority has about individuals' (*ibid.*: 2). Third, that registration officers would have unregulated access to all lists of local residents held by council departments – such as families registered with social services, local library card holders, and council house lists. Fourth, that individuals would have only limited access to the information held on them held by the local authority. Fifth, that the nationwide implementation of the poll tax would mean the creation, for the first time, of a complete list of the names and addresses of the whole adult population. Although the Government maintained that each local list was separate, there would be strong arguments, to maximize efficiency, for making the data in the registers compatible to allow transfers of information when people moved. In conclusion, the group requested further safeguards to protect personal privacy, but also identified an 'irreconcilable conflict between the need for the efficient collection of a tax of this kind and the protection of privacy' (*ibid.*: 4).

Franchise implications

Although ministers consistently refuted the proposition that the Community Charge was a tax on voting (Winetrobe, 1992), the right of Community Charge Registration Officers to draw on electoral rolls raised concerns about the impact the tax might have on voting behaviour. In particular it was feared that the linkage between electoral rolls and Community Charge Registers provided a powerful incentive for those unable or unwilling to pay the tax to voluntarily disenfranchise themselves in an attempt to avoid detection. Furthermore, given the structural regressiveness of the levy, such action would be most prevalent against those already marginalized from the political process, and most socially disadvantaged (who, coincidentally, were the type of voters least likely to support the Conservative Party).

Constitutional implications

It was also claimed that the reform package would seriously compromise the independence of local government. By centralizing control of business rate revenue, the proportion of local authority revenue met from local taxes would be reduced from around half to a quarter, which significantly increased the importance of grant assessments in the setting of charge levels (Blair, *op. cit.*). Whereas the Government saw this as a virtue – enhancing the financial accountability of local authorities by exposing charge payers to every pound their council 'over spent' – critics claimed that because all expenditure above Government assessments would have to be raised from only a quarter of the authorities revenue base (i.e domestic revenue), excess expenditure would have a powerful distorting effect on Charge levels, leading to disproportionate increases for marginal overspending (the so-called 'gearing' effect). This was seen to seriously compromise the accountability argument, and expose the exercise as a cynical attempt to use electoral resistance to higher taxes to force savage cuts in local expenditure.

Furthermore, the greater importance of central government assessments in determining local taxation levels inevitably raised concerns about the accuracy of these grant assessments. In particular, that 'simplifying' the needs assessment equation, would make them less sensitive to the particular needs and conditions of different areas.

A chronology of chaos: the rise and demise of the Community Charge

> 'The history of the poll tax illustrates how policies can have unintended consequences that give them a dynamic beyond the imagination of the original proponents. The Government became caught in a logic of events of which it lost control, and could no longer direct towards its desired ends' (Stoker, 1991: 203–204).

These then were the main criticisms and claims made for the Community Charge, and are important to bear in mind when appraising the terms of public and media debate on the tax. However, before addressing these matters one important contextual task remains. This is briefly to map the main events in the inglorious career of the Community Charge, from its first presentation in 1986 to its abolition in 1993.

Following the publication of the Green Paper in 1986, the Government moved quickly to introduce the legislation for Scotland. At the end of that year legislation for the accelerated introduction of the system in Scotland (The Abolition of Domestic Rates Etc. [Scotland] Bill) entered Parliament, and received its Royal Assent the following March. Unlike the legislation for England and Wales, this Bill passed with comparative ease, with no Conservative Party back bench rebellion.

Legislation for England and Wales was held in abeyance until after the

1987 General Election, which the Conservatives won in June with a barely reduced majority of nearly 100 MPs. In the post-election Cabinet reshuffle, Kenneth Baker, who had been one of the principal architects of the reforms, was replaced by Nicholas Ridley as Secretary of State for the Environment for England. Although initially Ridley had been sceptical about the feasibility of the poll tax option (Lawson, 1992), by the time of his appointment he was fully in favour of the proposals, and took to promoting the tax with all the enthusiasm of a convert (Ridley, *op. cit.*).

The triumphal post-election Conservative Party conference of that year marked a crucial turning point in the implementation of the policy. Party activists urged the Government to abandon the plan to run the poll tax alongside the existing system, and introduce the Community Charge in one go. By adopting the 'big bang' approach it was argued that those people exploited by the rates would benefit immediately from the redistributive effects of the new system. The Party leadership willingly acceded to this apparent unanimity of party opinion and agreed to introduce the tax in one go in 1990, apart from in those London authorities that would be hardest hit by the new arrangements.*

However, when the 1987 Local Government Finance Bill entered Parliament serious rifts opened up within the Conservative party. Its Second Reading was marked by an acrimonious debate on the fairness and effects of the poll tax proposal. While the proposing minister claimed the new system would 'be good for local democracy' (Hansard, 16/12/87: col 1119), the main opposition party described it as 'a threat to democracy itself' (Hansard, 16/12/87: col 1131). Senior figures on the left of the Conservative Party also voiced serious concerns – most noteably the ex-Environment Secretary, Michael Heseltine and ex-Party leader, Edward Heath.

The acrimony and internal dissent continued into the Bill's Committee stages, and by the time preparations were underway for its Third Reading had manifested in a proposed amendment which would have transformed the domestic tax proposals. The eponymous 'Mates Amendment' – championed by the Conservative back bencher Michael Mates, but the product of clandestine negotiations between Tory rebels and the Labour front bench – proposed that the single flat rate Community Charge be replaced

* The decision to introduce the tax over four years in London was also subsequently rescinded.

by a system of 'banded' poll taxes, that would link the system more directly to ability to pay. A vote on the amendment was held on the 19 April 1988, prior to the Bill's Third Reading, and fears of its success prompted the Government to announce an additional £130 million for rebates to cushion low income families from the impact of the new tax. The concession bought off a sufficient number of Conservative rebels to defeat the amendment with a reduced Government majority of 25.

As the Bill passed to the Lords, there was anticipation that the upper chamber might impede its progress to the statute books, or at least force the Government into major revisions. However, a rebellion headed by Conservative peer Lord Chelmsford was swamped by Government whips who dragooned various 'backwoodsmen' (Peers who rarely or never attended the House of Lords) into the House of Lords to support the Government. The Finance Bill passed through the Lords with a huge Government majority of 134, following the highest turnout of Conservative peers since 1971.

Although political controversy over the poll tax intensified in Scotland during 1988, there followed a hiatus in the political debate in England and Wales. However, the issue re-emerged once again in early 1989, with the introduction of the Community Charge in Scotland and the start of the registration process in England and Wales. Here again, major difficulties emerged for the Government. First, as we discuss in the next chapter, a major Government publicity offensive timed to coincide with these events went dramatically awry, causing considerable embarrassment to ministers. Second, concerns about the intrusiveness of the new tax system seemed to be borne out by the conduct of the registration process. Despite assurances from the Environment Secretary that 'strict limits' would be placed on the information which registration officers could obtain about individuals (*DoE News Release*, 17/3/89, No. 145), many local authorities requested excessive or irrelevant information on their registration forms. Out of the 403 forms examined by the Data Protection Registrar, only 37 were passed and 304 authorities were asked to clarify the purpose behind some of their questions (Liberty, 1989a). In response to the controversy the Secretary of State directed local authorities to avoid being too intrusive on their registration forms, but admitted he had 'no power to prescribe the content of any form' (*DoE News Release*, No. 344, 19/6/89: 2).

The third problem concerned the proposals for a self-financing system of 'safety nets' which were intended temporarily to cushion the profound redistributive effects of the new tax system. The scheme – where 'winners' had their gains redistributed back to authorities who lost out – had already been criticized as a smoke screen that would cynically obscure the full extent of the redistribution of income from poorer local authority areas to more affluent authorities (Esam and Oppenheim, *op. cit.*; Lee, 1989; LGIU, *op. cit.*). However, the thrust of the controversy on this occasion originated from the Government's own supporters, who criticized the system for apparently requiring parsimonious Conservative authorities to subsidize 'profligate' Labour councils. In the face of this criticism, even Margaret Thatcher publicly conceded that 'the transition period is flatly contradictory to the basic philosophy, so we have got to find a way through' (*Daily Express*, 7/9/89: 9), and at the Conservative Party conference it was announced that the safety nets would be dropped after the first year, and that the Treasury would fund the costs to losing authorities over the ensuing three years, at a cost of £600 million. Furthermore, a new system of transitional relief was introduced for households who were hardest hit by the new tax, at an additional cost of £375 million (Gibson, 1990).

A Cabinet reshuffle in July 1989 replaced the right wing Nicholas Ridley as Secretary of State for the Environment with the more moderate figure of Chris Patten, whose less combative political profile it was hoped would help ease the pathway to implementation. However, he had not been in office long before he was confronted by an escalating political crisis over the Community Charge which made all the preceding difficulties pale into insignificance.

The troubles seriously began in January 1990, following the announcement of the outcome of the revaluation of business properties and the first realization by many businesses of how much more taxation they would have to pay. Matters took an even more serious turn in late February, when local authorities were notified of their grant allocations and started setting the first Community Charges.

These initial charge levels greatly exceeded the Government's prior projections of probable taxation levels. In November 1989, the Government announced that the average Community Charge in England and Wales would be £278, provided local authorities met central government spending assessments. Although this figure itself represented a considerable increase on previous official estimates, the actual average charge level exceeded this projection by more than £80. Furthermore many Conservative as well as Labour authorities levied charges in excess of £400 per person.

The impact of these unexpectedly high charges were twofold. Firstly, the bitter wrangling on the policy within the Conservative Party over the policy turned into open warfare. Conservative backbenchers, from the right as well as the left of the Party, openly turned on the Government and exhorted them to repeal such an unpopular policy. At local Government level, anger was even more vociferous, and there followed a spate of high profile resignations and defections among Conservative councillors and activists.

Second, public demonstrations were held across England and Wales against the tax and its harsh impact. In Conservative as well as Labour areas, people demonstrated their disaffection with the policy and the Government. On several occasions there were serious breaches of public order, the most violent of which occurred on 31 March 1990, when a public demonstration in the centre of London disintegrated into a major riot which led to many arrests and injuries and millions of pounds worth of damage. So intense was the controversy over the policy, the Government was forced to make several immediate concessions, and instituted an internal review of the policy and its operation.

The combination of public outrage against the poll tax, internecine strife within the Conservative party, and a rejuvenated political opposition had a dramatic impact upon the Party's electoral fortunes. In March 1990 the Conservative stronghold of Mid Staffordshire fell in a by-election to Labour with a swing of 21 per cent. Nationally, Labour's opinion poll lead rose to unprecedented heights, and the Prime Minister's credibility sank to an all time low. In the May local government elections the Labour Party made sweeping gains at the Conservatives' expense, although they failed to secure two of the Tory's 'flagship' boroughs, which had levied particularly low Community Charges. In October 1990, another Conservative stronghold fell in a by-election. In Eastbourne a Conservative majority of nearly 17,000 was converted into a 4,500 majority for the Liberal Democrats. This was followed the next month by an appalling showing for the Conservatives in the Bradford North by-election, where they came in a poor third. In March 1991, the Conservatives also lost the Ribble Valley by-election, with a voting swing of 25 per cent to the Liberal Democrats.

The Government's persistent difficulties with the policy was a key factor behind the 1990 Conservative Party leadership contest. For, although Margaret Thatcher's stance on European policy was the catalyst for a serious challenge to her leadership, the main reason for her defeat lay in the parliamentary Party's concern about her dogged defence of a tax that was seriously compromising the Party's electoral credibility (Gibson, *op. cit.*; MacGregor, 1991).

Following John Major's victory in the leadership contest, the prospect of the repeal of the poll tax became a very real possibility. Michael Heseltine was appointed as Environment Secretary and embarked on a fundamental review of the structure and finance of local government. Over the ensuing months rumours circulated about the reform options under consideration and whether the poll tax would be abandoned completely. However, the Party's disastrous showing at the Ribble Valley by-election finally severed the Government's commitment to the policy.

Following the setting of the second year's poll taxes, a surprise blanket reduction in Community Charges of £140 was announced in the Chancellor's budget speech, which was to be funded by an increase in the standard rate of Value Added Tax from 15 per cent to 17.5 per cent. This was followed a few weeks later by a Commons statement from the Environment Secretary that the poll tax was to be abolished in 1993, and replaced with a new local tax. It took several further weeks for the Government to present the particular details of the replacement to Parliament. On 23 April 1991, after days of informed media speculation, Michael Heseltine let the House of Commons in on the worst kept secret in politics: that the replacement for the Community Charge would be a new property based 'Council Tax'.

Under these new arrangements, every domestic property would be assessed as to its capital value, and placed within several bands. The Council Tax would be levied according to the band in which a property fell (the more valuable the property, the higher the band, and the higher the Council Tax levied), and the number of adults living in the property (single adult households could claim a 25 per cent reduction in their Council Tax). The new business taxation and central grant arrangements remained essentially unchanged. The consultation period for the Council Tax was very brief and the legislation was forced through parliament where the proposals met with no back bench opposition. In March 1992 the Council Tax became law, and on 1 April 1993 replaced the poll tax in England, Scotland and Wales.

In the final two years between the announcement and actual repeal of the Community Charge, the financial pressure on local authorities intensified as large numbers of people continued not to pay. By April 1993, £1.5 billion was still owed in poll tax arrears (Broom, 1994). Furthermore, disturbing evidence emerged about the detrimental impact non-payment may have had on the electoral process. Official figures published by the Office of Population Census and Surveys (OPCS) in 1991 estimated a shortfall of 1 million people between those registered to vote and those eligible. Although a drop in electoral rolls had been apparent since 1984, it accelerated appreciably between 1988 and 1991, coincident with the arrival of the poll tax (*Population Trends*, 1991: 2). Over this three-year period, the proportion of adults eligible to vote and who had registered in Britain fell from 97.9 per cent to 95.6 per cent, with the decline most evident amongst young people who had just attained the right to vote (*ibid.*). According to one academic study, more than a third of this discrepancy was due to people not registering to avoid the poll tax (Smith and Maclean, 1992). Poll tax dodging also seriously affected the ten-yearly national census survey, conducted in 1991, with the initial canvas under-estimating the actual population by an estimated 1.8 million people (*Independent on Sunday*, 13/9/92).

Widespread concerns about the state of the electoral register in 1991 prompted many local authorities to conduct voter registration drives, which partially arrested the decline in electoral rolls before the 1992 General Election (Jenkins, 1992). For example, research by the Electoral Reform Society found that 229,064 voters in a sample of 300 local authority areas in England and Wales had surrendered their right to vote, against a projected decline (based on 1991 figures) of 280,000. Even so, the Society's spokesperson commented, 'It is still a sad day for democracy when people have decided to forego the right to vote because it would cost them too much money' (*Independent*, 25/3/92: 2).

The re-election of a majority Conservative Government in the April 1992 General Election, which confounded both political expectations and opinion poll projections, raised questions about the hidden influence poll tax disenfranchisement may have had on the election outcome by discouraging potential Labour supporters. According to Butler and Kavanagh (1992: 232) it isn't possible to argue that Labour lost the election through the deliberate non-registration of its supporters, because those areas where poll tax motivated deregistration was most apparent were already Labour controlled. However, a Warwick University study into the effects of non-registration for the poll tax on the election produced less sanguine conclusions. According to the study's 'central estimate', had poll tax disenfranchisement not been a factor during the election, the Conservative' majority would have been reduced to only five seats (eight less than its actual majority). This would have seriously increased the political vulnerability of the new administration (Smith and Maclean, *op. cit.*).

Beyond the possible influence that poll tax dodging may have had for the outcome of the General Election, the main opposition parties also expressed concerns about the impact the low registrations might have for the deliberations of the Boundary Commission, which by law had to base the parliamentary boundaries from 1996 onwards, on the figures from the 1991 electoral rolls (Jenkins, *op. cit.*; Smith and Maclean, *op. cit.*).

Concerns about local authority intrusions into personal privacy also remained, despite the earlier intervention of the Data Protection registrar. In 1988, it was announced that British Telecom had established a £4 million computer system to enable local authorities to exchange information about charge payers, and track individuals across local authority areas (Thornton, 1989). By late 1991, the Community Charge Information Exchange (CCIX) was used by 107 councils throughout England and Wales, and had handled in excess of 120,000 charge payer records in the previous year (British Telecom Print and Dispatch Bureau promotional literature [1992] *Customer Systems*). In 1990, in a flagrant disregard of conventions on petitioners' rights, Charnwood Borough Council cross referenced the names and addresses on an anti poll tax petition it received with its own Community Charge register to track down non-payees; and in 1991, the civil rights group Liberty challenged several local authorities who were threatening to withdraw services to persons not registered on their Community Charge register (Jenkins, 1991).

Summary and conclusions

In this chapter we have outlined the historical origins of the Community Charge and described its ignominious progression from inception through to abolition. We have also demonstrated how the political debate about the policy's practicality and propriety operated on a range of different levels, raising issues of local democracy, personal liability, equity, efficiency, macro-economics, and individual rights.

It is important to bear the complexity and breadth of this debate in mind when examining how this debate was publicly constructed by the policy's main protaganists and the local and national media, in particular when considering which aspects of the debate featured most prominently and which were marginalized. For it is by attending to these details that we can gain a sense of how journalists and political actors actively constructed and inhibited the structure of public debate.

Chapter 3

Selling Accountability: Government Promotion of the Community Charge

The more people know about the Community Charge, the more they will support it. The opposition are so frightened of the Community Charge that they are not even prepared to call it by its proper name' John Gummer, Minister for Local Government, 10/5/89, Hansard, Column 864.

As we survey the wreckage of the ill starred poll tax experiment, it is easy to forget the initial enthusiasm with which the Government promoted the Community Charge to the British public. In introducing a major fiscal innovation against a background of considerable public suspicion, the Government recognized the crucial importance of an effective public relations strategy in securing public acceptance of the policy. Accordingly it concentrated a considerable amount of time and expenditure on trying to promote the policy's merits to an unconvinced electorate. In this chapter we examine the main features of this strategy and how it developed in anticipation of, and in reaction to, broader political factors.

This discussion focuses exclusively upon central government: both in its role as the site of national executive power and as the dominant political party. This is because of the particular manner in which the policy was formulated and promoted. Marsh and Rhodes (1989) have observed that one of the defining features of the late Thatcher administrations was their autocratic, 'top down' approach to policy formulation and implementation. The poll tax was a classic example of this. Conceived in a conspiracy of clandestine meetings, from its first public presentation to its introduction in England and Wales, the Community Charge represented a political *fait accompli* (a few major concessions notwithstanding). And just as the Government circumvented the formal conventions of consultation, so its public relations work was organized and financed in a 'top down' manner (whether through Government departments or Conservative Central Office). Although local authorities were expected to assist in increasing public understanding of the change (largely in support of their own self interest), they never featured centrally in the Government's mission to explain.*

Preparing the presentation

From the first secretive discussions of the policy review team, the Government recognized that by replacing the existing rating system with a flat rate, personal levy, it was embarking on an ambitious and risky venture. Once the review team's proposals had been approved by the Cabinet, discussions began at the Department of the Environment as to how the policy could be most effectively promoted to the British electorate. Attention particularly focused on the brand image of the proposed tax. Although flat rate, individual levies have been known through history as 'poll taxes', there was an understandable concern about the negative historical connotations of such a name. In fourteenth century England every adult over fifteen years of age had been required to pay a series of poll taxes to fund the country's foreign wars. As the amounts levied gradually increased, and evasion became more prevalent, commissioners were sent out to forcibly collect the arrears from around the country. The ensuing peasants' revolt, led by Watt Tyler, resulted in a march on the capital, the storming of the Tower of London, and the execution of several ministers held responsible for the levy. This melodramatic and heroic ancestry was to be fully exploited by later opponents of the poll tax, linking the battle against the Community Charge with images of a down-trodden peasantry, resiliently resisting oppression.

* The only exceptions were the so-called 'flagship' Thatcherite authorities of Wandsworth, Westminster and Bradford that levied low poll taxes, and Conservative Central Office sought to use as illustrative examples of the direct linkage between cost efficiency and low local taxes. However, although council leaders from these authorities colluded closely with Conservative Central Office in promoting the political merits of the reforms, their councils' official publicity material pursued a more moderate line. In recognition of the deep public antipathy to the tax, their publicity material avoided endorsing its principals, and focused on the value for money the councils provided and how that reflected in the low charges levied (Deacon and Golding, 1993). As the Head of the PR department from one of these authorities put it in interview, 'Councillors have got to get themselves elected'.

In an attempt to distance the policy from such an unpromising historical precedent, a naming session was convened at the Department of Environment, where ministers and senior civil servants struggled to find a new title that would signify a more modern and positive image. Several options were considered, including Council Charge (dismissed as 'too bureaucratic'); Residents Charge ('too confusing'); and Residence Charge ('too bourgeois'), before it was decided to opt for the Community Charge (*Dispatches*, Channel 4, 11/3/93). Once this had been decided, the Government prepared to go public with its big new idea, which it was hoped would bring local government to heel and secure its political hegemony for years to come.

'You and the Community Charge': the Government goes public

An article published in the *Guardian* in early 1990, questioned whether the Government ever seriously considered aggressively promoting the poll tax through high profile publicity campaigns. Commenting on the anodyne quality of the last concerted Government publicity campaign on the poll tax in England and Wales, the article concluded:

> 'A measure likely to prove as unpopular as the Community Charge – as it will be called in all Government campaigns – can only be presented to the public in its most sanitized form, not piled high and sold cheap on our TV screens' (*Guardian*, 9/1/90: 25).

However, closer examination of the timing, content and expenditure of the Government's promotional work reveals a more complex picture. In particular, it shows that any reticence evident in later campaigning was not apparent in preceding campaigns, but reflected a timidity borne of consistent failure to elicit public, media and intra-party support for the policy.

There were two broad components to the Government's – as opposed to the Conservative Party's – promotion of the Community Charge. The first involved expensive public relations campaigns, encompassing the widespread distribution of publicity material, press adverts and information subsidies to local and national media. The second comprised more conventional and informal news management work with the media, that made particular use of parliamentary lobby briefings. The relative importance of these two strategies changed as the policy cycle proceeded, as did the nature of the messages conveyed. These changes were largely dictated by contextual political developments. Prior to the tax's introduction in England and Wales, the promotion of the Community Charge centred on formal, PR initiatives, that first stridently extolled the merits of the policy, but latterly became more reserved and descriptive. At the same time, news management work became far more significant, as ministers first strove to limit the crisis of confidence in the new tax, and then to find a publicly acceptable alternative. In the sections below we describe these developments in greater detail and consider critical questions about the propriety of many of their features.

Poll tax public relations: leaflets and booklets

The first poll tax publicity material was distributed at a very early stage. In January 1986, alongside the publication of the Green Paper, a 'popular version' was prepared for wider public consumption, entitled *Paying for Local Government: Proposals for Change.* 70,000 of these miniature versions were distributed within a year, after 'substantial demand' (Committee of Public Accounts, 1990: 14).

No further publicity material was distributed until after the Conservatives' victory in the 1987 General Election. However, on return to office, the Thatcher administration started to mobilize the considerable resources of Whitehall's public relations machinery to explain and promote their 'flagship' policy.

In October 1987, the Department of Environment issued a twelve page booklet to supplant the earlier summary of the Green Paper. Entitled *Paying for Local Government: The Need for Change,* it contrasted the perceived merits of a 'Community Charge' with the inequities and inadequacies of the rating system, local income tax, and greater central government control. It concluded with the confident prediction that the reforms would provide a 'greater say' and 'a fairer share' for all in local government. 53,000 copies of this leaflet were distributed before it, in turn, was supplanted by revised publicity material (*ibid.*: 14).

In December 1988 an attractive, twenty page booklet entitled *You and the Community Charge: Your Step by Step Guide* was released which again gave details of the reforms and their underlying rationale. ('No method of raising money is very popular but there has been a great deal of criticism of domestic rates for a long time ... At the moment, half the electors in England pay nothing directly towards the cost of their local services. With the Community Charge, this will no longer be the case. This will share the burden of paying for council services more widely and among almost all those who use them'.) The booklet was illustrated throughout with cartoons of people of different ages, occupations and ethnic groups, all smiling enigmatically. These euphoric citizens became something of a 'brand image' for a while, and were the object of considerable satirical comment.

Several additional back-up leaflets were also produced to provide more detailed information on individual aspects of the reforms; such as the business rate, exemptions from the tax, students and the Community Charge, the rebate scheme, the collective Community Charge, and the appeal system. ('You cannot appeal against the amount of Community Charge you are asked to pay. That is fixed by your local council, just as they used to fix the rates', *You and the Community Charge: The Appeals System*).

These booklets were followed up four months later with an even more comprehensive public relations offensive. In May 1989, 23 million leaflets entitled *The Community Charge (The So-Called 'Poll Tax': How it Will Work for You)* were distributed to every household in England and Wales at a total cost of £1.78million (*Guardian*, 11/5/89). In this brief leaflet the 'Step by Step' Guide was distilled into twenty three questions and answers. These were variously designed to explain the reforms ('Broadly, the following groups will not have to pay, i.e. will be exempt'); to promote its merits ('Only about half of all adults pay rates. So the Community Charge will share out the cost of local services amongst nearly everyone'); to dissuade people from attempting to avoid it ('It will not be easy to get out of paying the Community Charge'); to allay fears ('What if I have difficulty in filling in the form? The Registration Officer will be happy to help you'); and to refute criticisms ('The Community Charge has nothing to do with the right to vote'). Once again, readers were encouraged to apply for supplementary leaflets for more detailed information about the tax ('If the Community Charge is low enough, you may even be in pocket. But if your council sets a high Community Charge, then your extra income may not cover all of the 20 per cent you will have to pay', *You and the Community Charge: Rebates*).

In January 1990, the advertising agency Ogilvy and Mather were commissioned to design a nationwide 'How to Pay Less' advertising campaign on

Community Charge Benefits, that took in television, local and national press and magazines at a final cost of £3.1million (*DoE News Release*, No. 6, 4/1/90; *Campaign*, 6 April 1990). This final amount considerably exceeded the £1million initially projected for the account when tenders were invited in November 1989. The agency's chairperson, Mike Walsh, stressed the campaign would have 'no slogans, no gimmicks and no logos' (*Campaign*, 24/11/89), and there was a clear difference in its tone and content. Gone were the critiques of the rating system and the discourses about the political urgency of making every adult contribute something to local taxation, and in their place were straightforward exhortations to those on low incomes to apply for rebates to the tax. As Walsh later explained:

> 'Our strategy from the start has been informational. The kind of people we're talking to are pensioners and people on low incomes, who don't buy newspapers, so the advertising has to be on television. If they do read newspapers then they are free-sheets, so we have to be in those. There is no point in dressing the campaign up in jargon or flashy sell because these people find that kind of thing a complete turn-off. They need to see that there is something in it for them' (*Guardian*, 9/1/90: 25).

Also in January 1990, the Department of the Environment used Inland Revenue records to send literature to every business in England, explaining the operation and merits of the new Uniform Business Rate (*DoE News Release*, No. 30, 22/1/90). In a covering letter included with every booklet, the Environment Secretary explained:

> 'At present each local authority sets its own rate poundage. Some businesses face a poundage more than three times higher than others. This wide variation distorts business competition. And rates can rise steeply, and with little warning, from one year to the next, which makes it difficult for firms to plan ahead. Existing rateable values are also outdated ... The use of out of date values is another factor distorting competition between businesses.'

These latter two campaigns were the final major publicity initiatives conducted on behalf of the 1988 Local Finance Act reforms. This was partly because the moment of introduction had arrived, but also revealed the political difficulties the Government was confronting.* As the political debate gained its own momentum its publicity work became far more informal, covert and media orientated, as ministers strove to limit the damage the policy was having on their credibility.

In stark comparison, the introduction of the Council Tax was marked by only one limited public information campaign, comprising a series of five brief booklets, whose measured tone and understated graphics contrasted dramatically with those that heralded the implementation of the poll tax. In this literature the previous insistence that local taxation levels exclusively reflected local expenditure was also, quietly, laid to rest:

> 'The Council Tax is set by your local council. The amount set will depend on how much it and certain other public bodies in your area spend *and how much money they get from elsewhere*' (*Council Tax – A Guide to the New Tax for Local Government*, Department of the Environment, 1992, our emphasis).

Poll tax P.R. and the media: the two step flow

> 'You will almost certainly have read about the new Community Charge in the papers, or heard about it on television. You will probably have seen it called the poll tax, but the Community Charge is its real name' (*You and the Community Charge*, DoE Publicity booklet, January 1989).

Alongside the plethora of booklets, leaflets and press adverts produced between 1986 and 1990, the Government also directed a considerable amount of promotional material at the media. From the beginning ministers saw the media as being very important to their promotional strategies, both in informing the public and shaping public perceptions of it. Accordingly, the winning of editorial approbation was a prominent aspect of the

* A few modest Government public relations campaigns followed after February 1990. The Royal National Institute for the Blind was commissioned to reproduce the four main Community Charge leaflets on cassette tapes and in braille and moon writing (*DoE News Release*, No. 162, 9/3/90). Similarly, the British Deaf Association assisted in producing a sign language video for the deaf (*DoE News Release*, No. 166, 12/3/90; *DoE News Release*, No. 410, 11/7/90). In July 1990 a leaflet was published advising business rate payers how they might appeal against their new rating assessments (*DoE News Release*, No. 402, 5/7/90).

Government's publicity work. One particularly significant element to this was the attention on local media. The reasons for this were twofold. Firstly, it reflected the continuing political significance of local media, particularly in explaining a national policy with a clear local resonance. Second, it represented an attempt to talk over the heads of local authority sources, many of whom, as we discuss in the next chapter, were actively campaigning against the policy.

In September 1987 local government ministers Michael Howard and Christopher Chope embarked on a 'whistle stop tour' to impress on local worthies around the country the value and inevitability of the poll tax. Only one national press release was issued during the tour (*DoE News Release*, No. 369, 22/9/87), but great efforts were targeted at local newspaper editors, using a specially made video, fact packs and stylish presentations. Eight special fact packs were also produced to ensure, as Michael Howard's press release prior to the tour put it, 'that people should get a clear idea of how it will work' (*DoE News Release*, No 343, 8/9/87). The tour aimed at areas where political considerations demanded a careful and forceful marketing of the poll tax.

A later, and less ambitious news media initiative occurred in May 1989, and was timed to coincide with the blanket distribution of the 'so-called "poll tax"' leaflets. A 'ready made' article written by the Environment Minister, John Gummer, the Minister for Housing and Planning, was mailed and faxed by civil servants to local news desks across England. In this standard article, the minister extolled the merits of the Community Charge and sought to allay criticisms of its implementation,

> 'You will probably ... have heard or read many scare stories and half truths about the Community Charge peddled by those who oppose it. Today the Government begins to deliver THE FACTS ... These are some of the blatant untruths circulating about the Community Charge. 'It is a flat rate tax'. NOT TRUE. A generous system of rebates ensures that the charges paid by people with very low incomes reflects their ability to pay ... 'It is a tax imposed by Central Government'. NOT TRUE. It is a charge paid by most adults to pay for local services ... The level of that charge is set by Local Councils. 'It is unfair on the poor and the elderly'. NOT TRUE – it is designed to be fairer. The poor will be assisted by rebates and income support. Most elderly people are likely to pay *less* than they now pay in rates ... 'There will be an army of snoopers'. NOT

TRUE ... The information is largely confined to names, addresses and occasional dates. No-one's privacy need be threatened ... I am convinced that as people understand the Community Charge they will realize we have devised the fairest and simplest possible alternative to the rates' (*DoE News Release*, 5/5/89).

On several occasions the format of the Minister's article was tailored to include direct responses to criticisms made locally by opponents of the policy. In a feature article in the *Nottingham Evening Post*, the Minister condemned warnings from Graham Allen, a local Nottingham MP, as 'heartless scare mongering which conveniently ignore a crucial element of the new system' ('Truth on the Community Charge', 9/5/89). In the *Birmingham Evening Mail*, he attacked the 'groundless claims' made by Birmingham Councillor Roy Benjamin about the regressiveness of the tax, asserting he 'would do better pointing out to the people he represents that a generous rebates scheme will operate to help the poor' ('Community Charge – The Full Facts', 9/5/89). And in his article in the *Leicester Mercury*, he sarcastically suggested that 'someone should explain to the City's chairman of finance how the new system will work' ('City Rapped Over Poll Tax Fears', 9/5/89).

Apart from specific news management initiatives of this type, the Government also distributed a string of news releases to keep the media abreast of the progress towards implementation, and accentuate positive aspects of the policy. However, subtle changes were also evident in the tone and subject matter of these releases as the policy proceeded. These mirrored the progressive blandness of the Government's formal publicity campaigns, and suggested a growing realization that a crude 'good news' campaign would only exacerbate the Government's difficulties with the policy.*

As the 1987 Local Government Finance Bill negotiated its parliamentary passage, these releases frequently displayed a bullish optimism about the probity and likely popularity of the policy. A précis of a written answer by the Local Government Minister Michael Howard confidently predicted that

* In March 1990 disaffection with the policy in Whitehall had grown so intense that it was alleged that there had been 'no tears shed' by Bernard Ingham's team of information officers when the job of Head of Information at the DoE was given to a civil servant, 'For the principal task of the DoE Press office in the coming months will be to justify the poll tax. Not many Whitehall PR men see that as a rewarding task' (*Guardian*, 2/3/90: 6).

'most households will be better off with the Community Charge than they are now with the rates' (*DoE News Release*, No. 16, 13/1/88). In March 1988, a summary of a speech by the Environment Secretary confidently concluded the new system would 'enable the electorate, through the councillors they elect, to put local government under greater pressure to deliver value for money' (*DoE News Release*, No. 192, 28/3/88). The next month saw another environment minister congratulating the prudence of local authorities in making early preparations for the introduction of the Charge in England and Wales in 1990 (*DoE News Release*, No. 211, 11/4/88). Additional releases signalled the generosity of Government provisions for the transitional period ('Government Capital Allocations Will Help Councils Prepare For Community Charge', *DoE News Release*, No. 213, 13/4/88; 'More Help For People on Low Incomes to Pay Community Charge', *DoE News Release*, No. 214, 14/4/88). After the Bill had passed through the Lords, another release sought to allay concerns about the technical adequacy of the new system by highlighting a report from an independent consultancy firm that suggested the administrative costs of implementing the tax would not exceed those for the existing rating system (*DoE News Release*, No. 356, 23/6/88).* A simultaneous release provided projected figures for the tax in England and Wales based on 87/88 figures that revealed 'many of the highest Community Charges would have been substantially reduced this year had the Government's proposals for rate reform been fully in place' (*DoE News Release*, No. 357, 22/6/88: 1).

One of the two news releases that marked the receipt of the Royal Assent for the 1988 Local Government Act variously highlighted the munificence of the rebates and exemptions to the poll tax; the benefits of a national system for rating businesses; and the 'greatly simplified' new grant system that would 'take account of special local arrangements' (*DoE News Release*, No. 462, 29/7/88, 1–3). The other release emphasized how the new Act was 'an achievement for which millions will be grateful' (*DoE News Release*, No. 463, 29/7/88).

As the date for implementation in Scotland approached, and the Government geared itself for its major public relations offensive in England and

* The Minister's interpretation diverged tangentially from that of the Labour Party. According to the Shadow local government spokesperson on the same day: 'The Government has just paid Price Waterhouse £60,000 in order to confirm that the POLL TAX will be the worst 'value for money' tax in the UK' (Labour Party News Release [Jeff Rooker's Office], 23/6/88).

Wales, the advocacy of these news releases became even more explicit. In two releases later that year, local government minister, John Gummer, highlighted the key role local authorities would have in implementing the Community Charge (*DoE News Release*, No 543, 3/10/88), and claimed the new system was 'morally superior to the present system of domestic rates' (*DoE News Release*, No. 557, 7/10/88: 1). In the latter release, the Minister openly disparaged non party political opponents to the poll tax. In his words: 'the question I might ask in passing is why none of the moralizing clergy and lay people who have fulminated against the Community Charge has ever raised a whimper against the immorality of the rating system? No Bishops delivered petitions to No. 10 about the poor hit by the rates. Contrast that with the fairness of the Community Charge' (*ibid.*: 2–3).

However, as the Government's political difficulties intensified, the tone of these releases becomes far more measured in style and defensive in aspect. In March 1989, a reassurance was issued that the privacy of individuals would be completely protected under the Community Charge (*DoE News Release*, No. 145, 17/3/89). However, as criticisms increased about the conduct of certain local authorities during the registration process, an appended release was issued by Nicholas Ridley that urged local authorities to comply with data protection regulations (*DoE News Release*, No. 344, 19/6/89). In announcing an additional PR campaign on poll tax rebates, another minister acknowledged the growth of public concern, but predicted that 'this simple guide answers key questions about how rebates are worked out' (*DoE News Release*, No. 336, 15/6/89: 1).

The equivocation in the tone of the news releases increased as internal dissent within the Conservative Party intensified. In a news release detailing the changes in the transitional arrangements for the implementation of the policy, Local Government Minister, Lord Hesketh, acknowledged that 'the Government understands the concern which some have expressed about the arrangements for the safety net' ('Transitional Relief for Community Charge Payers', *DoE News Release*, No. 530, 11/10/89: 2). By the time the tax exploded on to the national political agenda in early 1990, and the Government's position became increasingly beleaguered, optimistic assessments of the policy's implementation became far rarer. The only exceptions were a flurry of releases from one junior minister ('David Hunt Hails Major Success for Community Charge Implementation', *DoE News Release*, No. 683, 13/12/89; 'Councils Forecasts of Community Charges Start to Come Down', *DoE News Release*, No. 36, 23/1/90; 'Community

Charge Will Improve Local Government Says David Hunt', *DoE News Release*, No. 61, 31/1/90). More typically, the releases accenuated the few positive aspects ('Larger Rate Reductions For Many Businesses From April', *DoE News Release* No. 692, 11/12/89, 'Sports Clubs to Gain From New Rates', *DoE News Release* No. 180, 19/3/90); reapportioned blame ('David Hunt Expresses Concern Over Standard Community Charge Levels' *DoE News Release* No. 183, 21/3/90); or reiterated the munificence and magnanimity of Government' support ('Charge Payers to Get £350million in Transitional Relief', *DoE News Release* No. 153, 7/3/90; '£21million grant to fund councils' cost of Community Charge Transitional Relief', *DoE News Release*, No. 178, 19/3/90; 'Minister Gives Camden More Time To Collect Rent', *DoE News Release* No. 231, 4/4/90). It was only from within the confines of this contained rhetorical logic that the Secretary of State could predict that local government in Britain 'now had the structure to operate competatively [sic] in a more complex and demanding world' ('Local Government Well Placed for the 21 Century', *DoE News Release*, No. 207, 28/3/90).

From April 1990, Government poll tax news releases focused on one particularly controversial aspect of the legislation: the decision to restrict (or 'Charge cap') poll tax levels in 22 Labour authority areas. However, these releases concentrated on the practice rather than the principles of these restrictions ('Chris Patten Caps Lambeth', *DoE News Release*, 250, 10/4/90; 'Camden Accepts Charge Cap', *DoE News Release*, No. 269, 26/4/90; 'Chris Patten Sets Hillingdon Charge Cap', *DoE News Release*, No. 350, 6/6/90; 'Chris Patten Sets Charge Caps For Basildon, Bristol and Doncaster', *DoE News Release*, No. 371, 18/6/90; 'Chris Patten Sets Charge Caps for 16 Councils', *DoE News Release*, No. 394, 2/7/90). Only one release indirectly addressed broader questions about the probity of these measures. Issued on behalf of the then Minister for Local Government and Inner Cities, the document warned local authorities that 'spending can't go on' and that the Government would not hesitate to use its powers more widely the following year should any authority, in the grip of 'leisure-centre-itis', seek to exploit public confusion and distrust of the poll tax by levying higher amounts than were entirely necessary. The Minister ignored rather than confronted the criticism that charge capping undermined the central principle of accountability, by concluding with the confident and dire warning to high spending authorities that 'in due course the electorate will find them out' (*DoE News Release*, No. 392, 29/6/90: 1).

Through the summer of 1990 the distribution of the releases became more intermittent and their focus shifted to the working of the new business rate system ('Business Rates Appeals Leaflet Published', *DoE News Release*, No. 402, 5/7/90; 'Small Shops Rates Bills Fall', *DoE News Release*, No. 433, 19/7/90; 'New Regulations on Business Rates Laid', *DoE News Release*, No. 477, 6/9/90). However, by the time the tensions in the senior levels of the Conservative Party spiralled towards open conflict and the deposition of the Prime Minister, official releases on local finance became exclusively concerned with expenditure targets of the Government and other macro-economic objectives ('Local Government Finance – England: Statement by Chris Patten, Secretary of State for the Environment', *DoE News Release*, No. 604, 31/10/90; 'Chris Patten Announces Department's Future Spending Plans', *DoE News Release*, No. 617; 8/11/90; 'Local Authorities Must Join Battle Against Inflation Says Chris Patten', *DoE News Release*, No. 628, 12/11/90), whilst occasionally stressing that the system was not as chaotic as was widely supposed ('Community Charge Collection Progress Encouraging, *DoE News Release*, No. 566, 16/10/90; 'Collection Figures Show That Nine Out of Ten are Paying the Community Charge', *DoE News Release*, No. 639, 14/11/90).

Following the accession of John Major to the post of Prime Minister and the appointment of Michael Heseltine as Environment Secretary with the brief to look at reform options for the poll tax, the principal purpose of these releases became that of signalling the Government's commitment to this review in response to public antipathy towards the system ('More Help for Standard Community Charge Payers', *DoE News Release*, No. 698, 13/12/90; 'Simplified Community Charge Bill for 1991/92', *DoE News Release*, No. 712, 14/12/90; 'Local Government Finance Settlement for 1991/92, Community Charge Reduction Scheme Announced', *DoE News Release*, No. 26, 17/1/91).

As the date for the Government's poll tax review approached, the tone of these releases became slightly more positive, albeit in a cautious manner. The Chancellor's shock announcement of a universal £140 reduction in all poll tax bills in March 1991 sparked a brief flurry of releases which gave details of these reductions ('Scheme for Reducing Community Charges for 1991/92', *DoE News Release*, No. 184, 19/3/91; 'Scheme for Reducing Community Charges for 1991/92', *DoE News Release*, No. 190, 20/3/91; 'Bill to Reduce Community Charge for 1991/92 is Published, *DoE News Release*, No. 194, 21/3/91;'Community Charge Reduction Scheme to Be

Extended', *DoE News Release*, No. 207, 26/3/91; 'Bill Reducing Community Charge Gets Royal Assent', *DoE News Release*, No. 216, 28/3/91), and strongly defended their legitimacy ('Criticism of Community Charge Reduction "Wrong Headed" Says Minister', *DoE News Release*, No. 191, 20/3/91; 'Government Announces That Over 14 Million People Will Get Full £140 Community Charge Reduction Scheme', *DoE News Release*, No. 246, 17/4/91; 'Average Community Charge in England £172 This Year', *DoE News Release*, No. 251, 23/4/91). A series of coincidental releases also assured the public that the tax would not penalize service personnel in the Gulf ('Gulf Crisis: Government Announces Special Grant to Local Authorities', *DoE News Releases*, No. 92, 19/2/91; 'Community Charge Compensation for Gulf Personnel', *DoE News Release*, No. 163, 14/3/91).

By comparison, the Council Tax was the subject of far fewer official DoE news releases, even during its legislative passage. When releases were distributed they tended to be descriptive and non-controversial ('New Local Government Finance Bill', *DoE News Release*, No. 333, 21/3/91; 'Royal Assent for New Bill Which Paves the Way for Council Tax', *DoE News Release*, No. 455, 25/7/91; 'Local Authorities Receive Guidance on Preparing for Council Tax', *DoE News Release*, No. 623, 17/10/91). Only one actively sought to open old wounds ('Councillors in Arrears Should Not Vote on Council Tax', *DoE News Release*, No. 617, 14/10/91).

From public relations to news management

> 'The poll tax has become a great big political problem for the Government. However presented, it has not worked out in the manner intended *and it has not been a surprise to hear that the Prime Minister's associates are now hinting in the heaviest manner, that major changes are going to be made in the next few months to the way the tax works*' (*6 pm News*, BBC Radio 4, 27 April 1990, our emphasis).

So what of the subtler forms of news management used by the Government in connection with the Community Charge? A considerable amount of the dialogue between the Government and national media élites is either unattributed or unreported, but nevertheless exerts a powerful influence upon the received wisdom of the media more generally. Did the Government exploit these hidden links in its attempts to promote support for the controversial policy or deflect criticisms of it?

Agenda-building is often most effective when achieved through surreptitious means (Gandy, 1982). In this respect the British Government is in an historically advantageous position. Not only does it have enormous resources available for publicity work, but as the locus of executive power and the pinnacle of the parliamentary system it can expect consistent and considerable media attention. At times such media attention can be seen as onerous and destabilizing, and a considerable amount of effort is made to conceal many aspects of government decision-making from media scrutiny. Nevertheless, the media's thirst for detailed inside information inevitably exposes them to political manipulation by governments through the selective and unattributed release of information and innuendo.

The routine mechanism for the covert diffusion of government information in Britain is the parliamentary lobby, a formal group of newspaper and broadcast journalists based at Westminster who receive almost daily briefings from senior government sources. Under Margaret Thatcher's leadership the lobby assumed an even more central importance to Government news management (Hennesy and Walker, 1987: 126). One consequence of this was that the Prime Minister's press secretary, Bernard Ingham, who was mainly responsible for the briefings, assumed an unprecedentedly influential position in government, and was frequently criticized for his use of the lobby to circumvent or undermine troublesome ministers, and even on occasion improvise Government policy (Harris, 1990).

Certainly, Ingham was a staunch supporter of the poll tax. Although he conceded in his memoirs that it 'did not take a genius' to identify the charge of unfairness that could be levied against the tax, he continued, 'Never can the Community Charge be cited as an example of Mrs Thatcher's uncaring nature. If she had not cared, she would not have tried to do anything about the value for money that citizens get out of their local authority' (Ingham, 1991: 244). All of the lobby journalists interviewed for the research confirmed his enthusiasm for the policy. In the words of one:

> 'Bernard always believed in it. And he believed in it in the same way as she did. And Bernard always thought that this is just, and that there's no reason why people earning different amounts, so long as they earn above level X, shouldn't pay the same because they are getting the

> same services. He believed that, lots of other people thought that was rubbish ... I mean he was a kind of, you know, playing the Geoff Boycott, forward defensive on it all the time. Hoping that in the end that we would just believe him' (Interview with authors).

Furthermore, Ingham was acutely conscious of the importance of effective public relations when implementing any new policy. Writing a few months before its abolition he commented:

> 'Policy formulated without regard for its presentation can come unstuck, too. Consider the poll tax. Leaving aside its alleged 'unfairness' in requiring the dustman to pay the same as the duke, little attempt was made in England and Wales to show, by specimen revaluations of property, that it could have been the lesser of two evils' (*The Times*, 22/9/92).

However, despite the loyalty and enthusiasm of this influential figure, the lobby, along with other more informal governmental briefings, were only very rarely used to ease the passage of the poll tax prior to its implementation in England and Wales. One notable exception occurred the weekend before the House of Commons vote on the Mates amendment, where lobby correspondents were briefed by unspecified senior Government sources about an alleged hidden agenda to the Conservative revolt: that Michael Mates was masking a future leadership challenge from Michael Heseltine (*Independent*, 19/4/88).*

However, with the tax's introduction in England and Wales, the lobby and other forms of informal news management became far more important. This was due to the intensity of the political crisis faced by the Government during this period. Damage limitation became the watch-word and ministers had to respond quickly to shore up the Government's diminishing credibility. Aside from their regular media appearances, which we deal with elsewhere, this centrally involved insinuating through more informal channels that the Government was seriously considering ways in which the worst excesses of the new system might be dealt with. In this way it was

* Ingham denied that the lobby had been the mechanism used to disseminate this smear. However, whatever its exact source, newspaper coverage on the eve of the vote on the Mates amendment clearly suggests there had been a high level, unattributed, Government briefing in which the question of Mates' real motives had been raised.

hoped to purvey the image of a government responding sensitively to public debate, as well as provide a convenient substitute for action.

However, these insinuations of action could on occasion damagingly backfire. In the lead up to the 1990 local government elections, the Prime Minister's parliamentary private secretary intimated to senior parliamentary journalists that the Government was considering further legislation in the summer that would significantly alter the operation of the new system. So intense was the resultant frenzy of media speculation that senior ministers were forced to publicly cool presumptions about the extent of any likely review and to deny the prospect of further legislation.

On occasions during this period, Ingham's 'straight bat' was replaced by a cross batted swipe at the Government's opponents. According to another lobby correspondent:

> '[The Lobby] was used very much to promote the story that what went wrong was that ... in the year in which the first poll tax bills were sent out, the year in which it came in, local councils increased their spending by a figure ... which from memory I think was 2 billion pounds. And obviously claimed that the reason the poll tax bills were so high was because councils had used the change from one taxation system to another as an excuse for raising their expenditure. Which I think is, was, a bit of a piece of sophistry' (Interview with authors).

Following the 1990 leadership contest, and the appointment of Heseltine and the announcement of the poll tax policy review, the lobby and other unattributed briefings became even more important. Before the announcement of the policy review these briefings were used to gauge political reactions to the various policy alternatives under consideration, confirming Sigal's point that 'the press is public opinion in the eyes of officials' (1973: 135). In the words of one journalist:

> 'There were kites flown. Certainly. There were various things talked about in the press about how to make the poll tax better ... I'm sure there was a lot of, you know, ideas tried out through the lobby to test the water ... The Heseltine stories on 20 per cent sound to me as though they are testing the water to see what reaction is like' (Interview with authors).

Or as another lobby correspondent wryly observed:

> 'Someone put it to me crudely as 'government by clapometer'. And in a sense that's true. You can be cynical about it, but you can also say, well listen that's why [Margaret Thatcher] got chucked out ... I think [John Major] was weak, and that he did too much to-ing and fro-ing and shillying and shallying and this and that, but having said that, it was really, yes he's bouncing it off us ... He was doing what any sensible politician would do, which is he was listening to what people thought' (Interview with authors).

Conservative Central Office and the Community Charge

We now turn our attention to the promotional work orchestrated nationally through the auspices of the Conservative Party's Central Office. Unrestricted by conventions of neutrality, one might have expected the Government to have used its party political resources extensively in promoting the poll tax. However, with one signal exception, the issue never featured prominently in the Conservative Party's official mainstream campaigning.

Despite the Community Charge's putative status as the 'flagship' of the Conservative Party's 1987 General Election campaign, the Party conspicuously avoided the issue during the battle. For example, this key note policy was mentioned in only two paragraphs of the Party's election manifesto, on the 62nd and 63rd pages of the 77 page document (*The Next Moves Forward*, Conservative Party Election Manifesto, May 1987) and was the subject of only one speech from the Environment Secretary during the campaign period, which was delivered to a constituency meeting in Streatham (Young, 1987). Instead, the principal emphasis of the Party's campaign strategy was to attack the deficiencies of Labour's defence and taxation policies (Miller, 1990), and when local government was mentioned in the Party's Election Broadcasts only two themes appeared: the success and popularity of the Government's 'Right to Buy' schemes (where people living in council accommodation could buy the property at a discounted rate) and the spectre of socialist extremism that, it was claimed, lurked behind Labour's modern new image. After the Election, the Conservative MP George Young observed, 'As a flagship, it did not appear to me to play much part in the hostilities, but perhaps there were sound nautical reasons for this' (*Guardian*, 14/9/87).

A *Guardian* editorial claimed this sin of omission was a deliberate one, and that ministers could 'scarcely believe their good fortune that the issue never really surfaced. When it briefly threatened to do so, Conservative Central Office was quick to counter claim that Labour, as the defender of the rating system, would carry out a comprehensive rates revaluation which would cripple householders in the wealthier parts of the country' (7/7/87: 10). It would seem this deliberate reticence was borne of a fear of stirring a damaging intra-party row and exciting public opinion in the pre-election period. Subsequent events confirm the astuteness of such a strategy. For example, in a leaked letter from the Environment Secretary's private secretary to one of the Prime Minister's private secretaries, during the parliamentary revolts of 1988, it was suggested that the reason for the intensity of the current controversy was that 'the issue is beginning to be understood by a number of back benchers' (*Independent*, 19/4/88: 2).

The spectre of internal dissent and the fear of public opinion inhibited all subsequent Central Office campaigning on the policy, with one exception: the local government elections in England and Wales in May 1990. In his book on the techniques and importance of political 'spin doctoring', Brendan Bruce, who was then Director of Communications for the Conservative Party (Bruce, 1990), provides an interesting insight into the underlying strategy of this particular campaign. Normally these elections would have been considered of secondary significance by the Conservative leadership. However, the growing support for Labour convinced senior party figures of the need for a high profile national campaign to wrest back the political initiative.

The campaign managers recognized that the election would be a rout, but were primed by 'psephological experts inside central office' that results in the model Thatcherite authorities of Wandsworth, Westminster and Bradford might buck the national trend. As it was clear the Party could not avoid the poll tax being the main issue, it was decided that the policy should be centre staged. The resulting communications strategy decided upon by Bruce and his colleague, Tim Bell, was predicated on three assumptions: that the tax would only bed down if people could be won round to the arguments about its fairness; that the real problem was the level of the bills; and that 'if we could prove that it was only under Labour-run councils that the charge was high, then we could rehearse one of our preferred general election themes: "Labour Cost You More"' (*ibid.*: 138).

The Party's national campaign strategy therefore focused on the three flagship councils of Wandsworth, Westminster and Bradford, briefing the media that should these low poll taxed areas remain Conservative, the Party would be highly satisfied regardless of their opponents' gains elsewhere. The adverts displayed in national and local press all focused on the central proposition that 'Conservative Councils Cost You Less'. (10 THINGS YOU SHOULD KNOW ABOUT THE COMMUNITY CHARGE [20/4/90)]; WHAT HAVE LABOUR DONE ABOUT THE COMMUNITY CHARGE? PUT IT UP [23/4/90]) and the Party Chairman, Kenneth Baker, toured the country wielding a 'Community Chargeometer' designed to demonstrate the disparities between poll tax levels in Tory and Labour councils (*The Times*, 19/4/90).

In Bruce's opinion their strategy was a complete success, for despite heavy losses across the country, when the Conservatives consolidated their control of Wandsworth and Westminster many media reported that Conservative prospects had not looked brighter for many months. Seeking to cultivate this train of thought the Party Chairman and his communications advisors immediately seized on each and every available photo-opportunity to perpetuate the image of party satisfaction with the election, and to deflect attention from 'the inconvenient statistics of Labour gains'. By the following Sunday:

> 'That night's television news and the following day's press were a director of communications' dream come true. Heseltine's ambition to thwart a Tory defeat had been abruptly terminated; the Prime Minister's position was strengthened; back bench morale improved; the polls reported we had cut Labour's lead by 7 percentage points; the poll tax argument had been shifted from one of principle to the size of the bill, and Central Office had proved that it could out campaign Labour' (*ibid.*: 140).

Although subsequent events proved these to be but phyrric victories, the Party leadership's successful redefinition of their 'worst ever local government results' (Butler and Kavanagh, 1992: 10) as a vindication of the tax, had important short term consequences by conveniently dampening debate about the future of the tax and Margaret Thatcher's premiership,

> 'The fact that the headlines were taken by the electoral triumphs in Wandsworth and Westminster ensured that the flat rate principle of the poll tax was retained and the results of the ministerial review ... promised only minor changes' (Gibson, 1990: 244–245).

After Margaret Thatcher's demise, and the announcement of the new Council Tax, the Party spin doctors worked strenuously to draw the sting out of the local finance debate. In tandem with the bland and low key Government publicity initiatives on the Council Tax, the Party played down the Council Tax in their campaigning, and in an ironic parallel with the 1987 General Election, conspicuously avoided the issue in the 1992 General Election. In the 1992 Conservative manifesto the Council Tax received a mention in one brief paragraph on the 38th page of the 50 page document:

> 'The Council Tax will be simple and straightforward to administer. It will be fair and will rightly reflect both the value of the property and the number of adults who live in it' (*1992 Conservative Party Manifesto*, March 1992: 38).

Information or propaganda? the propriety of the Government's information strategies

Throughout the 1980s concerns had increased about the Government's use of public funds to finance the promotion of politically controversial policies. It is one of the unwritten constitutional conventions of the British political system that publicly funded government publicity campaigns should not stray into the realms of party politics. A report by the Public Accounts Committee of the House of Commons, published in 1990, emphasized 'the importance of ensuring that government publicity campaigns are not, and are seen not to be, politically inspired' (Committee of Public Accounts, *op. cit.*: xii). Although the Committee stopped short of recommending legislation to ensure this distinction, it underlined 'the need to ensure propriety is made an explicit feature of campaign planning and implementation, *certainly for those campaigns identified as being particularly at risk*' (*ibid.*: xii, our emphasis).

With the introduction of the Community Charge, the conventional division between public information and party propaganda became very blurred, and many aspects of the publicity campaigns excited major controversies. Perhaps this was inevitable, given the extreme contentiousness of the proposals and the lack of any broad consensus as to their merits. Nevertheless, considering that the promotion of the policy was principally orchestrated through governmental rather than party resources, many of its aspects raised serious questions about the conflation of public and party interests by the Thatcher administration.

In October 1987, Labour's local government spokesperson complained that the booklet, *Paying for Local Government: The Need for Change*, contravened 1985 Cabinet Office guidelines that stipulated that Government publications should only be issued after the publication of a Bill or White Paper, or with the agreement of the Opposition Chief Whip (*Guardian*, 6/11/87). (At the time the booklet was produced only a Green Paper had been published.) Concerns were also expressed about the content of the leaflet, which it was felt overstepped the mark between information and promotion. A senior Civil Servant at the Department of Environment later conceded that the booklet was 'on the border line of overstepping the proprieties ... My recollection of that booklet was that it was too positive' (Interview with authors).

The *Step by Step Guide* was similarly denounced by the Opposition as 'a shameful use of taxpayers resources for propaganda to make [the] poll tax seem more acceptable ... This contrasts with the increased restrictions on local government publicity' (*Local Government Chronicle*, 20/1/89: 8).* However, objections were not only raised by parliamentary opponents to the tax. In 1989, the National Association of Citizen's Advice Bureaux refused to distribute the *Step by Step* guide through their offices because it was felt the booklet 'was setting out an essentially political argument about the Charge without giving the other side of the argument' (*Guardian*, 13/5/89).

However, these complaints about the propriety of the earlier publicity material paled in comparison to the furore over the blanket distribution of the leaflet *The Community Charge (The So-Called 'Poll Tax'): How it Will Work for You*, in May 1989, and the news management exercise that accompanied it.

The leaflet was launched on Monday, 8 May 1989 at a press conference attended by the Secretary of State for the Environment. However con-

* We are thankful to Bob Franklin for drawing our attention to this article.

troversy erupted before this occasion, when the Local Government Information Unit (LGIU) – a pressure group funded by the Labour Party and trades unions to campaign on behalf of local authorities – obtained an advance copy and distributed a detailed critique to national and local media which identified twelve 'errors of fact and misleading information'. These errors, it claimed, revealed the leaflet to be 'politically biased in its phraseology, and in what it includes, and what is left out' (LGIU News Release, 8/5/89: 3). When challenged about this on the day of the launch, the sponsoring minister completely refuted the claims of the LGIU, explaining:

> 'The intention was to get a leaflet which was just a straight factual leaflet. We've gone to great trouble to do that. It's even coloured yellow, so that it can't possibly be thought in any way to be party political ... And even so, after all this effort, one body of a rather extreme kind, suggests that it's biased. But I don't think the public will think it when they get it' (*Today*, BBC Radio 4, 8/5/89).

However, the dispute escalated the next day when Greenwich London Borough Council was granted an *ex parte* injunction in the High Court restraining the Environment Secretary from further distribution or publication of the leaflet. The focus of the Council's action was question 16 of the leaflet, which stated 'filling in the form does *not* mean you will have to pay the Community Charge for anyone else'. This, the Council's solicitors claimed, was a manifest piece of misinformation as it failed to refer to section 16 of the 1988 Local Government Act which stated that spouses and cohabitees were 'joint and severally liable' for their partner's charges. As such, the publication 'did not accord with the Government's conventions and standards for publications of this sort' (*The Times*, 17/5/89). The seriousness of this omission was compounded by the discovery that the equivalent literature distributed by the Welsh Office contained the caveat, 'in the case of husbands and wives living together, and couples living together as though they were married, each partner could be held responsible for the arrears owed by the other' (*Independent*, 11/5/89: 2).

The Government's embarrassment increased the following day when it emerged that distribution of the leaflets had continued in spite of the injunction, and ministers had to explain to enraged parliamentary opponents that news of the court's judgement had come too late to prevent the Post Office from continuing with their distribution.

At the full High Court hearing on the case, Lord Justice Woolf found for the Environment Secretary, concluding that the leaflet was not literally inaccurate. 'The worst that could be said about it was that it was misleading by omission. However, there had to be a selection and a selection was made. As a matter of law it could not be said that the department was not entitled to exercise its judgement in the way indicated' (Law Report, *The Times*, 17/5/89). When Greenwich Council decided not to appeal, distribution of the remaining 11 million leaflets continued.

The furore over the content and distribution of the poll tax leaflet was mirrored by controversy over its accompanying news management exercise. A spokesperson for the Department of the Environment insisted the main purpose of John Gummer's articles was 'to put right mistakes and misunderstandings and to ensure that the public had the correct information about the Community Charge' (*Guardian*, 13/5/89: 2). Another asserted: 'These are not political articles ... Where the Minister corrects misinformation, then attribution to local individuals is necessary' (*Independent*, 12/5/89). However, the targeted criticism of political opponents of the Government created considerable outrage. Leicester City Council was stung into releasing its own news release which complained about '... the possible misuse by the Government of civil servants and public money to run a politically biased campaign on the new poll tax' (Leicester City Council News Release, 11/5/89). David Blunkett, then Labour's shadow spokesperson on Local Government went further, claiming, 'the fact that civil servants are not only being used to promote propaganda, but also to attack individual opposition politicians takes the issue on from the abuse of taxpayers' money and into the realms of constitutional impropriety' (*Labour Parliamentary News Release [David Blunkett's Office]*, 12/5/89). In the House of Commons another Opposition MP questioned, 'is it one of the supreme ironies of history that at the same time as the Tory benches are praising President Gorbachev for trying to separate the party from the state, they are doing the same in Britain?' (*Hansard*, 16/5/89, col. 186).

Even the later 'toned down' Community Charge Benefits campaign attracted criticism. For example, confidential correspondence between Local Authority Associations and the Department of the Environment expressed concerns that the adverts would amount to a 'soft, subliminal selling of the poll tax', by giving a false impression of the actual availability of rebates under the new system. Similarly, Labour's Local Government Spokesperson spoke of the 'justified anxiety as to the exact nature of the Government's publicity campaign ... Soft selling the poll tax would be a gross misuse of taxpayers' money' (*Guardian*, 15/12/89). On the eve of the launch of the campaign in February 1990, the Local Government Information Unit complained:

> 'Once again, Government publicity spells out the good news, but leaves out the bad, People who are not eligible but who are misled by the campaign into thinking that they may get rebates will have to be told by their councils what the true position is ... No mention is made of the fact that it is central government which is the main determiner of poll tax levels' (*LGIU Briefing*, No. 36, Jan/Feb 1990: 1).

Overview of the Government strategy

From our discussion we can discern six key features in the Government's promotion of the Community Charge.

First, the promotion of the Community Charge was principally organized and funded at a *governmental* rather than *party* level. Second, in view of this and the intensely controversial nature of the policy, the tone and quality of these publicity initiatives challenged the conventional distinction between public information and party propaganda, if not in law, then in spirit. Third, from the outset the Government identified the media as a crucial factor in the battle for public opinion, and directed a considerable amount of attention towards them in its publicity work. Fourth, the public promotion of the tax was organized at both party and governmental level in a 'top down' manner; which in turn reflected the particular way in which the tax was conceived and implemented. Fifth, the timing of both governmental and party publicity initiatives were specifically determined by broader political considerations. The description of the Community Charge as the Conservatives' electoral flagship could not have been more inappropriate. Rather, there was a deliberate conspiracy of silence on the issue during the 1987 General Election. Sixth, the tone and management of the Government's public relations work altered dramatically as events proceeded. As the policy derailed, the tone of formal publicity material and news releases became more measured and defensive, and greater emphasis was placed on conventional strategies of news management to limit the political damage.

In the following chapters we compare these strategies with those of the main opponents of the tax, and consider their respective influence in shaping the terms of public and media debate on the issue.

Chapter 4

Promoting Dissent: Anti Poll Tax Campaigning

The political opposition to the Community Charge did not conform to conventional party political divisions or confine itself to the arena of party politics. Whereas all the main opposition parties trenchantly opposed the new tax, the policy also opened up wide divisions within the Conservative Party. Furthermore, many non party political institutions openly campaigned against the tax, including influential opinion leaders from the trade unions, the voluntary sector, the business community, and the clergy.

In this chapter we identify the campaigning strategies of some of these main protagonists. Given the diversity of political opposition, this review is necessarily selective. However, through these case studies, we intend to demonstrate both the variety of this political opposition, as well as the internal tensions that divided it. For the political battle over the poll tax was not just a contest between supporters and critics of the poll tax, but also among its opponents.

Labour Party opposition

It is inappropriate to talk about Labour Party opposition to the poll tax in any unitary sense. This is partly because Labour opposition mobilized at both local and national level. However, even more crucially, although the consensus within the Labour Party against the Community Charge was absolute and implacable, there was no equivalent agreement as to how much emphasis should be placed on the issue, what methods of resistance should be advocated, or what aspects of the policy's shortcomings should be consistently brought to the public's attention. Therefore it is necessary to differentiate between Labour's *national* campaigning against the poll tax, as sanctioned by the Party's National Executive Committee; semi-autonomous, *local* initiatives (most significantly those authored by Labour municipal local authorities); and the activities of Party *mavericks*, who not only sought to oppose the tax, but also the terms of political opposition recommended by the Party's leadership. In this section we focus on Labour's national and local campaigning. The activities of Party mavericks are addressed in our examination of the anti poll tax movement, because of the central role they played in its formation and campaigning (Lavalette and Mooney, 1992/3).

Labour's national campaigning

There were clear parallels between the timing and intensity of Labour's national campaigning against the poll tax and the Government's promotional timetable. Just as Conservative Central Office sought to exclude the issue from the 1987 General Election, so Labour neglected the topic during the campaign. The poll tax received one fleeting mention in the Party's Election broadcasts (*Observer*, 26/3/91: 25); was mentioned in only three sentences in the Party's official manifesto; and was referred to incidentally in one national newspaper advertisment at the end of the campaign ('If you're thinking of voting Conservative, here's a final cheque-list', 11/7/87).

However, after the Conservatives' emphatic electoral victory, and as moves began to promote the new tax, the Labour Party launched its first concerted, extra-parliamentary campaign on the issue in England and Wales. In September 1987, at the Party conference, the Shadow Environment spokesperson announced the campaign would variously draw attention to the harshness and unfairness of the poll tax; the preponderance of losers under the new arrangements; the 'massive increase in Whitehall control over local communities'; 'the sinister implications for personal and civil liberties'; the inadequacy of the rebate provisions; and the undermining of electoral and democratic processes by driving people off the electoral register. Campaign leaflets were drawn up for public distribution and a comprehensive advice note was sent to all Labour groups, local parties and affiliated organizations (*Labour Party News Release* [Campaign and Communications Directorate], 23/9/87).

In Scotland, the Party had mobilized earlier against the policy and initially adopted a more combative approach. In early 1987, the Scottish Labour

Party launched a 'Stop It' campaign, which used petitions, information briefings and legal challenges to draw public attention to the issue and pressurize the Government. One of the major initiatives was a 'send it back' campaign which advised the public, through leaflets and press advertisments, to query their registration forms and thereby overburden the registration process. The Party also urged councils not to collect the tax (Barker, 1992). However, this flirtation with a virtual non payment stance was soon abandoned, and after September 1988 the Scottish Party's campaigning conformed more closely to the national strategies employed in England and Wales.

In January 1988, at a national press conference, the Labour Party leader announced the launch of a nationwide anti poll tax petition. The collection continued until 1990. A few months later, in the local government elections held during the parliamentary passage of the poll tax, the Party attempted to focus public and media attention on the likely inequities of the new tax. For example, one national advertisment enquired:

> 'What would you say about a tax that cost a couple in a small flat twice as much as a millionaire in a mansion?'

At a national press conference marking the launch of Labour's election campaign, the Shadow Environment spokesperson revelled in the 'huge and growing embarrassment' of the Conservative Party over the poll tax, and the Shadow Women's spokesperson highlighted the particularly severe impact the tax would have on women (*The Morning Star*, 14/4/88).

In February 1989, the Party's National Executive Committee produced a new campaign strategy comprising four key elements: to ensure that the responsibility for the policy was blamed on the Government and not local authorities; to give people the 'facts' on the poll tax and dispel public ignorance; to help people avoid its most punitive aspects; and to argue for a system of local taxation which would relate to people's ability to pay ('Poll Tax Facts', Labour Party, 1989). Aside from releasing a further swathe of campaign packs and briefings, it was decided to try to get the Party's poll tax protest sponsored. Newspaper advertisments urged the public to sign their name to the Party protest, and also contribute to Party funds. These initial advertisments were financed through an appeal to Party members that raised £80,000 in 5 days (*Guardian*, 31/3/89) and continued into 1990. Also in February 1989 a 'weekend of activity' at local level was announced which was to form the start of two months of campaigning activity prior to the May local county council elections.

Throughout that year, pressure increased from some back-bench MPs and Party activists, for the Party to adopt a more aggressive stance in its campaigning. This largely focused on urging the Party to organize a national demonstration against the tax. In personal correspondence to the shadow local government spokesperson, one back bench MP wrote:

> 'I cannot stress too much the strategic importance of the Party backing a demonstration in London as a way of boosting the morale of the campaign. It would also enable the Labour Party to be the centre of attention for all the many people who would want to do something about the tax once they realize the enormity of its unfairness' (23/8/89).

However, Labour's National Executive Committee resisted these calls, preferring to focus their national campaigning on sponsored advertisements, parliamentary activity and media appearances.

In September 1989, further national guidelines were distributed to all Labour controlled councils, advising them of their duty to implement the tax, and the need to deflect the blame on to the Government. One of the key additional recommendations was that Labour councils should conduct high profile public information campaigns, to ensure a high take-up of poll tax benefits (*Guardian*, 29/9/89). In March 1990, this directive resulted in a series of local 'Claim It' campaigns, which particularly targeted young people as concerns grew that the tax would encourage large numbers of potential Labour voters to voluntarily disenfranchise themselves in an attempt to avoid paying the tax (*Guardian*, 30/3/90).*

Also in early 1990, the Labour Party moved to take advantage of the Conservatives' disarray by producing a 'dossier of dissent', entitled 'A Political Cyanide Pill', which listed critical comments against the tax made by Conservative politicians (*Guardian*, 2/4/90). However, as the fierce

* The concern about the detrimental impact poll tax non-registration might have on Labour's prospects in key marginal constituencies intensified over the next two years. In early 1992 Labour Party headquarters issued a campaign pack to local parties, highlighting this pernicious effect of the tax and encouraging them to assist in voter registration drives ('The Right to Vote: A Guide to Electoral Registration', *Labour Party Campaign Pack*, February 1992).

controversy over the tax intensified prior to the 1990 local government elections, Labour also attempted to broaden the political agenda. Whereas Conservative Central Office orchestrated a single issue campaign on the Community Charge, Labour's strategy organized itself around the unifying theme of the Party as 'The People Who Can, Not the People Who Con', and highlighted the discrepancy between Conservative Party promises and its performance (*The Times*,19/4/90). This formed part of a new tactic to try to implicate a wider range of senior Tories in the policy failures of the Government, rather than just the then Conservative Party leader (*The Sunday Times*, 29/4/90). And just as Margaret Thatcher was marginalized in Labour's political attack, so her flagship policy was relegated in prominence (*Independent*, 14/6/90). In a series of newspaper adverts and campaign booklets, a litany of Conservative failures was listed – from the inadequacies of the youth training provision, to the growth in interest rates, mortgage repossessions, and general levels of poverty. In this list, the poll tax and the Uniform Business Rate were relegated to fifth and seventh place ('Don't Fall for the Con', Labour Advertisment, *The Times*, 18/4/90).

Like the Government, the opposition saw the media as playing a highly significant role in framing and informing public perceptions of the policy. For example, the centrally produced campaign and publicity material distributed to Party activists repeatedly emphasized the importance of spreading the bad news via the media. In the 1989 'Information and Campaign Pack' local activists were urged:

> 'Organize a survey in your local shopping centre using the following question: 'When poll tax starts next year who do you think will control most of the money your council gets to run services like refuse collection, schools, libraries and street sweeping – councillors or the government ministers?' Arrange for the local press to take pictures of you conducting your survey. Issue a press release containing the results of your survey along with the true answer ... Find out how much the poll tax is costing your council to implement ... Send a letter to your local newspaper – a suggested model letter is provided ... Set up a Labour Party hot line – it just needs a telephone line and a recording machine. Advertise the phone number in your local papers, on radio and in newsletters. Ask people to leave their name and address if they want advice on civil liberty issues ... Organize a photo-call of party members of different ages submitting their rebate applications. Talk to the editors of local papers asking them to run special features on claiming

rebates and transitional relief ('Poll Tax Facts', *Labour Party Campaign Pack*, 1989: 2–9).

However, at a national level, there was a clear disparity in the Party's media strategy on the issue. Throughout the 1980s, the Labour Party had become increasingly sensitive to questions of political marketing and the agenda-setting power of the national media, and in 1985 appointed Peter Mandelson as their first ever Director of Campaigns and Communication. Over the next few years, Labour's Shadow Communications Agency (SCA) – a team of volunteer advertising agents, media professionals and marketing consultants convened by Mandelson, who operated independently of the paid staff at Labour's headquarters – exerted a considerable influence on the direction and presentation of Labour activities, redesigning 'Labour's campaigning strategy and its political priorities' (Hefferman and Marqusee, 1992: 210). However, the SCA was only rarely used during the policy's early stages to transmit Labour's message of dissent about the poll tax. Rather, the Party's national media news management on the issue initially relied upon the individual initiative of those junior shadow spokespersons – and their researchers – most closely connected with the parliamentary debate on the tax. These sources experienced two problems in generating media attention to the tax and its implications. First, because they weren't senior shadow spokespersons, their proclamations weren't invested with equivalent status by journalists, and therefore had less assurance of gaining media attention (as one told us, 'Things received the media's attention when they were pushed by the press office of the Labour Party ... We were battling against the tide'). Second, being denied the services of the Party's main publicity resources, they had only limited secretarial and research resources at their disposal to disseminate information.

Nevertheless, 'by press-releasing everything' (as one shadow spokesperson put it) these politicians did provide the national media with a fairly intensive stream of negative information about the tax during its parliamentary stages. For example, after Jeff Rooker's appointment as shadow spokeperson for local government in 1987, he distributed a string of news releases on the poll tax as the prospect of legislation approached. One of his earliest releases (21/7/87) questioned 'Is the Poll Tax Racist?', and provided evidence that Asian households would lose heavily under the new system. Two months later he distributed figures which suggested that over 56 per cent of adults would be worse off under the new system (14/9/87). He also distributed the text of a speech which described how the poll tax would accelerate the erosion of local government autonomy (21/9/87). Three days later he listed twenty eight Conservative MPs in whose constituencies single adult households would pay more under the poll tax than they would under the rates (24/9/87), and the next day highlighted the structural inequities of the new system, its constitutional implications and the threats it posed to individual privacy (25/9/87).

Once the legislative process had begun Rooker produced specific illustrations of how the tax might detrimentally affect particular localities (3/11/87); examples of Government propaganda abuses (5/11/87); and evidence about the structural regressiveness of the tax (12/11/87). On the eve of the Bill's Second Reading he published the findings of a survey he had conducted in his Perry Barr consituency which suggested that 75 per cent of adults would lose under the new tax (14/12/87). As the Bill entered its committee stages, and the Government moved to guillotine the process, he condemned its undemocratic actions and highlighted 'crucial technical questions' that remained unanswered due to the foreshortening of the committee stage (20/2/88 and 26/2/88). A fortnight later he claimed that a million single pensioners would lose under the tax, and in a footnote warned journalists,'Remember every time Tory minister[s] talk of "households" instead of "people or adults" be very careful about taking the figures at face value' (8/3/88).

Two days later he drew attention to the likely complexities of the registration process (10/3/88), and in a release the following month highlighted a 'misleading gallup poll' conducted in his constituency, which he suspected might be used to challenge his independent projections of poll tax levels in the area (10/3/88). As the Local Government Finance Bill completed its parliamentary passage, these releases became far more intermittent. In June, he focused on the high cost of the tax compared with the rates ('Poll Tax Costs to be Double the Rates', 23/6/88), and the next month he drew attention to the civil liberties issues raised by the new tax (14/7/88), as well as the naïveté of an influential national radio programme in uncritically accepting a minister's claims about the generosity of poll tax rebates,

> 'Most unusually the BBC *Today* programme were appallingly badly briefed for the item on the poll tax rebate issue in respect of poor disabled people broadcast this morning' (*Labour Party News Release* [Jeff Rooker's office], 20/7/88).

Alongside news releases, Labour's environment team also staged a variety of parlimentary pseudo-news events to attract media attention. As Rooker explained:

> 'We tried to manipulate the poll tax Bill programme so that when we were raising a key issue like student nurses, we'd have a public gallery full of nurses in uniform. When we did carers, David Blunkett organized a whole wodge of young carers, this that and the other to come in. We were photographed outside ... We had to manipulate our own timetable so that we finished where we wanted to finish. So it was always good to start on a Tuesday and Thursday morning with something really good, because the media would be better on a morning than they would in the afternoon ... We actually, actively sought to manipulate the media, and to say, look here is a good point that we're doing today, and let the press gallery know what was on this morning on the poll tax, and this is what's on on Thursday ... We weren't passive about it at all. Because we knew the more people knew about the poll tax, the less they liked it' (Interview with authors).

As the poll tax's introduction in England and Wales approached, a similar shift occurred in the Labour Party's media strategy to that of the Government. No longer required to draw media attention to the issue, Shadow spokespersons became less involved in formal PR stunts and more actively engaged in news management work. Although principally aimed at exerting maximum pressure on the Government over the policy, this work also involved damage limitation – whether in defending their preferred reform option or challenging Government accusations about their responsibility for violence at poll tax demonstrations,

> 'We had to handle ourselves very carefully around the time of the mass demonstration that turned into a riot [Trafalgar Square, 31 March 1990]. We had to be careful that we were able to maximize the impact of people's frustration and worry, and minimize anything that turned on us in terms of being associated either with the riots or with the non-payment campaign' (Shadow spokesperson, interview with authors).

Once the abolition of the poll tax had been announced, and legislation for the Council Tax was pushed through, the media became the principal means by which the Labour party sought to challenge the Government in this policy area. Whereas the Government sought to stifle continued debate about local taxation as the prospect of a General Election loomed closer, the Labour front bench strove to maintain media attention on the issue. However, this proved an increasingly frustrating task. As David Blunkett complained during the committee stages of the Council Tax Bill:

> 'We are here, 16 hours a day, plugging away and the world is going on outside. And everybody's interested in anything but what we're saying and doing. We're trying to raise the same kind of issues about the anomalies, the unfairness, the critical, technical questions which falls on the Council Tax, but its proving very difficult' (Interview with authors).

During the 1992 General Election, Labour again sought to revitalize the poll tax issue in the final week before polling, by featuring the issue in two of its daily news conferences, and making it the central issue in a keynote address by the Shadow environment spokesperson five days before the Election (Deacon and Golding, 1992; Berry, 1992). However, here, once again, it found media attention to the issue conspicuously elusive.

Inhibitions on Labour's national campaigning

> 'Revolution cancelled due to shortage of free rail passes' (Labour MP's memorandum to his political researcher, July 1989).

The tone and intensity of the Labour Party's national campaigning against the poll tax attracted considerable criticism from within and outside the Party. For many, the Party's national campaigning displayed an unfortunate insularity, timidity and passivity (Donnell, 1990; Peck, 1987; Burns, 1992). In March 1990, the Chairman of the Party's Scottish Local Government group openly chastised the Party's National Executive for its inertia on the issue in England and Wales:

> 'The NEC let us down, they let Scotland down, and they refused to organize the mass demonstrations and rallies that were necessary ... We asked you to lead and you refused to lead, and the National Executive's duty is to pick up our challenge' (*Guardian*, 10/3/90: 2).

Questions were also raised about the interpretative dimensions of Labour's campaign agenda. While it is true the Party's campaign material often addressed the constitutional and democratic issues posed by the poll tax, these complex but significant issues became less prominent in the Party's front line campaigning as the political debate developed. For example, one Labour MP who consistently sought to focus public attention to the detrimental impact the tax would have on the franchise, complained:

> 'I've raised the matter in parliamentary Labour meetings ... But I haven't found it being picked up in people's speeches. And I have always had the feeling that it was felt a bit dangerous to stress the *poll* tax bit of it' (Interview with authors).

Certainly, hindsight raises some major questions about the conduct, content and timing of the Party's national campaign. Why did the Party collude in a conspiracy of silence on the policy during the 1987 General Election? Why did the NEC persistently resist calls to organize national demonstrations in England and Wales prior to its introduction? And what factors might have progressively inhibited the breadth of the Party's campaign agenda?

Undoubtedly, pecuniary restrictions played their part. During the late 1980s the Party's funds were under severe pressure, and the resources were not readily available for organizing widespread public campaigns. In February 1989, the Party's Director of Campaigns and Communication stressed that the Party's 'Poll Tax Protest' adverts could only be financed 'if sufficient funds are generated' (*Guardian*, 15/2/89: 25). Later that year, in personal correspondence to a member of the Campaign Group of Labour MPs, the Party's Local Government spokesperson explained 'the major reason' why the NEC had rejected calls for a national anti poll tax demonstration was 'lack of funds' (31/7/89). Certainly, the Labour Party could not match the glossy and very expensive information subsidies, so central to the Government's promotional activities. Would-be, anti poll tax activists had to pay £2 for Labour's 1989 campaign pack.

However financial limitations, in themselves, do not adequately explain the often reticent nature of the Party's national campaigning. There was also a failure of political imagination at senior levels of the Party as to the likely unpopularity of the issue. This was most evident before the 1987 General Election. As Pimlott (1988) explains, at that stage the likely impact of the tax was not fully understood, particularly as the initial proposals were for a ten-year phasing in period, which would have meant a radically different tax to the one eventually imposed in 1989 and 1990.

The Party's initial insensitivity to the issue was further exacerbated by factionalism within the ranks of the parliamentary Party. As one former shadow spokesperson conceded:

> 'I went through the general election like the majority of Labour MPs in England [did], and never referred to it in public ... In '88/'89 I realized the biggest mistake the Labour Party ever made was treating the Scottish legislation [The Abolition of Rates in Scotland etc. Act, 1987] as a piece of Scottish legislation and not British legislation. We should have had a bigger input ... But the fact is that the Scottish legislation was treated by English Labour MPS as Scottish. We didn't interfere, we didn't take any notice, we knew it was horrible and everyone was having a rough time, but it didn't affect us' (Interview with authors).

Furthermore, Labour's low profile on the issue reflected a failure of political nerve. This was particularly evident before the 1987 General Election, when the Party was under greatest pressure from Conservative Party and media attack over the excesses of the 'Loony Left' in local government (Goldsmiths' University Media Research Group, 1987). In response to this problem, the Party leadership had distanced themselves from the activities of several high profile Labour authorities, and purged them of insurgent influences. The coverage given to this continued conflict convinced many senior figures within the Shadow Cabinet that local government was an issue that the Party debated at its peril, particularly during election campaigns, where political stereotypes exert a powerful influence on electoral preferences. Accordingly, it was decided that the Party's interests were best served by avoiding the issue at such a sensitive time. This decision was not universally popular. As one Labour politician explained:

> '[The Labour leadership] believed that local government was bad news. They believed that local finance was even worse news and therefore you steered clear of it. Whereas many of us realized that it wasn't "bad news", there was a battle to be had. The Conservatives had managed to create an atmosphere which we certainly had to change, and we'd do so by revealing what the poll tax was all about. Not merely its financial disadvantages to individuals, but the philosophies and

values behind it which would lead to all the kind of problems and difficulties that it eventually led to' (Interview with authors).

After the 1987 General Election, and as the prospect of local financial reform became unavoidable, these general concerns about the Party's difficulties with the local government issue distilled into two specific problem areas that continued to inhibit the Party's campaigning up until the tax's implementation.

The first concerned which method of opposition to the policy the Party should advocate. Although there was initial indecision as to how closely the Party should participate in a non-payment campaign, by 1988, the Party's leadership had firmly rejected the non-payment stance and committed itself to legal methods of opposition. This reflected a 'new realism' in the Party about the need to pursue electability, whatever the cost to the Party's radical credentials (Lavalette and Mooney, 1989). Such a position was not popular with many Party activists and these tensions came to a head in 1990, when thirty Labour back bench MPs announced their intention not to pay the tax, and Labour councillors from Liverpool, Haringey and Islington initially refused to set a poll tax and advocated a policy of non collection (*Guardian*, 29/3/90). At a keynote speech at the Scottish Labour Party's annual conference, Neil Kinnock railed against the 'Toytown revolutionaries' who suported non-payment and exhorted them to 'examine their consciences' (*The World Tonight*, Radio 4, 9/3/90).* The Party's difficulties on this issue were exacerbated by coincidental violence at several of the poll tax demonstrations held at that time, which the Conservatives sought to conflate with the illegal act of non-payment and the defiance of the thirty Labour MPs.

The second problematic area for Labour was in deciding on a policy alternative either to the Rates or the Community Charge. On his appointment as shadow local government spokesperson, Jeff Rooker warned:

> 'I am not prepared to see the Labour party walk naked into the debating chamber, which is what a crude and negative opposition to the poll tax will amount to, if we are seen only to be defenders of the present unfair rating system. We shall need to use our brains so that we are seen to be

* Ultimately this disagreement resulted in the deselection of two Labour MPs (Hefferman and Marqusee, *op. cit.*).

positive, by seeking to offer workable, popular alternatives – which can be understood' (News Release [Jeff Rooker's Office], 27/7/87).

However, deciding on a workable, popular alternative, proved a difficult task. Initially the Party proposed a twin tax system which combined a property tax based on capital values with a local income tax. The Government's response was to produce 'selective comparisons' of the amount paid under the poll tax and Labour's proposals. As the Environment Secretary challenged:

> '[The Shadow Environment Spokesperson] does not want [Labour's alternative] to be exposed, but we are going to expose his little wheeze. I invite all MPs to put down questions; there is a lot of good material here' (*The Times*, 26/1/89: 10).

By 1989, Labour retreated from this option, and recipients of the new campaign pack were told they would receive 'a more detailed briefing on Labour's alternative to the poll tax once our proposals have been refined' (*Poll Tax Facts: Information and Campaign Pack*, 1989: 1). In September, at the NEC's pre-conference meeting it was decided to abandon this two tax system, and invest more energies in exploring other options (*The Times*, 27/9/89). By early 1990, the provisional, preferred option became a single property tax based on capital values. Although Labour avoided being too specific on the details of their proposals, the Government sought to deflect media and public scrutiny on to the deficiencies of Labour's 'roof tax'. In response, the NEC initiated a further high level policy review (*Guardian*, 25/5/90), which addressed whether the property component of the tax should be based on capital or 'notional rentable' values, and whether its linkage to ability to pay should be effected by extending rebate provisions, or linking local taxation to income tax codes (*Guardian*, 19/6/90). Eventually it was decided to support a return to thc previous rating system on the old valuations and an improved rebate system, with a revaluation to be based on house prices, building costs and private market rents to be conducted after two years (*Guardian*, 24/7/90).

What is significant about both these problematic policy areas for Labour, was how centrally the media featured in their political calculations. When the Shadow local government minister warned of the dangers of Labour 'walking naked into the conference' chamber, he was also keenly aware of the dangers of entering the media arena in a similar state of undress:

> *'Labour supporters and least of all Labour MPs, do not want to be in the position of having to cringe each time a shadow minister appears on the box, knowing the first line of attack on the POLL TAX will be converted rapidly into a defensive position on the illegality argument.* Overseas Labour Parties are incredulous at the prospect of the British Labour Party showing an outstanding degree of political incompetence, by wasting energy on the illegality argument at the expense of the real issue of the POLL TAX itself. *Those who think they can get away with both on the media are deluding themselves'* (News Release [Jeff Rooker's Office], 14/9/88, our emphasis).

The Party's prevarication and evasiveness over their policy alternative were borne of a similar anxiety. According to *The Times'* Chief Political Correspondent, Labour's renunciation of the twin-tax option reflected concerns in the senior echelons of the Party that 'the value of the propaganda weapon which they believe the poll tax represents to them should not be undermined by Tory charges that it wants to replace one tax with two' (*The Times*, 27/9/89: 2). Similarly, the later decision to discard a 'capital value' property tax system, was based 'more on presentational problems rather than on practicality' (*Guardian*, 19/6/90).

The problems Labour faced in deciding upon and defending a coherent stance on the non-payment issue also had a knock-on effect in terms of the issues the leadership was prepared to emphasize in their parliamentary and media campaigning. As one Shadow Spokesperson explained:

> 'The problem for us, and there's a real issue here, is that the more we pressed the question of the register and its intrusiveness, the more we knew we would accelerate the existing non-payment campaign, non-registration, non-voting campaign. And there was a genuine ambivalence. That we had to be extremely careful that we didn't discourage people from registering to vote. As it is 4 million disappeared off the census, so that was something that we were right to be concerned about. So it did temper a little the way we described the likely intrusiveness, into people's relationships, into who lived in the household, on the grounds that this could be a major disadvantage to the Labour

> Party in electoral terms, and I think that's proved to be the case' (Interview with authors).

Labour's local campaigning

> 'Above all, this booklet gives you the facts you need to make up your mind on the poll tax. An informed debate needs an informed public.' (*Paying the Poll Tax in Liverpool*, booklet distributed by Liverpool City Council, 1989).

Our analysis of *local* Labour Party's campaigning focuses on the communication strategies of Labour local authorities, not only because their elected status made them the most significant sources of local Labour opposition,* but also because their opposition created tensions with their executive responsibilities. Although profoundly antagonistic to a policy specifically designed to expose them to the wrath of a vengeful electorate, they nevertheless shared an interest in securing high levels of payment, to maintain their levels of service provision.† Therefore their public relations activities had to achieve two diverging objectives: on the one hand, to inform the public of how and why they should pay, whilst, on the other, drawing attention to the inequity and inefficiency of the policy and the culpability of central government.

In 1987, several Labour authorities conducted pre-emptive publicity campaigns that clearly signalled their antipathy to the poll tax. In September 1987, Leicester City Council produced a sixteen-page brochure,'How the Poll Tax Affects Leicester', which variously explained the tax; its problems ('It is unfair ... It is undemocratic ... It is costly and difficult to adminster ... It will increase house prices' *How the Poll Tax Affects Leicester*, 1987: 6–7); its likely redistributional effects; and its limited support. This main brochure was supplemented by several shorter leaflets which summarized its main points, and targeted specific sections of the community.

Sheffield City Council's, 'Beginners Guide to the Poll Tax', published at the

* When Stoker observes that 'Government ministers lost the propaganda battle with local authorities' over the introduction of the poll tax, he is primarily referring to the high profile campaigning of Labour controlled local authorities (1991: 186).

† The 1988 Local Government Finance Act also contained provisions which placed a legal obligation on levying authorities to collect the tax.

same time, drew attention to the huge discrepancy between Government and Council estimations of likely charge levels in the Sheffield area; the preponderance of likely losers under the new system; the exorbitant administrative costs; and the potential threat posed to individual privacy. Eight 'supplementary sheets' were available on request, which gave more detailed expositions of the policy's defects and refutations of Government claims.

In December 1987, Reading Borough Council ran a publicity campaign through the local media which invited local residents to ring a telephone hotline and receive an information pack delivering 'Plain Facts On The Poll Tax' (*PR Weekly*, 10/12/87). Initially it was intended to run the adverts on local independent radio but they were barred by the Independent Broadcasting Authority. The IBA's ban did not reflect the content of the adverts but rather their subject matter, which it was claimed put the adverts in contravention of the Broadcasting Act which prohibited adverts of a wholly or mainly political nature (*Local Government Chronicle*, 11/12/87).

The following year, Liverpool City Council distributed a glossy booklet: *The Poll Tax: What it is and What it Means to You*, and in its introduction clearly stated the council's stance: 'Liverpool City Council is opposed to the poll tax. It believes that it will make poor people poorer, and will drive many more people into poverty for the first time' (1989: 2). Alongside explanations of the origins and details of the policy, the document drew attention to the potential threats posed to personal privacy, the fallaciousness of Government Community Charge projections; and the 'cynical' nature of the safety net arrangements. It concluded with a so-called 'ready reckoner' – sets of tables which highlighted the likely redistributional impact of the tax on a ward basis – and a discussion of how the new system would systematically discriminate against disadvantaged sections of the community.

As the date for the tax's implementation drew closer, a second feature became more apparent in this type of publicity material. Although this material continued to signal the levying authorities' antipathy to the poll tax, more emphasis was placed on the rebates available to those unable to pay the tax. This shift reflected three factors. Firstly, it was a response to NEC directives for Labour authorities to conduct local rebate campaigns. Second, the increasing detail available on the rebate package coupled with the Government's *volte face* on the transitional relief arrangements, made the need for revised information all the more urgent. Third, these authorities' recognized it was in their own self interest to secure a high take up of rebates, as the greater administrative burden placed upon them by the new taxation arrangements would only be exacerbated should a significant number of potential claimants apply once enforcement proceedings had begun (Convention of Scottish Local Authorities, Executive Committee Meeting Item, 3/3/89).

Sheffield City Council's revised publicity material comprised a series of leaflets which variously explained the benefit system ('What is poll tax benefit?... Who can't claim? ... How does the council pay poll tax benefit?... Where can I get more information?'); its implications for various sections of the community ('Poll Tax and Young People', 'Poll Tax and the Black Community'); and the impact of the uniform Business Rate on the business community ('Poll Tax [sic] and the Business Community'). Liverpool City Council's revised booklet, *Paying the Poll Tax in Liverpool*, included an expanded section on poll tax benefits, how they could be claimed and a negative assessment of the system's first year of operation in Scotland.

From late 1990, the informational aspect of these campaigns became more apparent. Rather than criticizing the principles of the policy, the publicity mainly focused on the need for people to pay the tax, the sympathetic hearing they would receive from the local council if they were experiencing difficulties, and the legal obligation of the authority to pursue those who persistently refused to pay. For example, in February 1993, Leicester City Council launched a concerted television, radio and newspaper advertisement campaign assuring those in arrears that they would receive a sympathetic hearing from the council. As one of the advertisements in the council's own freely distributed civic magazine put it:

> 'We know that some people are having difficulty paying their Poll Tax. But, as a local authority we have a duty to collect it and will do so. If you are on a low income and are worried about Poll Tax arrears we can offer you a way out. Talk to us. Together we can agree how much you can afford to pay off each week' (*Leicester Link*, February 1993).

The reasons for the change in emphasis were threefold. Firstly, by mid-1990 it was clear that the local authorities had won the propaganda battle with the Government, and that the public blamed the Government for high poll tax levels. Second, the tensions between these councils' wish to communicate their antipathy to the tax, and their need to ensure widespread payment to protect their revenue yields, became increasingly severe. As non-payment levels remained stubbornly high, and the pressure on these authorities' finances increased, a more unsympathetic attitude to non-payees came to predominate in ruling groups. Third, as the controversial process of legal enforcement began, these authorities found themselves under attack from local anti poll tax groups who sought to encourage non-payment and condemned council complicity in enforcing the tax's implementation. As a consequence of this, the political aims of these authorities' publicity work during the tax's final period became more concerned with refuting the claims of anti poll tax groups about the levels and advisability of non-payment, than in responding to the rhetoric of a government that had long accepted it had lost the argument.

Not surprisingly, the local and regional news media featured centrally in the communication strategies of those Labour authorities who mobilized against the poll tax. To some degree this reflected the general trend towards greater investment and professionalism in local government news management. As one internal local authority document summarized it:

> 'Good relations with the media are not an 'optional extra' for the City Council; they must be an integral part of the Council's attempts to improve its image. A "good image" is not a goal in itself. But it can help in attracting investment, improving relationships with outside bodies, and *reducing unnecessary and unwarranted hostility from the public we serve*' (Guide to Relations with the Media, Liverpool City Council, May 1991, our emphasis).

However, the political controversy over the Community Charge made these contacts even more crucial, both in informing the public and presenting the councils' views (Dale, 1989). Interestingly, the significance of the local media in the introduction of the poll tax was not lost on the Audit Commission either, who stressed the need for all authorities to attend to their media work when administering the system: providing hypothetical scenarios where local authority court actions could either be displayed positively in the local media, as an illustration of local efficiency, or negatively, as an example of local bureaucratic insensitivity (Audit Commission, 1990).

Our different local sample areas exposed a great diversity in the sophistication and organization of media work by councils. Whereas several local authorities had invested in press offices employing experienced ex-journalists, others operated on a far more *ad hoc* basis. And it appeared that party political factors played a part in determining the extent of investment in this area. Whereas most of the Conservative authorities we spoke to tended to favour a more individualistic approach to media relations – with senior figures in the ruling group adopting sole or main responsibility for media liasons – all of those Labour authorities we contacted who actively campaigned against the tax preferred a more *systematic* approach to press relations, seeking to channel all press contacts through their press offices.* An example of this political difference was provided in one authority, where political control of the City Council shifted from the Conservatives to Labour in 1990. Under the Conservative group, press and publicity work had been directly controlled and organized by the Council leader. With the shift to Labour, the council's press and publicity operations were completely transformed. A formal press office was established and a directive was passed to all authority departments that they should direct all future press contact via it.

Labour authorities also tended to invest more in *ersatz* local media – free magazines, newspapers or news inserts authored by local press officers and designed to provide a one-step communication flow from the authority to its residents. These were also widely used to disseminate information and opinion on the Community Charge:

> 'We [put information] in the Council newspaper. I hesitate to call it a newspaper ... It's sent out every two weeks. It's sent out with one of the local free newspapers ... It goes to every house. You would usually have the front page for purely editorial. We did quite a lot of poll tax stories. So that was going out to all homes' (Council Press Officer, interview with authors).

Prior to the introduction of the tax, many Labour authorities had found it difficult to attract consistent media attention to the issue. However once it had arrived, they found themselves deluged with requests for information

* In many cases, this systematic approach was more of an ideal than a reality, with local journalists preferring to contact local councillors and professionals directly rather than going through the press office, and with influential figures within certain departments proving reluctant to relinquish their direct contact with news media.

and interviews. As one press officer put it, 'The poll tax is a never ending source of fascination to the media ... It's definitely added a new dimension' (Interview with authors). Although a considerable amount of this contact concerned straightforward information provision, or facilitating access to senior local government officers, press offices were also used to refute charges of administrative incompetence and where appropriate to make a political point. For example, after the Chancellor's surprise blanket reduction in poll tax levels in March 1991, one authority expressed its pique by inviting the local media to photograph and interview their senior finance officer astride a mountain of now redundant poll tax bills.

Inhibitions on local Labour authority campaigning

It should be stressed that not all Labour local authorities chose to conduct high profile anti poll tax publicity campaigns. For example, in Nottingham, whilst Labour councillors were always willing to castigate the Government and the policy in the local media, the council itself distributed very little publicity material on the tax, and when it did so the literature focused either on how people could apply for rebates ('We'll help when you've been Poll Taxed', Nottingham City Council Leaflet, 1990) or offering incentives for regular and efficient payment ('Pay your Community Charge/Poll Tax by direct debit and you could WIN a fabulous £2,000 holiday for two', Nottingham City Council Leaflet, 1990). Similarly, Easington District Council's formal publicity merely amounted to a series of press adverts and posters informing the public of where to apply for rebates. While this difference in the nature and extent of publicity produced by Labour authorities sometimes revealed the differing public relations capabilities of these authorities, it also reflected political considerations. It was no accident that those Labour councils who conducted the most controversial publicity campaigns and mobilized most precipitatively against the tax, were those larger municipal authorities who expected to lose most under the new system.

However, in challenging central government so directly, these authorities were embarking on a potentially hazardous course. Apart from the contradictions created by denigrating a tax they also had to collect, these dissenting authorities confronted a more immediate threat. In Britain, local government publicity is governed by statute. The 1986 and 1988 Local Government Acts laid down regulations which prohibit councils from producing 'political' publicity, which is discerned from a test set down in section 2 of the 1986 Act: whether the material 'appears to be designed to affect public support for a political party'. Although there has been widespread confusion about the extent of these powers, as well as some of their central operating definitions, these regulations could have considerably inhibited these Labour authorities in their publicity work. Certainly, those authorities who formally campaigned against the tax were highly conscious of the dangers of falling foul of the law. As a council press officer from one of these authorities explained:

> '[The Council's publicity material] had to be very legally vetted ... Anything that I wrote that was interesting and had a little bit of style about it got taken out basically' (Interview with authors).

Such caution was not ill founded. Throughout the policy's implementation, the Local Government Unit at Conservative Central Office carefully monitored Labour council publicity, and on one occasion had unsuccessfully tried to get the Audit Commission to pursue a prosecution against one Labour authority for contravening the legislation.

However, if these regulations inhibited the style of presentation, they did not significantly prevent these councils from communicating their preferred message. As one commentator pointed out in 1988:

> 'The restrictions ... should not really inhibit the conduct of any campaign about the poll tax. It may require the adoption of a different style to that which an authority may otherwise prefer. But where, as here, the facts themselves are so damning, it should be easy to devise lawful, but effective, publicity' (Willmore, 1988).

Nevertheless, even if the practical effects of the regulations were negligible, the legislation may have been a significant factor in encouraging some authorities to focus their campaigning against the tax through the local media, which apart from having the benefit of being considerably cheaper than large scale information subsidies, was not covered by the legislation (Dale, *op. cit.*).

Conservative Party opposition

The Labour Party – and other opposition parties – were not the only source of party political opposition to the Community Charge. The tax also antagonized a wide range of Conservative Party opinion, which eventually grew to such an extent that it proved a crucial factor in the deposition of the Party leader (McGregor, 1991). Given the vehemence of this opposition, and its profound influence on the conduct and evolution of this policy debate, it is important to consider its nature and how the message of insurrection was communicated within the Party and onwards to the general public.

There was an important qualitative change in Conservative opposition as the policy cycle proceeded. Prior to mid-1989, Conservative opposition was mainly located among 'critics' on the Left of the party who objected to the *principles* of the policy (Norton, 1990). However, as the prospect of implementation loomed, opposition spread to other sections of the Party, who balked at the effects of the tax. By March 1990, the sound of Conservative Backbenchers applauding the idea of the Community Charge but condemning its practice was a familiar refrain around Westminster. As we discuss later, this shift in intra-party opposition to the Community Charge held major implications for the conduct and construction of public debate on the policy, particularly by the media.

Furthermore, the timing of the public expression of this internal dissent was highly significant. Despite the vehemence of some in their opposition to the Tax, no influential figures within the Party went public with their objections until after the Conservative Party's success in the 1987 General Election. (Indeed, Michael Heseltine, Michael Mates and other high profile critics voted *for* the Scottish legislation in 1986/87.) There were several reasons for this additional absence of comment on the issue before the 1987 Election. As we have explained, opposition within the Party was not as broadly based as it was to become. As one of the most influential right wing back-bench critics, explained:

> 'The principle which I accepted – and still accept – that just the same as the American revolution was 'no taxation without representation', we had representation without taxation, which is still to me politically immoral, and I still stand by that. The nitty-gritty I did not look at. And at the 1987 Election, on platforms I defended it, because it was immensely popular in Conservative circles' (Interview with authors).

Furthermore, there was a basic lack of awareness among many back benchers as to the salience of the issue. In a revealing exchange with the authors, one of the most prominent Conservative opponents of the Tax during its legislative passage offered the following explanation as to why he failed to address the issue before the General Election and before the Bill was presented to Parliament:

> 'Because Mrs Thatcher – entirely on her own – threw it into the manifesto, without consulting anybody. None of us knew about it before it appeared in the manifesto ... It was specifically excluded from the Green Paper as not being a way forward ... There was an '81 [Green Paper], there was an '83 [White Paper] and there was an '86 [Green Paper], all specifically said – oh, and the Layfield report – all specifically said the poll tax is not the answer. And then it got slung into the manifesto' (Interview with authors).

However, given the political astuteness of several Parliamentary critics of the Community Charge, it is unlikely that political myopia alone provides a sufficient explanation for the absence of dissent in the pre-election period. Rather, their silence also probably reflected a tactical decision to hold fire until the election had been won, after which they could exert their greatest influence over the direction of Government policy.

One unifying feature of all Conservative Party opposition to the poll tax was its media-centredness. Indeed, the media were the principal means by which Conservative disaffection found public expression. This is not surprising, for no matter how deeply felt the antagonisms among Tory ranks, party loyalties and obligations made it unthinkable that Conservative dissenters would disseminate formal, anti poll tax publicity material.

Briefings given to the media by Conservative dissidents were both overt and covert. One particularly influential overt media briefing was delivered by the ex-local government minister, Rhodes Boyson, who in 1989 approached *The Times* with projections about the likely impact of the tax on low rated properties in the north of England and expressed his concerns about the threat they posed to the Conservatives' electoral prospects. He explained his motives thus:

> 'Presumably *The Times* comes out every day and I am told people read it. I may have been misled, but I'm told people read it. *And if you can't*

> *get government to see sense* then you go there. When it was written up in *The Times* afterwards [about what had happened] – the *Sunday Times* did a big write-up which you'll have seen which said I leaked [the figures]. I didn't leak anything at all. I just made public what was public. What I did was interpret what it meant' (Interview with authors, our emphasis).

Boyson's point about using the media to make the Government 'see sense' is highly significant. In our previous chapter we noted the autocratic nature of the Government's promotion and decision-making on this policy. It is clear that as internal dissent within the Party grew, and as its leadership stubbornly refused to respond to these criticisms, 'going public' with criticisms became the principal mechanism for exerting pressure upon it. This approach was especially evident among grass roots Conservative opinion, which had been particularly alienated by the introduction of the policy. For example, in March 1990, at the height of the political furore over the tax, there were several high profile Conservative council resignations in connection with the issue. At least one of these – the resignation of Conservative councillors in Beverley, Humberside on Budget Day – was deliberately timed to attract maximum media attention and thereby optimum political embarrassment for ministers.

This media orientation also reflected the reciprocal interest of the media in Conservative critics. Those Conservatives who voiced their concerns publicly had little difficulty in gaining access to the media to air their views, recognizing that the inherent newsworthiness of their message obviated the need for sophisticated news management. Whereas a Labour frontbench spokesperson spoke of the 'very hard work in the back room, of the job of convincing people that [the poll tax] mattered, and then convincing them of our credibilty and then keeping up the flow of information to them', Conservative dissenters were able to adopt a far more relaxed approach to news management:

> 'I'm not one of these people who puts a press release out every two minutes, or even once a week. I put it out as and when I've got something particular I want to say, which I suppose is maybe four or five times a year. So I don't have 'press work' as such. When the poll tax happened, it was *all* done by talking to journalists' (Conservative MP, interview with authors).

Beyond these public articulations of Conservative opposition, our research uncovered another, hidden, dimension in the communication of Conservative dissent via the media. At the height of the poll tax crisis there was a surreptitious but highly significant breakdown in collective responsibility in the Cabinet over the issue. This principally involved certain senior ministers conveying to trusted media confidants their private antagonism towards the Community Charge. But whereas other Party objectors 'went public' with their concerns to the media, these senior government figures went privately: providing information that was not to be reported, but which the reporter should use as the pinch of salt to season any public proclamations the minister might make. As one lobby journalist recollected:

> '[A senior minister] went to the offices of one national newspaper, just for a sort of lunch thing, and the editor was there, the political editor, local government correspondent et cetera et cetera, and he said in categorical terms – and you've got to bear in mind that these are "deep throat" off the record occasions – he said he thought it was an awful idea, and he really didn't want anything to do with it' (Interview with authors).

Although these 'confidential' briefings were mainly only divulged to very senior lobby journalists, they were clearly intended to filter out for broader, unofficial consumption by journalists, to create a 'received wisdom' as to the private views of the politician, whatever his public rhetoric might suggest. As another lobby correspondent explained:

> 'I'd bump into people at the bar, you know at the end of a long day, and I'd say "oh god, [names minister] wasn't very good today was he?" And they'd say 'well you know about him, you know he hates the poll tax'. And you'd say 'What do you mean he hates the poll tax?' And that's, it's all drip,drip, drip and it sort of oozes out like that' (Interview with authors).

The deposition of Margaret Thatcher and the announcement of the poll tax's abolition, effectively drew the sting of Conservative disaffection. However, as the prospect of the next General Election loomed closer, the Party spin doctors also actively sought to stifle any remaining public expressions of disquiet within the Party. As one high profile Parliamentary critic explained:

> 'I have been silenced!' (Interview with authors).

Other arenas of political opposition

So what of other sources of political opposition to the Community Charge, beyond the party political arena? For the rest of this chapter we explore how a range of professional organizations and pressure groups publicly mobilized against the tax, and the factors that influenced their campaign strategies. We begin by examining how local authority associations and pressure groups responded to the new policy, as they played a crucial role in constructing and co-ordinating the broad response of local government to this highly significant constitutional reform.

Local government organizations

Not surprisingly, all local authority associations identified the salience of the reforms at a very early stage (DoE, 1986b), and expressed a considerable exasperation at the inertia of the main political parties and the media over the issue. As a senior finance officer from one association explained:

> 'Our leading members were instructed to raise [the Community Charge] and get a high profile with their colleagues and in the parliamentary field. And it was just a sort of total surprise to us that not a lot was made of it until immediately after the General Election. And then the contrast between July 1987 onwards and the previous eighteen months was just amazing ... Suddenly, Wham! It took off. People realized it was for real, it was coming, and the media was full of poll tax stories, which then began to feed off each other. Life was very interesting here, thereafter' (Interview with authors).

Although these different organizations were unanimous in their opposition to the tax, there were clear disparities in the nature of their opposition. For example, the Labour controlled Associations (such as the Association of Metropolitan Authorities [AMA], the Association of London Authorities

[ALA], and the Convention of Scottish Local Authorities [COSLA]) assumed a more oppositional position: highlighting how the system eroded local government autonomy and regressively redistributed central grant from deprived to affluent regions. By comparison, the lobbying and campaigning of the Conservative controlled Association of District Council (ADC) had a more revisionist stance: identifying practical problems with the legislation which would prove particularly disadvantageous for its constituent authorities. (For example, the ADC played a very significant role in the political furore which forced the Government to rescind the 'self-financing' safety net proposals in 1989.)

There were two reasons for this difference. First, as it was recognized that the municipal authorities would be hit hardest by the new system, it was inevitable that their representative organizations would adopt a more combative posture. Second, the political complexion of different Associations exerted an obvious influence over the type of political posture it could assume. Because general Conservative disaffection with the Community Charge in local government only began to appear towards mid-1989, the ADC had to be cautious in their campaigning on the tax during its Parliamentary passage in 1987/88. As one officer explained:

> 'We had the continual tension that you get when you've got a local association ... controlled by the same political party down the road ... [The Association's Chair's] attitude was: the Conservatives have got a big majority, we can jump up and down and scream as much as we like, but the Government majority has the right and the power to push it through. So there comes a point when it's silly just to go on and on opposing ... We should really be spending our time looking at ways of amending details' (Interview with authors).

Interestingly, as the political debate developed, the focus of each Associations' campaigning and lobbying subtly altered. For example, whereas the groundswell of Conservative disaffection with the poll tax from 1989 permitted the ADC a freer hand to attack the principles as well as practicalities of the tax; the worsening financial privations experienced by member authorities of the AMA led it to place less emphasis on issues of principle and more on the practical issue of getting people to pay. Whereas before 1990, the AMA had frequently highlighted questions about the dangers the tax posed to the franchise and the threats posed to privacy, by the end of 1991, one of their main objectives was to persuade the Government to conduct a 'Pay Up' promotional campaign. As a senior finance officer from the Association explained '[before 1990] we could take a principled view and be upset about information gathering ... [By 1990/91] we started to have to take a less than principled view, and accept we had to get on and do the job' (Interview with authors).

All associations perceived the media as being very important in the developing political debate on the policy, and engaged in news management work as an adjunct to their lobbying in Whitehall. As one press officer put it: 'we use the media whenever we can to promulgate our line, obviously. It's one of our major weapons'. As with other political actors in the debate, their press work was both proactive – highlighting issues and parading their concerns – and reactive, deflecting criticisms and castigating other sources 'when we think they haven't got it quite right' (Interview with authors). On another level, they were a significant source of comment and technical expertise for the media, which provided another opportunity for them to present their concerns and opinions.

An example of an early and prominent exercise in staged news management by one association came in December 1988, when the *Daily Mirror* ran a front page story under the rather improbable headline: SEX AND THE POLL TAX (*Daily Mirror*, 8/12/88), which was followed by another item the next day – GAYS GET BETTER DEAL ON POLL TAX (*Daily Mirror*, 9/12/88: 18). Both stories originated from a seminar organized by the AMA and the National Council for Civil Liberties on the privacy implications of the new system. The first story related to the power of local authorities to acquire information about the marital status of charge payers (hence the 'SEX' dimension); the second, to the rules governing joint and several liability, which did not apply to homosexual couples (hence the 'Gays get better deal' angle):

> 'We tried it in the *Mirror* and spent the best part of the day talking them through the story and finally at the end of the day [the journalist] said "I ought to go and run this, I think I'll get it on the front page". Watching *Newsnight* that night, it was the same day that Roy Orbison had died, so all tabloids were leaping on Roy Orbison, and then they finally got to the bottom the of the pile, and Peter Snow, I think it was, said "I see the *Mirror*'s got something about the Poll Tax". There was a

> huge splash. It kept Orbison off the front page' (Interview with authors).

Although delighted with the initial splash, the Association was less pleased with the subsidiary piece:

> 'The follow up story next day, which we sort of hastily disowned. First we concocted it and then I got into some trouble on this from our equal opportunities guys' (Interview with authors).

Apart from the campaigning of local authority associations, the views of certain councils were also forcefully represented by the pressure group, the Local Government Information Unit (LGIU). As this group was initially established in the early 1980s as part of Labour councils' political response to attacks from central government, it was not surprising that the Community Charge came to dominate all aspects of its work for a considerable period of time.

Throughout the debate, the Unit distributed a considerable amount of publicity material on the Community Charge. Aside from their monthly newletters, which often covered poll tax issues ('How Will The Cap Fit?'*LGIU Briefing*, No. 38; 'Poll Tax Package: the Real Story', *LGIU Briefing*, No. 43), from March 1989, the Unit distributed a monthly 'Poll Tax Focus' briefing, which was superceded in October 1991 by a monthly 'Council Tax Facts' briefing. It also produced a guide to the poll tax, which outlined its details and deficiencies (LGIU, 1989). This material was distributed to registered members, and also to national and media outlets. Furthermore, it published, in conjunction with the Child Poverty Action Group, a very influential analysis of the redistributive implications of the tax, which directly challenged the optimistic veneer of DoE projections (Esam and Oppenheim, 1989).

As a pressure group, the Unit paid particular attention to the media in their publicity work, investing a considerable amount of resources in distributing information to national and local media. In doing so they made at least two significant interventions in the reporting of the policy. The first was a reactive exercise, where, having obtained copies of the Government's 'So-Called Poll Tax' leaflet before its launch, the Unit briefed national and local news media of its deficiencies well in advance of its official launch (LGIU News Release, 8/5/89). The second significant contribution was in co-ordinating the legal appeal by several Labour authorities against the Government's capping decision in April 1990. Apart from providing legal and technical advice for the councils' defence, the Unit was also responsible for ensuring the councils' arguments were clearly presented through the media. In all, twenty five news releases on poll tax capping were distributed by the Unit between the capping announcement on the 3 April 1990 and the House of Lord's rejection of the councils' appeal on the 16 July 1990. These highlighted iniquities and anomalies in the capping criteria ('Political spite' in making cap fit, *LGIU News Release*, 3/4/90; 'Poll Tax capping: power without responsibility' *LGIU News Release*, 16/7/90) and informed the media of future news conferences and media events ('Poll tax capping – Media Events, June 4 & June 5. 11 am. Council Chambers, Camden. Opportunities for film crews to meet capped councils', *LGIU News Release*, 1/6/90; 'Press conference of capped councils. 3 pm. Legal officer present to answer detailed questions', *LGIU News Release*, 4/6/90; '10.15–10.30. Outside High Court. Photo-Opportunity', *LGIU News Release*, 5/6/90). As the capped authorities awaited the outcome of the first High Court judgement on the 14 June 1990 the LGIU sought to ensure that, even if the councils' did lose the judgement (which they did), then their viewpoint would still be adequately represented in the media:

> 'We booked God knows how many rooms at the L[ondon] S[chool] [of] E[conomics] for a press conference for the media to hang around and do interviews in ...That was very good because they were actually trapped there most of the morning, waiting for judgement. So they had background papers to read. It was quite effective. I remember a couple of journalists say, "God! I didn't know that. That's not fair, is it?" ... We were concerned that if we lost, then you'd have the Secretary of State in his office, looking very smart and, you know, "statesmanish". As it happened, Chris Patten [Secretary of State for the Environment] was in ... Bristol, I think it was, and he was followed round by people with "Down With The Poll Tax" banners. So we did quite well out of that' (Interview with authors).

However, although specific interventions of this type were quite effective in securing media attention to problematic aspects of the new system, the Unit frequently experienced difficulties in being prominently and regularly quoted in the media, particularly at national level:

> '[The media] run their quotes – The AMA, the ADC, the Association of

County Councils, and that's probably it, and possibly Tony Travers, you know or similar. For us to get a quote in, it's either got to be extremely good, or they've not been able to get hold of other people. Just because they go for the establishment ones first, because we're recognized as a sort of pressure group' (LGIU press officer, interview with authors).

Anti poll tax organizations

One of the most remarkable effects of the Community Charge was the way it mobilized large sections of the community to express their opposition through impressive gestures of collective action, be it in a stubborn refusal to pay the tax, or via large scale public demonstrations. The Anti Poll Tax movement – a generic term we use here to encompass the plethora of formal, single issue, unions, alliances, groups and federations established to fight the poll tax – first emerged in Scotland, and then spread southwards. By November 1989 there were over 1,000 Anti Poll Tax Unions (APTUs) in Britain.

The movement emerged from a growing frustration with the political responses of the mainstream parties – particularly the Labour Party – for their failure to place sufficient emphasis on the issue; their insufficiently radical methods of resistance; and their disinterest in building a community-based campaign (Lavalette and Mooney, 1990).

As previously mentioned, 'maverick' sources within the Labour Party, including a significant rump of the parliamentary Party, played a crucial role in establishing this protest movement. In March 1988, the Campaign Group of Labour MPs produced a 'Statement on fighting the poll tax' which emphasized the need for 'a broad protest movement prepared, in the final instance, to use civil disobedience to make this 'Tory Tax' unworkable'. This would include 'send it back' anti-registration campaigns, mass appeals against registrars' assessments and the occupation of council buildings (*Labour Party News Release [Campaign Group of MPs]*, 30/3/88). As a 'symbolic action', the signatories declared their intention neither to register nor to pay the tax.

These dissenting factions within the Labour Party and other political pressure groups on the Left, mobilized far more precipitatively against the tax than the mainstream of the Party, convening several early meetings and conferences to discuss strategies for opposing it (Independent Labour Party, 1988). The first Anti Poll Tax Unions in Scotland were established before the 1987 General Election (Burns, 1992).

However, although the movement was unified by calls for a more concerted and radical means for opposing the Community Charge, it was also riven with disagreements as to the best method of opposing it, and how the movement should be structured.

Many activists asserted that the tax could only be defeated by engineering a mass non-payment campaign and that Labour councils and trades unions should actively obstruct its non-implementation (Scottish Anti Poll Tax Federation, 1989; Sewell, 1989; Burns, 1992; Labour Party Young Socialists, 1989). Others expressed doubts about achieving a sufficent 'level of resistance' through non-payment (because of the 'serious costs for the people undertaking it') and recommended instead the pursuit of 'collective civil disobedience allied to mass demonstrations' to 'significantly raise the political temperature' (Independent Labour Party, *op. cit.*). The particular strategy preferred by different anti poll tax factions had direct implications for their relationship with other sources of political opposition to the tax. Whereas those who recommended non-payment had no compunction about publicly condemning the 'pay up brigade' in the Labour Party, those advocating the latter approach still sought to keep the channels of communication open with the Party's leadership. For example, in a news release following Labour's defeat at the Govan by-election, one Labour MP urged the party to adopt the mass protest option as a means of circumventing 'the sterile debate between simple non payment and simon pure legality' (*Labour Party Press Release [Harry Barnes's Office]* 16/11/88).

There were also disagreements as to how formalized the movement should become, and who should exert control over it. In November 1988, a conference at Oxford established a national federation of anti poll tax groups in England. The next month the Socialist conference established a competing national forum. In November 1989, the All British Anti Poll Tax Federation was launched, whose immediate aim was 'to organize these millions [of non-payers] into an army of mass non-payment' (*Militant*, 24/11/89). The increasing tensions between these national federations focused on questions of strategy and political control. For example, a newsletter released by the first national federation criticized the 'sectarianism' of those endorsing a straight non-payment strategy, dismissing the Socialist Conference as 'an ultra-leftist jamboree' and the All British Federation as 'Militant dominated'* (*National Federation Newsletter*, January 1990). Militant's involvement was to prove an increasingly tendentious issue, both within the movement itself, and in external evaluations of its mandate and credibility. According to a member of the Federation's first national committee, Militant's domination both seriously compromised the Federation's credibility with the movement as a whole, and generally served to obscure the devolved nature of the anti poll tax movement (Burns, *op. cit.*).

Despite this factionalism, all anti poll tax groups recognized the importance of establishing effective communication strategies, to publicize their existence and encourage people to participate in the campaign. However, they were far less media-orientated in their publicity work than other political sources involved in the debate, often preferring more traditional methods of public meetings, grass roots campaigning and leafleting. For example, The Strathclyde Federation distributed a quarter of a million copies of its first newsletter, and Anti Poll Tax Unions in Haringey claimed to have delivered over 1 million leaflets door to door by 1991 (Burns, *op. cit.*).

However, the more marginal significance assigned to the mainstream media in their campaigning didn't reflect a perception that the media were politically irrelevant. For example, the Scottish Anti Poll Tax Federation attributed a lull in the non-payment campaign in Scotland in late 1988 to 'Tory spokespersons supported by the big guns of the popular press [who] have created a crescendo of propaganda to suggest that the high percentages now registered mean there will be no campaign of non-payment' (Scottish Anti Poll Tax Federation, *op. cit.*). Rather, the less media centric approach of anti poll tax groups reflected a recognition that any extra-legal stance was unlikely to receive a sympathetic response from journalists. Furthermore, they often had difficulty in getting the media – particularly at national level – to recognize them as legitimate forums of political activity (a problem often experienced by political pressure groups [Hansen, 1991]). As one APTU representative complained:

* Militant Tendency is a far Left, Trotskyite group, which was expelled from the Labour party in the mid-1980s. It had pursued 'entryist' methods, 'a classic tactic of the revolutionary Left, which involves infiltration of the mainstream Labour Party in order to push it into more hard-line Socialism, win converts to its cause and provoke divisions and possible splits from which it might benefit' (Coxall & Robins, 1989).

> 'We might have initiated a story, but then [the local media] will go to the Council for confirmation of it, and quote the councillor or councillors, rather than use the story we've given them. So its difficult to get anything actually directly in, especially direct quotes or information in that sense ... For every story we give the media, they'll ask the Council for their statement. The vast, in fact all council statements will be unchallenged by the media. They won't actually come to us unless we coincide – deliberately coincide – with one that we're expecting from the Council' (Interview with authors).

When anti poll tax groups did receive coverage, it was principally achieved through public gestures: commanding media attention through demonstrations or imaginative publicity gimmicks:

> 'On Monday 17 June ... Members of Oxford Against the Poll Tax will present a cheque to the City Council. The cheque will be made out for the sum of 'absolutely nothing' and signed on behalf of the people of Oxford. It will symbolize the extremely low level of payment that we expect the poll tax department to receive in this coming year' (*OAPT News Release*, 14/6/91).

Most significantly, local groups focused their news management exclusively on local media, partly because of their greater proximity, but also because they perceived their principal political opponents as being the local authorities who were enforcing the charge. National media contacts, on the other hand, were almost exclusively dealt with via the Militant dominated All British Federation. As we discuss later, this differing contact was to prove highly significant in the respective evaluations made of the anti poll tax movement by these different media sectors.

Voluntary sector voices

Over recent years, charities and voluntary organizations have assumed an increasingly prominent political and social role in Britain, whether supplementing or replacing statutory provision, defending and expressing the needs of marginalized and disadvantaged sections of society, or campaigning for change (Deacon & Golding, 1991; NCVO, 1990).The Community Charge held serious implications for the sector. First, it had a major impact upon the resources of the sector: in the prospect of increased liabilities and responsibilities under the new system (for example, the new arrangements for charitable rate relief); reduced local government funding (Mabbott, 1992); and increased demand for voluntary sector services as financial pressures forced cutbacks in statutory provision (NCVO, 1987; Entezari, 1988; Davis-Smith, 1988). Second, the tax seriously affected the living standards of clients or members of these organizations (NCVO, 1987). Third, the policy raised contentious political and social issues, with which many organizations were directly concerned; for example, the erosion of civil liberties in Britain and the growing inegalitarianism of opportunity and reward.

The British vountary sector is extraordinarily heterogeneous, and different types of voluntary organizations tended to focus on different aspects of the policy in their public campaigning. Many conducted public information campaigns to increase public understanding and inform people of their rights. For example, in October 1989 the Information and Policy department of Age Concern distributed an information briefing on 'The Community Charge (Poll Tax) and Old People' which gave general details on the system and when and how people should pay. On occasions, these informational initiatives were conducted in tandem with Government.*

However, given the policy's major ramifications for the sector, many organizations went far beyond passive information provision in their publicity work on the policy. Campaigning on the resource implications of the tax was principally conducted by *intermediary organizations* – those organizations who provide training and advice for a wide range of organizations, and represent the generic interests of the sector (e.g the National Council for Voluntary Organizations and regional Councils for Vountary Service). Campaigning on behalf of specific sections of society was mainly conducted by *caring or service providing organizations*. For example, Age Concern sought to bring the Government's attention to the particularly penurous effect the tax would have on the elderly, particularly with regard to the rebate arrangements. Issue based campaigning, which explicitly addressed the broader political implications of the system, was principally conducted by *issue based pressure groups*. For example, the most significant source of comment about the privacy implications of the new arrangements was the pressure group 'Liberty' (previously known as the National

* For example the Royal National Institute for the Blind and the British Deaf Society co-operated with the Department of the Environment in producing braille and sign language versions of Government Community Charge information.

Council for Civil Liberties). In 1987, the organization distributed a booklet which highlighted the potential threats posed to individual privacy by a more intrusive system of personal taxation (NCCL, 1987). In 1989 it played a pivotal role in highlighting the often spurious nature of many of the questions being asked by local councils when compiling poll tax registers (Liberty, 1989a). Furthermore, in conjunction with the Association of London Authorities, it produced an explanatory booklet answering questions about how people could control the details and accuracy of personal information collected about them (Liberty, 1989b) and two 'best practice' guides for registration officers and councillors (Liberty, 1989c, 1989d). By 1990, it became embroiled in the controversy over the policing of the Trafalgar Square riot, and conducted its own independent observation of the policing of a subsequent national demonstration in October 1990. From early 1991 onwards, its attention focused on the legal enforcement of the tax, in particular, the threat to civil rights posed by the unregulated use of bailiffs and instances where courts were denying peoples' legal rights (Liberty, 1991).

This distinction between resource, client and issue based campaigning wasn't always absolute, reflecting a general blurring of distinction in the funtions of voluntary organizations (NCVO, 1990). For example, the Manchester Council for Voluntary Service convened an Anti Poll Tax Forum which campaigned on both a resource and client basis. Aside from attempting to produce a more concerted response from the sector, the Forum specifically campaigned against any further undermining of voluntary sector funding, and for residents in short stay accomodation to be exempted from the tax (*Greater Manchester Poll Tax Forum Leaflet*, 1989). Another organization that campaigned on two fronts – in this instance on a 'client' and 'issue' basis – was the Child Poverty Action Group. Although the organization's initial attention to the issue reflected a recognition that the tax would seriously affect their client group (in this case, poor people), their campaigning and publicity material frequently attacked the policy on an issue orientated basis, focusing on the political implications of such a structurally regressive system. In the words of the Group's Director:

> 'We believe that the poll tax proposals are undemocratic. CPAG has for many years been concerned not only about the incomes of the poor but also their ability to participate fully in society' (Quoted in Oppenheim, 1987).

One of the most significant collective sources of voluntary sector campaigning at a national level was the Poll Tax Forum, which integrated resource, issue and client based campaign work. The Forum's founding membership included leading charities such as MENCAP, NCVO and the Salvation Army, as well as members of the clergy, professional associations, trades unions and political pressure groups. It was established to 'research and publicize the effects of the Community Charge and related matters' (*PTF Newsletter*, 1, April 1989). One of its main contributions was to issue a 'charter for a fair local tax', which listed a set of criteria against which any local tax should be evaluated (*PTF Newsletter*, 2, June 1989).

Once again, the media featured prominently in the communication strategies of those voluntary organizations who publicly entered this policy debate. For example, a 'constituency action pack' produced by the CPAG in February 1988 highlighted the regressiveness of the tax, the twin threats it posed to local government autonomy and provided a 'model press release' which would draw local media attention to the organization's concerns ('Poll Tax: 'Hitting Poor Hardest'', *CPAG Model Press Release*, 30 February 1988). Similarly, the Poll Tax Forum urged all its affiliated organizations to 'issue a press release in support of the Charter. Make sure your local papers and radio know about the Charter and the arguments in support of it' (*PTF Newsletter*, 2, June 1989). Not surprisingly, issue based pressure groups revealed the most explicit media orientation in their campaigning:

> 'One way of reaching the public, of course, is through the media. Every week we issue press releases or make statements to journalists. Staff members are frequently interviewed on local and national television and radio. As well as giving interviews, we are constantly called upon to brief journalists preparing stories with civil liberties implications' (*Liberty Annual Report*, 1988: 15).

However, although voluntary organizations sought to engage actively in the evolving political debate over the policy, there were factors that potentially inhibited them in this aspect, and discouraged some from conducting issue orientated campaigns. First, those organizations who had charitable status, and depended upon all the financial benefits thereby accrued, had to be very cautious about how they publicly participated in a highly charged political debate. Beyond these specific restrictions, many organizations avoided addressing the political implications of the reforms because they feared participation would compromise their long cherished apolitical position (as the director of a Citizen's Advice Bureau put it in interview, 'we are an impartial service and do not comment upon Government policy').

Second, many organizations, particularly those operating at a local or regional level, found themselves tilting at two windmills: the Government on the one hand, and the local authorities whose expenditure decisions directly impacted upon them. Interestingly, whereas voicing criticisms against the tax via the media tended to be a first resort in organizations' strategies to influence central government decision-making, it was generally a last resort in their dealings with local authorities, where it was feared that a high profile complaint about funding cuts might hinder, rather than help, delicate financial negotiations.

Summary and conclusions

In this chapter we have described the political and public responses of a diverse range of political and institutional actors to the introduction of the Community Charge. It should be stressed that this review was necessarily selective, and as such did not include the active contributions made by other political parties, the trades union movement and the business sector. Nevertheless, through the cases presented we can discern several general principles about the construction and articulation of critical discourses against the policy.

First, the sources of political opposition to the policy were disparate, and extended well beyond the party political arena. Even more significantly, the distribution of this critical opinion did not conform to traditional political divisions. Indeed, there were no other sources of support for the policy apart from the Government, even from within its own Party. Second, the battle for 'primary definition' in the political debate on the poll tax debate was not just between the Government and its detractors, but also between opponents of the policy. Different sources highlighted different issues, and recommended different strategies, and these were the product of broader political factors. Furthermore, their issue agendas were not always constant, but changed as the debate developed. Fourth, different oppositional sources mobilized against the tax at different stages of the policy's implementation. Again, this timetable was underwritten by a range of complex political accidents and considerations. Fifth, all of these policy protaganists identified the media as playing a significant role in the evolution of the political debate. Indeed, because of the divisive nature of the policy, and the particularly autocratic manner in which it was introduced, the media assumed an even more central role in the political lobbying of many sources. As the Government closed its ears to the various concerns, and circumvented conventions of negotiation and consultation, the media became the principal forum by which political sources – even those closely allied to the Government – sought to exert pressure upon ministers. Sixth, media considerations appear to have been a major factor in shaping the campaign agendas and strategies of key oppositional voices.

Having described the main sources and strategies of political advocacy for and against the Community Charge, our attention now turns to how the media reported this complex and controversial policy debate, and the factors that influenced the generation of these accounts.

Chapter 5

Policy Made Public: Media Coverage of the Community Charge

We have seen that the plan to introduce the Community Charge generated an intense and far reaching political debate, in which the main protagonists identified the media as playing a key role in shaping public opinion. This raises the question of how the media reported this complex and controversial policy throughout its turbulent history. In this chapter we explore which preferred readings of the Community Charge were offered in local and national media coverage, and, in particular, how these readings varied across media sectors.*

A rogue by any other name? The media and the so-called 'poll tax'

It is somewhat inappropriate to talk of media coverage of the 'Community Charge', when the media themselves so overwhelmingly preferred the more familiar, and deliberately pejorative label, 'poll tax'. Less than 1.5 per cent of the 3,165 poll tax focused items published in the *Guardian*, *The Times* and the *Sunday Times* between 1986 and 1991 used 'Community Charge' in their headlines, and the term was mentioned anywhere in only 29 per cent of all national poll tax items (focused and related) between March and May 1990, and 33 per cent in the local media.

We have discussed elsewhere the Government's strategic and political reasons for preferring to label the new levy as a 'charge', yet these findings expose its spectacular failure to promote the term into the nation's political lexicon via the popular media. Subsequent interviews with journalists revealed the media's resistance to the Government's label reflected several

* Please refer to the appendix for details of the content analysis sampling and method.

factors: in particular, the unwieldiness of the term 'Community Charge' (which is over twice as long as 'poll tax'), and the recognition that 'poll tax' had a wider public currency (a point conceded in the Government's own publicity). However, journalists' preference was also informed by a particular value position on local taxation – i.e. that the new levy should be seen as a tax not a 'charge', and that its fairness should be assessed in relation to ability to pay. Clearly, we have here a basic and conspicuous failure by the Government to control media definitions in the way that it would have liked, which, according to one author, may have been a key reason behind the policy's failure (Winetrobe, 1992). While such a claim may be overstated, when we consider other features in poll tax coverage, the symbolism of the media's resistance on this point becomes particularly apposite.

So what of the broader features of media coverage of the poll tax? Our analysis divides into three broad sections. The first describes how the policy was reported in the national media, from inception through to abolition. The second provides a comparative analysis of the coverage of the issue in local media during the introduction of the tax in England and Wales. The third considers which aspects of the broader political debate about the tax were marginalized in media coverage.

National media coverage of the Community Charge

The poll tax attracted varying amounts of national media coverage during its passage from inception to abolition. As Fig. 5.1 shows, its news worthiness varied considerably and consistently during this six year period. Although we later identify clear thematic differences in press and broadcast coverage, this chart demonstrates the consistent *tenor* of coverage between media sectors throughout the policy cycle.

When we consider the main themes of Community Charge focused coverage in the national press during the different stages in the policy cycle (see Table 5.1), it is also clear that the *interpretative* agenda of national press coverage did not remain stable throughout the policy cycle. However, these figures only provide a crude measure of the fluctuations in media discourses, and it is necessary to look more qualitatively at the changing terms and tone of reporting to properly capture how the interpretative and evaluative dimensions of the debate shifted over time.

Table 5.1 Main themes of poll tax focused coverage in the *Guardian*, *The Times* and the *Sunday Times* (January 1986 – September 1991)

Presentation	Consultation/ formulation	Legislation	Preparation	Introduction	Evaluation	Abolition
1/86–2/86	3/86–10/87	11/87–7/88	8/88–12/89	1/90–4/90	5/90–2/91	3/91–9/91
Legislative process (28%)	Other government/ parliament decision-making (15%)	Conservative Party responses (24%)	Other government/ parliament decision-making (24%)	General public responses (24%)	Other government/ parliament decision-making (25%)	Other government/ parliament decision-making (28%)
Other government/ parliament decision-making (12%)	Conservative Party responses (14%)	Other government/ parliament decision-making (16%	Local government implementation (18%)	Other government/ parliament decision-making (18%)	Local government implementation (21%)	Local government implementation (14%)
Previous local financial reforms (12%)	Legislative process (11%)	Legislative process (12%)	Labour Party responses (9%)	Local government implementation (13%)	General public responses (12%)	Alternatives to poll tax (11%)
Increased accountability for local government (8%)	Winners and losers (8%)	Local government implementation (10%)	Conservative Party responses (7%)	Conservative Party responses (6%)	Cuts in local government services (7%)	Conservative Party responses (9%)
Winners and losers (4%)	Impact on civil liberties and franchise (6%)	Labour Party responses (6%)	Winners and losers (6%)	Negative economic effects (5%)	Conservative Party responses (6%)	General public responses (8%)
25 items	251 items	440 items	440 items	692 items	822 items	543 items

Figures relate to news, feature and leader items (poll tax focused) only. Percentages = appearance of theme as main theme/number of poll tax focused items during each period.

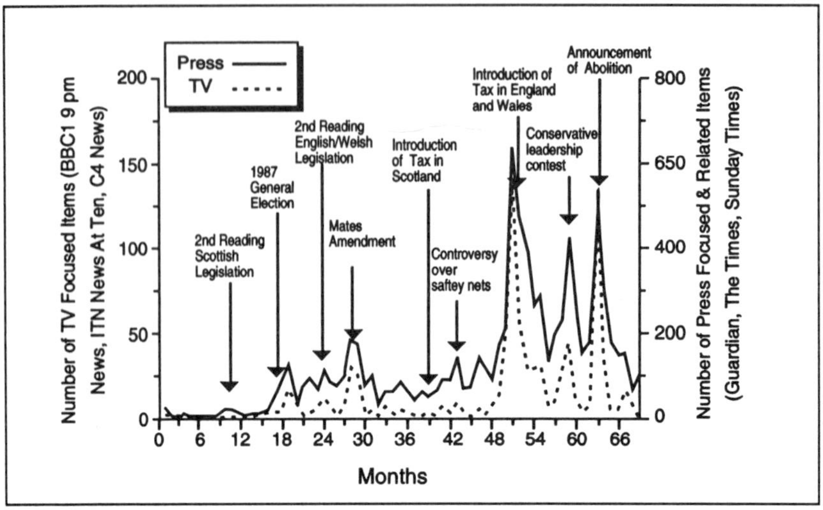

Fig. 5.1. Comparison of national TV and broadsheet poll tax coverage (January 1986 – September 1991).

Inception (October 1984 – December 1985)

Despite the clandestine nature of the initial Government discussions about the reform options, it didn't take long for the media to discern the direction of the Government's thinking. Three months before the Green Paper's publication, *Channel Four News* accurately predicted that the Government's rate reform plans would be a 'combination of property tax and poll tax' (23/9/85). Several of the broadsheet papers anticipated the Government's plans even earlier. In July 1985, the *Guardian* reported dissent within the Cabinet over the poll tax option ('Cabinet balks at early reform of rates system', 1/7/85), and *The Times* ran a piece warning about the potential unpopularity of the poll tax option ('Poll Tax flaws that could see Tory heads rolling: the basic arithmetic of Mrs Thatcher's rates alternative', 15/7/85). Throughout the remainder of 1985, the *Guardian*, *The Times* and the *Sunday Times* ran twenty-two additional poll tax focused and related stories, which either speculated on the Government's plans ('Ministers may press for extended discussion on plan to reform rates', *The Times*, 24/12/85) or recorded negative reactions ('London stores could face rate rises of £1.4m: calculations of Chartered Institute of Public Finance and Accountancy', *The Times*, 2/8/85; 'Poll Tax rejected by boroughs', *The Times*, 2/8/90; 'TUC at Blackpool: No to a poll tax', *Guardian*, 5/9/85; 'CBI Conference: Rates Plan "dangerous"', *The Times*, 20/11/85).

This coverage reveals three points about coverage during the inception period. Despite the initial secrecy of the Government's decision to adopt the poll tax option, by mid-1985, the secret was out. In addition, the accuracy of media predictions suggests the information was released by the Government itself, via covert disclosures. Finally, despite the enormous significance of what was being proposed and the furore over the rating revaluations in Scotland, the national media showed little initial interest in the fundamental reform in prospect.

Presentation (January – February 1986)

The first, formal public presentation of the Government's plans, in the Green Paper of January 1986, sparked a brief flurry of media coverage which quickly tailed off as the formal consultation process began. In their respective political memoirs, both the then Environment Secretary and the Chancellor of the Exchequer recalled that the initial press reactions to the poll tax proposals were favourable (Baker, 1993; Lawson, 1992). However, closer examination reveals a far more mixed evaluation of the proposals. In the tabloid press, the Green Paper was largely welcomed. The *Daily Mail* wholeheartedly endorsed the Government's arguments, discerning that 'the big advantage of the change will be that, far more than the present system, the benefits people receive will bear a logical relation to what they pay' ('Bold Reform', Editorial, 29/1/86: 6). Similarly, the *Daily Express* commended 'a bold attempt to bring sanity and fairness into local financing' ('A bold and fair reform', Editorial, 30/1/86: 12). Although the *Sun* neglected to editorialize on the proposals, the tone of their news report conveyed at least a modicum of approval for the change ('Rates to face axe at last', 29/1/86).

In the broadsheet press, support was less conspicuous. Only the *Daily Telegraph* welcomed the Green Paper, describing it as 'quite the cleverest way yet devised' of resolving the need to control expenditure and secure local accountability ('Light on Rates', Editorial, 29/1/86). On the other side, the *Guardian* identified a cautionary tone to the Paper due to the poll tax's likely unpopularity, and argued that a local income tax would have been a far preferable reform option ('Green Paper, Yellow Lines', Editorial, 29/1/86: 12). The *Financial Times* applauded the Government's aim to increase the accountability of local government, but concluded that the redistribution of the domestic tax burden that would occur would only excite public antipathy and erode Conservative Party support for the measures ('The Wrong Way to Help Rate-Payers', Editorial, 29/1/86: 18). *The Times* criticized the publication from a localist stance, concluding that 'The Green Paper's plans will convince only those who trust the central government, right down to the nitty gritty of parochial decision-making' ('Benefits of Rates', Editorial, 29/1/86: 11). The next day it presented 'The Case for a Local Income Tax' (Editorial, 30/1/86).

Consultation and Formulation (March 1986 – October 1987)

If initial media evaluations of the Green Paper were somewhat mixed, their attention to the issue was quickly deflected. During the formal consultation process for the policy in England and Wales – which concluded in December 1986 with the publication of a terse summary of responses (DoE, 1986b) – the Community Charge received minimal TV and press attention. This disinterest continued through most of the formulative period, despite several significant related developments. For example, the passage of the Scottish legislation was almost completely neglected. Similarly, the Community Charge was also curiously absent from national media agendas before the June 1987 General Election, despite its ostensible status as the flagship of the Conservative's campaign. Indeed, the issue received considerably more media comment in the month after the ballot, than in the month before it.

Following the election, national media attention gradually increased as the prospect of legislation loomed and discussions at the Conservative Party conference produced a profound revision in the manner of the policy's implementation ('Tories reject plan to phase in poll tax', *Independent*, 7/10/87; 'The charge of the rates brigade', *Daily Mail*, 7/10/87; 'Poll Tax: Maggie names the day', *Sun*, 18/11/87).

Although governmental decision-making remained the principal focus of coverage during the consultation and formulation periods, Conservative Party reactions received more attention – in particular critical responses – as did projections of the likely redistributional effects of the domestic tax reforms ('Assessing your poll position. *The Times* answers the key questions about the new poll tax and shows how much each adult will be expected to pay', *The Times*, 13/7/87: 10; 'A price on your head ... Maurice Chittenden takes a look at the effects of the proposed Community Charge', The *Sunday Times*, 25/6/87: 25; 'Winners and Losers, a guide to the poll tax', *Guardian*, 7/7/87). In addition, debates about the potential threats posed by the tax to individual privacy and the franchise were far more prominent during this period than they were ever to be again ('No representation without taxation?', *Sunday Times*, 19/7/87; 'Big Brother won't be watching say the new poll tax planners', *Daily Mail*, 9/9/87; 'Privacy row over poll tax computer plan for Scotland', *Independent*, 9/9/87; 'NCCL Warning of poll tax national surveillance', *Guardian*, 5/10/87).

Although editorial press comment on the policy during this period was sporadic, some of it was highly critical. The *Sunday Times* echoed the localist concerns of *The Times*, condemning 'a sinister threat to councils' created by the 'drift to centralism' in the British constitution, of which the poll tax was but one example (Editorial, 12/4/87), and after the General Election spelt out its unequivocal opposition to the policy by urging the Government to re-vamp the rating system ('A Pox on the Poll Tax', Editorial, 5/7/87: 26). In late 1987, the *Independent* castigated the Environment Secretary's 'poor defence of a bad tax' at the Conservative Party conference, and highlighted how the tax would increase Whitehall's control ('To spend an extra pound, a local authority will have to raise about four. This may be an admirable way of controlling spending, but it strengthens central power, not local democracy' [Editorial, 7/10/87: 16]). The *Guardian* remained consistent in its support for a local income tax and opposition to a tax 'which is bad in principle ... which is bad in practice ... and which has appalling electoral consequences for the Tories' ('A black hole of an issue', Editorial, 7/7/87: 10).

Only *The Times* significantly shifted its position. In two editorials in late 1986, the paper commended the Government's aims of increasing the accountability of local government ('The rating game', Editorial, 14/11/86), but concluded that 'this well-meant change will be much more damaging to the Government than even its former attempts to reform local government' ('Community charge', Editorial, 17/12/86: 21). However, in an editorial during the General Election, it abandoned its previous localist concerns by urging: 'The radical approach to local government would be to transfer to the Exchequer the cost of those services which are essentially national and are laid on local authorities by the central government ... A flat-rate Community Charge for the rest would be much more acceptable' ('Rates and the Tory voter', Editorial, 25/2/87: 16).

Legislation (November 1987 – July 1988)

The introduction of the Community Charge legislation for England and

Wales in late 1987 was the first trigger for concerted national media attention to the issue. In stark contrast to the lack of interest in the Scottish legislation, the 1987 Local Government Finance Bill stirred up significant waves of media attention; first with the Second Reading of the Bill in the House of Commons, and then the Commons vote on the Mates Amendment and the passage of the Bill through the House of Lords, in April and May 1988.

Apart from the increase in coverage, there were also shifts in the interpretative agenda of press coverage. First, political rifts within the Conservative Party dominated the coverage of the Bill's parliamentary passage ('Insurrection', *Sunday Times*, 17/4/88; 'A nasty attack of mid-term indigestion', *Sunday Telegraph*, 17/4/88; 'Thatcher poll tax majority may fall to 20', *Independent*, 18/4/88; 'Maggie faces poll tax war', *Daily Star*, 20/4/88). Second, projections of how local government would implement and administer the new taxation arrangements, and discussions about its redistributional effects, gained greater prominence.

Clearly, the Conservative Party rebellion provided the personality conflict previously missing from the issue, a point underlined by the primacy given to the critical views of the ex-Conservative Leader, Edward Heath, and the disaffected, ex-cabinet minister, Michael Heseltine, who were both known to harbour profound grievances against their Party leader ('Heseltine Leads Poll Tax Rebels', *Daily Telegraph*, 17/12/87; 'Heseltine Heads Attack on 'Obdurate' poll tax', *Guardian*, 17/12/87; 'Now Tarzan Swings in for a blast at the poll tax', *Today*, 17/12/87; 'Heath Savages Maggie's Poll Tax Plan', *Daily Star*, 18/12/87; 'Thatcher treats us like scum of the earth', *Daily Mirror*, 19/12/87). The prominence of these two politicians in media reports of the Second Reading, far exceeded the sum of their contribution to the Parliamentary debate.*

This in turn triggered a recurrent subtext to reporting of the Conservative rebellion: that the tax was a stalking horse for those on the left of the Party to challenge the Conservative leadership ('Heseltine adds fuel to rebel ringleader claim', *Sunday Telegraph*, 17/4/88; 'Heseltine in dirty tricks row', *Daily Mail*, 18/4/88; 'The desirable residence [10 Downing Street] at the heart of that poll tax revolt', *Daily Mail*, 20/4/88: 6). In November

* A scrutiny of Hansard during the Second Reading shows that in a five hour debate, devouring 216 columns of Parliamentary report, Heseltine had provided just four columns and Heath, one and a half.

1987, the *Sun* vilified Heseltine for his hypocrisy in attacking the poll tax in England after supporting legislation for Scotland ('Many Faces', Editorial, 18/12/87) and the following day attacked Heath for 'act[ing] like the scum of the earth' ('Up the poll', Editorial, 19/12/87: 6). Similarly, the *Daily Express* asserted that 'it is not hostility to the Community Charge that animates most [Conservative rebels] but hostility to the Prime Minister' ('Quiet, Please, We're rebels', Editorial, 19/12/87: 8). Prior to the vote on the Mates Amendment, the *Daily Mail* warned that Michael Mates was 'just as surely doing Mr Heseltine's work as if he were a ventriloquist's dummy ... That is a very powerful reason for ensuring that the amendment fails' ('Travails of a rebel', Editorial, 18/4/88: 6). This debate was not just confined to the Conservative-aligned press. For example, the *Independent* asserted after the Second Reading, 'In everything Mr Heseltine says and does, he makes plain his ambition to succeed Mrs Thatcher. It is in that context that Mr Heseltine's Wednesday night contribution to the debate on the rate reform Bill must be seen' ('A Salutary Ambition', Editorial, 18/12/87), and the *Today* newspaper observed that 'naked ambition has been [Heseltine's] undoing' ('Calm down Tarzan', Editorial, 18/12/87: 8).

By this stage, national editorial enthusiasm was starting to wane. A terse editorial in the *Daily Express* welcomed the tax as 'a radical and well-overdue reform. It is right that we should not have to wait for it a minute longer than necessary' ('Instant reform! A first rate move', Editorial, 18/11/87: 8), but the *Daily Mail*'s support was appreciably more equivocal: initially suggesting the root of the Government's problems lay with the poor presentation of their case (Editorial, 19/12/87: 6), and later, only tacitly endorsing the poll tax by deriding the rates as 'a rotten tax', and the Mates Amendment as 'a fiscal mongrel' ('Ridding Britain of the rates', Editorial, 20/4/88: 6). The *Sun* avoided making any specific editorial comment about the merits of the policy during its legislative passage. Of the broadsheet press, The *Daily Telegraph* continued in its support, if in a more muted vein, commenting on the eve of the Mates Amendment 'the Government's proposals at least have a certain simplicity and a sort of flat rate fairness. Mr Mates' amendment appears to be neither simple, workable, nor particularly fair' ('Flat rate fairness', Editorial, 18/4/88: 16). *The Times*, too, in a major change of stance, commended it for establishing a clear linkage between the cost of services and local taxation levels ('Cost of local democracy', Editorial, 19/12/87: 11), and described it as a 'preferable substitute for the present unfair system of local finance' ('To the Lords', Editorial, 20/4/88: 15).

In contrast, the clamour of editorial condemnation became far more insistent, and was not exclusively restricted to the non-aligned or Labour supporting papers. The *Mail on Sunday*, a staunchly Conservative tabloid, urged the Government to adopt 'a progressive tax based as much on ability to pay as on demand for services' ('Nought out of three for poll tax targets', Editorial, 24/2/88: 8). Meanwhile the *Sunday Times* – which had been noted for its increasingly explicit support for the Conservative Party during the 1980s – remained 'unconvinced by the case for the poll tax', because it threatened 'to cripple the proper functioning of local democracy' ('Advances against inertia', Editorial, 22/11/87: 34), and urged its defeat ('Poll tax should not pass', Editorial, 17/4/88). Similarly, the *Independent* encouraged the rebel Conservatives forces to 'press ... with all courage' for a banded poll tax ('Positive alternative to the poll tax', Editorial, 14/12/87: 16), and later excoriated the Government for becoming 'complacent to the point of arrogance' ('Mrs Thatcher's moral dilemmas', Editorial, 16/4/88: 10). The *Guardian*, too, expressed support for the Mates Amendment ('The rebels still have a good cause', Editorial, 16/4/88: 22) and its absolute opposition to the flat rate charge ('Flagship Futility', Editorial, 19/2/88: 20; 'Still up the poll', Editorial, 25/3/88: 22). *Today* concluded that 'when [Mrs Thatcher] looks at the alternatives, she will find that rates are not so bad after all' ('Tax that's not worth revolt', Editorial, 18/4/88: 8). Not surprisingly, the Labour supporting *Daily Mirror*, after ignoring the issue during its Second Reading, later attacked the poll tax for its manifest regressiveness ('No Prime Minister', Editorial, 18/4/88: 2).

By the time the Bill moved to the House of Lords the editorial concerns of the press shifted to the constitutional repercussions of a defeat or amendment of the legislation at this stage. The *Daily Mail* ('The Peers should know their place', Editorial, 23/5/88), the *Sunday Times* ('Time to break the spell', Editorial, 15/5/88) and *The Times* ('Vote of the Lords', Editorial, 24/5/88: 15) warned against the Lords amending or defeating 'an historic tax reform approved by the Commons' (Editorial, *Daily Mail*, 20/4/88: 6). The *Guardian* took a different view of such constitutional protocol, attacking the Government's strategy of filling the Lords with 'backwoodsmen' as 'a form of gerrymandering which has drawn attention once again to the anomalous place of hereditary Lords in our democracy' ('The sheep troop in from the shires', Editorial, 25/5/88: 18). The Labour affiliated *Sunday*

Mirror expressed similar sentiments, reviling those peers who 'abused their privilege to help a Government which didn't deserve that help' ('Low life', Editorial, 29/5/88: 2).

Preparation (August 1988 – December 1989)

Following the passage of the 1988 Local Government Finance Act, a hiatus in national media coverage of the tax ensued, revealing, once again, a conspicuous disregard for the policy's impact in Scotland, where the Charge's introduction in April 1989 brought only a minor increase in coverage of the policy.

Instead, the main triggers to coverage during the preparatory period were unforeseen political crises that interrupted the transition towards implementation in England and Wales. The first was the political furore over the Government's controversial Community Charge publicity campaign in May 1989. The second, the rebellion in Conservative party ranks following the announcement of the self financing safety net arrangements, in July 1989. The third, the Government's decision to completely change the Charge's transitional arrangements, from a self-financing redistribution towards a centrally subvented system, in October and November 1989.

During the preparatory period, coverage of central government and parliamentary decision-making once again came to the fore (the dominant theme in a quarter of the coverage), principally concerning governmental promotion and publicity of the tax (8 per cent of all items) and the safety net arrangements (7 per cent). Furthermore, coverage of issues related to local government implementation of the tax attracted more attention (18 per cent): especially related to the registration process (7 per cent), and local enforcement procedures (4 per cent).

When we examine the evaluative tone of the national press coverage of these areas, it is clear that the seeds of doubt sowed during the legislative period, were rapidly germinating into outright scepticism, even among those papers that had recently endorsed the tax during its legislative passage ('Poll Tax: the nightmare that won't go away', *Daily Express*, 14/9/89). When opponents of the tax halted the launch of the Government's Community Charge mass leafleting campaign, press ridicule of the Government, and particularly the ministers responsible, was merciless. The *Daily Mail* on its front page likened the local government minister to a children's cartoon character, lampooning a 'Whitehall farce over Postman Pat' (11/5/89), and in its editorial condemned 'political arrogance of the kind that is in danger of turning a mighty department into a public relations disaster' ('Gummer's grin', Editorial, 11/5/89: 6). The *Daily Telegraph* noted 'the marks of, shall we say, carelessness' in the publicity, and observed how the principle that Government publicity should not be used for party political purposes 'has frequently been winked at, particularly by this Government. All the more reason for a warning shot' (Editorial, 11/5/89: 16). The *Guardian* too attacked the 'biased' nature of the leaflet ('Getting fair play on the poll tax', Editorial, 10/5/89: 22).

However, this controversy was soon superseded by media attention to the political battle over the Government's safety net proposals, announced on 19 July 1989. The anger these arrangements evoked among Conservative back-benchers, generated another intense bout of news coverage, much of which patently editorialized about the competence and prospects of the Secretary of State. The *Daily Mail*'s front page urged 'Ridley has to go now' (20/7/89); the *Mirror* noted 'It's another fine mess, Mr Ridley' (20/7/89); and the *Sun* described how 'Ridley drives commons up the poll!' (20/7/89). *Today* was in no doubts about the consequences of the announcement: 'Poll-axed Ridley signs his execution warrant' (20/7/89), and the following day pictured the minister adjusting his spectacles alongside the headline: 'I don't remember precisely what I've done today' (21/7/89). Even the staunchly loyal *Daily Express* scathingly attacked the minister as 'the unacceptable face of Thatcherism' for alienating 'Tory rebels who object to their constituents paying a penny to bail out voters, mainly in Labour areas, from facing the full penalty for electing a spendthrift council' (Editorial, 21/7/89: 8). Ameliorative statements from the Prime Minister were also seized upon, for signs that the Government was about to change tack on the policy ('Thatcher juggling act on poll tax', *Sunday Telegraph*; 23/7/89; 'Thatcher tries to defuse row over poll tax', *Daily Telegraph*, 21/7/89), and the Cabinet reshuffle which promptly followed, which saw Chris Patten appointed as the Secretary of State for the Environment, produced considerable media speculation as to what this change in political emphasis might mean for the progress of the policy ('Patten opens with poll tax pledge', *Guardian*, 26/7/89; 'Patten moves to defuse Tory anger on poll tax safety net', *Daily Telegraph*, 26/7/89).

The issue resurfaced later in the year, when it was announced at the Conservative Party conference that the Government would centrally fund the transitional arrangements after the first year. This major policy revision was widely welcomed in many sections of the national press, although much was made in the news reporting of the additional expense of these subsidies ('Government will spend £1bn to smooth poll tax', *Independent*, 12/10/89; 'Tories unveil £1.3bn poll tax cushion', *The Times*, 12/10/89; '£1.5bn Tory bid to buy off poll tax revolt', *Daily Mirror*, 12/10/89; '£1bn escape on poll tax', *Daily Mail*, 12/10/89). The *Daily Telegraph*, having reconsidered its initial opposition to a centrally financed transitional system ('Poll tax pain', Editorial, 6/10/89), commended the Government's 'poll tax ingenuity' in producing transitional arrangements that were 'much fairer – as well as more saleable politically – than those of his predecessor' (Editorial, 12/10/89: 12). In contrast, only the *Guardian* detected 'a certain awesome amorality' in the Government's decision to buy their way out of their trouble ('Baling in Billions', Editorial, 12/10/89: 22).

Despite the intensity of media deliberations on the safety net issue, the alternative critique of the safety net arrangements – that they helped to obscure the extent of the redistribution of resources from poorer to more affluent areas (Lee, 1989; Esam and Oppenheim, 1989; LGIU, 1989) – was almost completely absent from national press debate. Rather, what reflective discussion there was either accepted the formulation that the parsimonious were being penalized for the sins of the profligate ('Ridley's Riddle', Editorial, *Daily Mail*, 20/7/89: 6) or expressed concerns about how changes in the funding of the system would impact upon the Government's macro-economic policies ('Poll tax blues', Editorial, *The Times*, 10/7/89; 'Mr Ridley's Safety Net', Editorial, *The Times*, 20/7/89).

The preparatory period was also the only time when attention to the political response of the Labour Party exceeded coverage of Conservative responses ('Labour heads off Party fear', *The Times*, 27/9/89; 'Kinnock also threatened by poll tax fight', *Daily Telegraph*, 2/9/89; ''Confused' plan for local taxes causes concern', *Daily Telegraph*, 6/10/89). In mid-1988, the *Guardian* noted Labour's 'mangled disarray' over how to oppose the tax, and the Government's probable delight in the mess the poll tax 'seems to have landed its enemies' ('Politics of dissent', Editorial, 31/8/88). All the national press, regardless of their political orientation, cautioned Labour against adopting a non-payment/implementation strategy. In 1988, the *Daily Mail* attacked the Labour Party leader's 'silly advice' in encouraging voters to snarl up the registration process, asserting that 'any political leader who dallies with illegality, shoots his own party in the foot and trots out such foolish advice does not deserve respect' (Editorial, 16/4/88: 6). A few months later this point was echoed, in detail, if not in tone, by a *Daily Mirror* editorial which attacked those Labour MPs – including the shadow spokesperson, Robin Cook – who supported non-payment. It concluded that Cook, 'as a democrat ... should set an example to others' (Editorial, 25/8/88: 2). This hostility towards non-payment remained throughout subsequent reporting of the tax.

Media attention also focused on Labour's 'twin tax' reform options. The idea was predictably savaged by the Conservative press ('Labour planning double rates burden and council free-for-all', *Daily Mail*, 24/9/88), as was their decision to reconsider this option ('Big brother tax threat ... Labour is devising a controversial new tax on homes ... Tories raised the spectre of spendthrift Left wing town halls being given free rein to snoop into people's private financial affairs', *Daily Mail*, 18/9/89: 1). However, even the pro-Labour *Daily Mirror* expressed serious reservations about the twin tax proposals, describing it as a system which penalized 'the couple who invested their capital in a private pension' rather than 'those who invested in a spree in the Caribbean' ('Labour's Loser', Editorial, *Daily Mirror*, 22/7/88: 2). Only the *Guardian* showed any enthusiasm, asserting: 'Labour's proposals may well have more attraction in the way they provide a financial framework for giving local authorities back to people' ('If not the poll tax ...', Editorial, 30/9/88: 22).

Introduction (January 1990 – April 1990)

In quantitative terms, the introductory period was the most intensive phase of media comment on the Community Charge. During January and February 1990, local government finance began to move up the press and television agenda; however, once local authorities started to set the first poll tax levels, in late February, coverage increased exponentially. Indeed, there were more poll tax related items in the national media during March and April 1990 than in the whole of 1989.

In our description of the thematic details of national media coverage prior to its introduction in England and Wales, we have focused on the main themes in national press coverage of the policy. Although this provides a useful barometer of the shifting emphasis of media coverage over several years, it is but a crude measure, as it ignores *poll tax related* coverage (where the issue was mentioned in a secondary context in items which focused on other matters) and doesn't quantify subsidiary themes within items. Furthermore, we have no formal basis for comparing divergence in press and broadcast news agendas. In this section, we analyse these issues more directly by drawing on data from the more intensive sampling conducted between 1 March and 5 May 1990.

Table 5.2 shows the relative prominence and stance of the main organizations and individuals in poll tax focused and related national coverage during this crucial period. Despite the policy's explicitly local implications, the views and activities of national politicians were favoured over local politicians by a ratio of more than two to one. Furthermore, attention focused on the élites of the two main political parties, and conspicuously marginalized representatives from other political parties. Non party political actors were also infrequently featured. For example, local authority associations appeared in 3 per cent of items across all media sectors; representatives from the voluntary sector in under 2 per cent; and local government professionals – whose responsibility it was to administer the new system – 2 per cent. Even those single issue pressure groups established to fight the tax – the Anti Poll Tax Unions and Federations – received a proportionally insignificant amount of coverage (less than 3 per cent). Indeed, the only arena of debate and activity beyond parliament that attracted any significant coverage was among the general public (reflecting the widespread reporting of public demonstrations against the tax that occurred at this time). However, greater media prominence did not, in itself, guarantee a definitional advantage. For example, although the Government was the dominant political actor in national coverage, it was consistently more defensive in its stance* than its political adversaries. Government representatives only offered support for any aspect of the policy in a minority of instances, whereas other spokespersons displayed a consistently critical stance towards the policy. The cumulative picture this produces is of the Community Charge as a controversial policy initiative with a wide range of critics, and with few supporters willing, or able, to convey their support via the media. For example, although Margaret Thatcher received nearly twice as much coverage as the Labour leader, she

* Only those individuals or institutions who were active participants in a news item were coded. That is, they had some independent status in the reporting of an item, and were not just referred to by another actor. The stance of each actor towards the Community Charge and related reforms was then noted ('critical', 'neutral', or 'unstated/neutral') and was exclusively determined by the explicit views he or she conveyed, or was attributed with, in the item.

was reported making explicitly supportive statements in less than a quarter of her appearances.

Table 5.2 Political actors in national Community Charge coverage (1 March – 5 May 1990)

		Disposition of Actors	
	Proportional presence in all items Col. 1 %	Critical Col. 2 %	Supportive Col. 3 %
Party political actors			
Government	46	2	14
Other national conservative politician	15	55	8
Local Conservative politician/authority	11	35	5
Other Conservative party actor	6	23	9
Labour shadow cabinet	21	67	–
Other Labour national politician	8	78	–
Local Labour politician/authority	11	41	–
Other Labour party actor	7	31	–
All other party political actors	10	63	–
Party political actor (party not stated)	7	19	–
Non party political actors			
Local government associations/pressure groups	3	88	1
General public	21	71	1
Anti poll tax groups	3	73	–
Other voluntary organizations	2	47	4
Local government professionals	2	33	–
Trades unions	5	62	–
Research Agencies	7	10	1
Business & business federations	7	53	1
Other actors (other professionals, journalists)	19	18	–
Total of national TV/press/radio items	2224		

Figures relate to news and feature poll tax items only (focused and related). Column 1: percentages = proportion of items which featured at least one actor in category. Columns 2 and 3: percentage = disposition displayed of each actor/frequency of appearance. Percentages are separate and do not add up to 100.

The defensiveness of the Government's posture becomes even clearer when we analyse the primary and subsidiary themes of all poll tax coverage during the introductory period (see Table 5.3). Generally, all national media shared a disinterest in the historical reasons for the policy's development (such as the failings of the rating system and the problems of controlling local expenditure), but paid considerable attention to the negative responses to the policy from the general public (see below) and the Conservative Party ('Baker's panic plea to Tories on poll tax', *Observer*, 25/2/90; 'Stop the hysteria', *Daily Mail*, 8/3/90; 'War in the Tory ranks', *Daily Mirror*, 24/3/90).

Table 5.3 Themes in national Community Charge coverage (1 March – 5 May 1990)

	TV %	Radio %	Broadsheet %	Tabloids %
1. Origins of policy				
Iniquity of rating system and other	5	4	5	4
2. Implementation of policy				
governmental/parliamentary decision-making	13	17	15	10
Local government administration	9	8	11	14
3. Responses to the policy				
public responses	15	14	15	16
Conservative party responses	4	7	7	7
Labour party responses	3	3	4	4
Other actor responses	2	5	3	2
4. Effects of policy				
Inequities/anomolies of new system	6	8	5	5
Electoral detriment of the Government	12	8	9	9
Winners and Losers	2	2	5	6
Negative impact on local services	3	4	3	2
Other negative economic effects	4	3	6	3
Culpability for high poll tax levels	5	4	2	6
Inefficiency of new system	1	2	1	1
Equity of new system	4	3	1	1
Other effects	5	5	3	5
5. Other themes				
Explanations about aspects of the reforms	2	1	3	2
Alternatives to the reforms	4	3	3	2
Total themes coded	876	559	2491	940

Figures relate to news, feature and editorial items (poll tax focused and related). Up to four themes could be coded for each item. Percentages = frequency of appearance/aggregate of themes coded. All figures are rounded. $x^2 = 230.41$; df = 51; $P < 0.00$.

Coverage of local government implementation roughly balanced attention to parliamentary decision-making during this period, with most local interest focused on the exceedingly high charges initially levied by councils, particularly in Conservative areas ('Labour councils' charge only marginally higher than Tories', *Observer*, 11/3/90; 'Comparing the figures: 'High spender' jibe misfires', *Guardian*, 12/3/90). Coverage of parliamentary decision-making mainly centred on speculation about Government attempts to resolve the political crisis ('Climb down over poll tax blunder', *Daily Mail*, 22/3/90; 'Rethink of poll tax begins', *Daily Telegraph*, 12/4/90; '10 ways Maggie can help us like poll tax: She's ready to try new ideas', *Sun*, 28/4/90; 'Thatcher U-Turn in poll tax chaos', *Daily Mirror*, 28/4/90).

Coverage of the effects of the Community Charge was almost exclusively defined as contradicting the Government's interests: in electoral terms, eroding their support; in economic terms, harming the immediate prospects of businesses and the economy; and in redistributional terms, unfairly shifting the taxation burden from Duke to Dustman.There were also significant thematic variations between the reporting of different media sectors. These differences mainly related to the reporting of the implementation of the tax and its effects. In coverage of the implementative process the tabloid press gave less attention to parliamentary decision-making and more to local government implementation of the tax. In the reporting of effects of the tax, a more varied pattern emerged. Firstly, television and the tabloid press paid proportionally greater attention to the issue of which tier of government was culpable for the high charge levels. Second, the broadsheet press gave more coverage to the negative economic effects of the tax, whereas television news gave it far lower prominence. Third, television news focused more attention on the negative electoral implications that the tax was having on the Conservative Party, whereas this issue was more marginal in broadsheet coverage. Fourth, radio news and current affairs coverage paid more attention to questions regarding the inequities of the new system (such as the inadequacy of rebate provisions, and the failure of the system to take into account ability to pay).

Several interacting factors produced these variations. On a most basic level they reflected the different physical constraints and demands placed on news media sectors. Both television news and tabloids have far less potential news space than either the broadsheet press or radio, which seriously limits the opportunity for contextual or reflective discussion. In addition, they are far more mindful of the visuality of a story when selecting their news. In the tabloid press, these concerns are compounded by a deep commitment to strident populism and the prioritization of entertainment over information (Golding, 1993) which creates an obvious impatience with the complexities of the legislature and economy.

Another important reason for the variation relates to the activities of key news sources. For example, the Government's damage limitation news work – which sought to blame high poll tax levels on councils and then promote the theme that 'Conservative Councils Cost You Less' – was principally targeted at television, because of its greater ubiquity and perceived influence. This would explain the greater prominence of the culpability issue in TV coverage, as Government ministers strove to turn every sound-bite into a tirade on local government profligacy.

Finally, political partisanship also influenced news priorities. The strong pro-Conservative affiliation of most of the tabloids, coupled with their historical vilification of the' loony left' in local government, made them the most receptive to the Government's argument that high poll tax levels were the fault of local authorities. This would explain the proportionally greater attention paid by the tabloids to local government implementation and culpability for high charge levels. However, as we see below, by this stage, any attempts to demonize local government proved very hard to sustain.

The introductory period marked the virtual eradication of the last vestiges of national media support for the policy, even among the pro-Conservative press. Although the *Daily Mail* briefly maintained that 'the principle of the poll tax ... is sound', it criticized 'the pathetic failure of the Government ... to put its case across' ('Rough passage for the poll tax' Editorial, 2/3/90: 6), and later conceded the poll tax was 'plainly a loser' ('About-turn on the poll tax', Editorial, 28/4/90: 6). *The Times* asserted that the case for reverting to a property based system of taxation was 'overwhelming' ('Tinkering with error', Editorial, 28/4/90: 11). The only concerted support came from the *Sun*, which heartily endorsed the Government's arguments that excessive poll tax levels solely reflected local profligacy by declaring 'War on poll tax wasters'. Readers were invited to call a poll tax hotline with examples of 'barmy burghers' 'who fritter away YOUR cash' (1/3/90), and throughout March a litany of articles was printed citing examples of wasteful local expenditure ('Council cash was going to pot! Grant went to pay for drug farm', 1/3/90; '£18,000 to look after lesbians', 2/3/90; 'Everyone a loony! Leftie council waste £68-a-head poll tax on 300 daft dole-outs', 20/3/90). However, the *Sun* soon tired of this line, partly because it became increasingly evident that it had been seriously misinformed in many of the 'facts' it cited (*Observer*, 25/3/90), but also because the paper realized it had seriously misjudged the public mood, and had placed itself in a dangerously isolated position in comparison with its national press rivals. (For example, the *Daily Mirror* ran a counter campaign asking 'Is your Council under attack from the *Sun?*').

However, despite the chorus of condemnation against the tax, it would be mistaken to assume that the Government was consistently on the defensive during the introductory period. If it signally failed to generate journalistic support for its policy, the media's interest in reporting antagonistic public responses to the Community Charge, afforded an opportunity to divert the focus of political debate away from the tax and on to the issue of the far left's insurgency of the constitutional Labour Party. It is important to look more closely at this aspect of media debate, not just because disagreement about the political meaning of the poll tax demonstrations constituted a key moment of ideological contestation in the debate, but also because the way in which the media explained and adjudicated upon their significance provides a revealing insight into how they define the parameters of legitimate dissent in our political culture.

'We're not paying the poll tax': national media and public dissent

When the first public demonstrations occurred in rural and suburban areas, and the middle classes of 'Little England' took to the streets to vent their wrath against the Government, they were universally reported as being problematic for it, with both press and broadcast media emphasizing the unforeseen and unlikely nature of the rebellion:

> 'This countryside is the countryside of the middle class England of myth. You almost expect to meet Winnie the Pooh and Piglet in the woods ... The creator of Alice in Wonderland lived just down the road from here. 'Just down the road' nowadays, means the M25: the fast track through the Conservative heartlands of the home counties. But it's in towns around this motorway that some of the fiercest criticism is coming of the inequalities of the Community Charge' (*Newsnight*, BBC2, 29/3/90).

This formulation was exemplified in a Channel Four documentary which followed an outraged resident on an ambling tour of an idyllic rural village in Kent, in which she invited friends and neighbours to share their anger against the tax with the viewing public:

> 'We're here to look round the village to see exactly the problems which have been worrying me, at any rate, and I don't think it's only me. I think a lot of people feel the same as I do. That some questions are there and they need to be answered. And, hopefully, if we enquire politely enough, we'll get some answers' (*A Polite Enquiry*, Channel 4, 29/3/90).

However, as the demonstrations spread to inner city areas and became more violent, a second interpretation emerged, keenly fanned by Conservative Central Office. This was that the demonstrations compromised Labour more than the Government; or as one television news bulletin put it: 'Although this protest was aimed at Mrs Thatcher's poll tax, there's no doubt that it's Mr Kinnock who will dislike these scenes most' (ITN *News at Ten*, 1/3/90). Intrinsic to this political interpretation was the notion that the violent outbursts were deliberately orchestrated by political extremists on the left, who were hi-jacking the anti poll tax protests for their own subversive purposes ('Dumped militants stir up poll tax violence', *Daily Mirror*, 8/3/90; 'How militant plotted the campaign: A *Sunday Times* investigation team exposes the secret methods of the Trotskyite travelling circus', *Sunday Times*, 11/4/90; 'How the activists use hotlines to mobilize armies of protest', *The Times*, 9/3/90; 'Return of rent-a-mob', *Daily Mail*, 7/3/90). The possibility of far left sedition alarmed the liberal media as much as the Conservative press. For example, the *Guardian* attacked 'the playground revolutionaries of Militant and the SWP, maintaining their long tradition of polluting every cause they espouse' ('The mobs move in', Editorial, 8/3/90: 18), and the *Daily Mirror* attacked Militant as a 'pestilential nuisance' on the constitutional Labour party ('Vote this tax away', Editorial, 8/3/90: 2).

As the violence of the demonstrations increased, the news reporting increasingly adopted familiar inferential frameworks evident in earlier reporting of urban unrest (Halloran *et al.*, 1970; Murdock, 1984; Solomos, 1986; Hansen and Murdock, 1985). Making sense of troubling and unusual events requires their interpretation by the media into terminology and narrative readily understood by audiences. Here two competing 'stories' were available for this task – the sturdy resilience of the British people in the face of potty authoritarianism, and the dangerous sedition of marginal wastrels, flouting acceptable standards and exploiting decent goodwill. In the event the latter narrative, readily nourished by generations of copy denouncing the dangerous classes of urban Britain, prevailed, not least because of its insistent elaboration by authoritative sources. One classic feature of this was in the widespread use of 'binary oppositions' (Eco, 1979) to demarcate permissible and unacceptable protest action. On one level this involved contrasting the spontaneity of the earlier demonstrations with the alleged premeditation of the riots:

> 'This is all a far cry from the initial English poll tax protests, when the style was more umbrella and green welly than nap-sack and bicycle cape. In the last week or so the agitprop left have seized on an issue they know to be massively unpopular in the hope of riding it to respectability' (*Newsnight*, 6/3/90).

On another level, juxtaposing the bewilderment of bystanders and victims with the knowing cynicism of the rioters:

> 'One elderly resident of Hackney condemned the looters who smashed into shops during last night's protests. She said, "why do they break things? They can speak to each other in a nice way, and have it out"' (Closing trailer, BBC1 *6pm News*, 9/3/90).

And, finally, comparing the fragility of the rule of Law, with the powerful, lurking forces of anarchy:

> '"He was holding a metal bar. He used it. He must have known that he might even kill me": How a policeman suffered in the defence of democracy' (*Daily Mail*, 17/4/90).

All of these features were particularly evident in the coverage of the most serious violence in Trafalgar Square on 31 March 1990. After the riot, several sections of the tabloid press conducted their own brand of trial by media, asking the public to identify the faces of rioters photographed during the trouble ('Nail the Poll Tax Thugs', *Sun*, 3/4/90; 'Wanted: Help Hunt Down Tax Riot Thugs', *News of the World*, 13/5/90). And if the broadsheet and broadcast media avoided such excesses, the same underlying emphasis on criminality and conspiracy exerted a powerful influence over their analyses. For example, the day after the riot, a Radio 4 news presenter asserted it was 'generally agreed that the street violence had nothing to do with local government reform. This was no act of civil disobedience in a noble cause. It was an excuse for hooliganism or worse' (*World this Weekend*, Radio 4, 1/4/90). *The Times*, meanwhile, looked back nostalgically to the anti-Vietnam war marches of the 1960s,

> 'The British have learnt to take street disorder more seriously since then ... The songs they bellowed were nonsense jingles without a breath of politics in them. If there were deeply angry people among them nursing a heartfelt political grievance, they kept a low profile. Street protest was a gentler game twenty years ago' (2/4/90: 3).

The *Sunday Times* linked the poll tax violence with the emergence of an alienated British 'underclass' ('The fighting underclass', 8/4/90), a theme which the *Daily Mail* subsequently developed in a sustained and vitriolic abuse of the disadvantaged and dispossessed ('The bloody birth of an underclass', 9/4/90; 'A class to fit the crime', 10/4/90; 'Idleness of the shirking class', 11/4/90; 'Where does society go from here?', 12/4/90).

Although serious questions later emerged about the role that over-zealous and incompetent policing may have played in escalating the violence,* the reporting displayed a marked deference to police interpretations of the causes of the riot: firstly, in the privileging of police commentators in reports ('The Metropolitan police have begun a high level investigation into the riot. At a news conference a short while ago, the Deputy Assistant Commissioner, David Meynell, talked of the savage violence used against the police', BBC1 *1pm News*, 1/4/90), and, secondly, in a tendency to portray the police as victims of, rather than participants in, the violence ('Victims in blue risked death in line of duty', *Daily Mail*, 2/4/90). Where representatives of anti poll tax groups and maverick Labour MPs questioned the police's tactics, these issues were consistently subordinated within a dominant framework of criminality. For example, the *Guardian*'s full page account of the demonstration provided a 'protester's view' which

* The civil liberty group, Liberty, was so concerned about police tactics it agreed to monitor the policing of another national demonstration against the poll tax in October 1990. In March 1991, an internal report by the Deputy Assistant Commissioner of the Metropolitan Police on the policing of the riot identified a serious breakdown in police communications during the riot, with officers unaware of tactics used by other units. It also acknowledged that the precipitative use of riot shields and the frequent movement of speeding police vehicles had 'raised the temperature of the crowd' (*Guardian*, 5/3/91: 4).

questioned the heavy handed and disorganized policing ('Police "broke guidelines"', 2/4/90). However, this account was balanced by the police's description of 'A simple brutal assault', and set within a larger piece with the headline: 'Black flags signalled violence to come'. Alongside it a contextual piece explored the 'Shadowy source of violent revolt'.

This discursive closure was not absolute, but what critical reflectiveness there was about the frameworks and assumptions of mainstream reporting, was confined to the peripheries or the letters pages (e.g. the *Guardian*'s letter pages, 2/4/90 & 7/4/90). For example, on BBC2's *Late Show* (12/3/90) a journalist asserted that 'by dramatising the poll tax through images of riot and violence, the press endangers the democracy it purports to defend'. And in the *Guardian*'s youth section, another commentator observed how the simplistic stereotyping of 'mindless militants or mindful mutants' obviated the need 'to go through the dreary business of thinking about things' (14/3/90: 16).

The shifting interpretation of the public demonstrations by the media had a powerful influence on the campaign strategies of the main protagonists in the debate. Apart from the Government, who actively encouraged debate around the hidden motives for the demonstrations and Labour's culpability, the coverage prompted a swift response from the Labour leadership, who derided the non-payment strategy and unequivocally condemned the public disorder. After Trafalgar Square, the Party's Deputy leader, Roy Hattersley, stated 'the people responsible simply have to be prosecuted and punished very severely indeed' (BBC1 *1pm News*, 1/4/90), and in Parliament condemned 'without reservation or qualification the violence that took place in and around Trafalgar Square last Saturday ... All democrats will combine in demanding the rooting out of the threat to our free society which was perpetrated by individuals and organizations who were responsible for the disgraceful scenes and conduct in the capital last Saturday'* (*Hansard*, 2/4/90, columns 894–895). The effect of this strategy was twofold. Firstly, as opinion polls demonstrated the resilience of Labour's lead throughout early April, it helped to further dampen media

* Journalists played a key role in drawing the responsibility of far left groups for the violence to the attention of the Home Secretary and Shadow Home Secretary. After the riot they presented both with leaflets distributed at the demonstration by the Anarchist group 'Class War', which stated 'Scraps with the cops may not stop the poll tax, but ... who needs an excuse for a fight with the Bill?' (*Hansard*, Column 895, 2/4/90).

interest in implicating Labour with the violence. Second, by deferring to the inferential frame provided by the police and the Government about the riot and its causes, it reinforced the denial of their political significance and the discursive closure around the exacerbatory influence of over-zealous or incompetent policing.

Evaluation (May 1990 – February 1990)

Although media interest in the Community Charge started to wane as the debris was cleared from Trafalgar Square and the first bills were delivered, media attention fell away most dramatically from May onwards. The main reason for the decrease in coverage was the political inferences drawn from the results of the 1990 local elections, held on 3 May. In Chapter 3, we described how the campaigning strategy of Conservative Central Office deliberately focused media attention on their performance in their three 'flagship' boroughs of Wandsworth, Westminster and Bradford, with their pruned services and low poll tax levels, to deflect attention from their poor performance in other councils. This political strategy proved highly effective in media terms. In the lead up to the ballot, the flagship authorities were consistently at the forefront of media attention, and when the Conservatives' consolidated their power in two of the three authorities (despite catastrophic losses elsewhere) the result was generally interpreted by the national media as inconclusive. According to *Newsnight* it was 'a day on which honour could be salvaged on all sides' (4/5/90). Or, in the words of the lead item on *Channel Four News*, a result that afforded 'the tax and Mrs Thatcher herself some breathing space ... Labour will insist the idea of the poll tax was generally rejected. In the end, though, it's likely to be interpreted both ways' (4/5/90).

Throughout the summer months of 1990, the Community Charge was temporarily relegated in national news agendas, but re-emerged in November 1990, as coverage of the Conservative leadership contest heightened speculation about what would happen to the policy in the event of a new leader securing office. After Mrs Thatcher's deposition and a fundamental review of the policy began, media attention waned once more, only to increase again in anticipation of the announcement of the policy review.

The interpretative focus of the press agenda also shifted during this period:

away from public opposition and back towards Governmental decision-making, in particular, the concessions and revisions being contemplated to offset the political difficulties the tax had created. Local government enforcement of the tax also attracted more coverage, as did the impact of the tax upon local service provision. In addition, the issue of Conservative Party disaffection remained a significant, if subordinated, subtext during this period, particularly during the leadership contest. When Michael Heseltine announced his intention to stand against Margaret Thatcher, a lot of media commentary focused on what her defeat would mean for the future structure of local finance and the electoral prospects of the Conservative Party ('Labour's Poll Lead Shrinks In Ballots', *Sunday Times*, 11/11/90).

Although media interest reduced after the excitement of the leadership contest there was sporadic evidence of governmental 'kite flying' undertaken to assess the likely popularity of different reform alternatives via the media ('PM rules out abolition of poll tax', *Guardian*, 7/1/91; 'Major backtracks on Poll tax gaffe: TV statement ruling out abolition a contingent thought', *Guardian*, 16/1/91; 'Major refuses to rule out return to rates', *Guardian*, 31/1/91).

Abolition (March 1991 – March 1993)

The final intensive period of national media coverage of the Community Charge came in March and April 1991, when media speculation about the results of the poll tax review reached a fever pitch. After the Government's disastrous showing in the Ribble Valley by-election in early March, the lobby was given formal notice that the poll tax was to be completely abandoned ('Major decides the poll tax must be scrapped', *Sunday Times*, 10/3/91). Later that month, these covert briefings became the subject of media attention themselves, as senior Government sources leaked details of the Environment Secretary's statement to Parliament three days in advance, apparently without the prior knowledge or consent of the Prime Minister ('MPs bemused by the leak of Heseltine Plans', *Independent*, 20/3/93; 'Westminster leaks outlined the course of poll tax successor', *Today*, 20/3/91; 'Heseltine on the No. 10 carpet over poll tax leak', *Daily Mail*, 20/3/91). The reasons for the leaks were never made clear, although the political editor of one national paper speculated that 'senior sources' had sanctioned the disclosure to out-manoeuvre those within the Conservative Party who wished to see the tax retained ('Tarzan to probe the great poll tax leak', *Daily Star*, 21/3/91).

This minor storm was immediately superseded by reports of the Chancellor's decision to finance a universal £140 reduction in all poll tax levels by increasing Value Added Tax. Most of the tabloids, appropriating Gulf War terminology, approved of the surprise decision and speculated about what the move might mean for the timing of the next General Election ('£140 poll tax is slashed, June election looms', *Sun*, 20/3/91; 'Stormin' Norman to the rescue', *Daily Mail*, 20/3/91; 'VAT missile takes £140 out of the poll tax', *Today*, 20/3/91; 'Storming Norman's poll tax massacre signals early elections', *Daily Express*, 20/3/91). Only the *Mirror* and the *Daily Star* considered the hike in the VAT rate to be a price not worth paying ('Tax on kids' sweeties: "it's the poor who'll pay for this bill CON!"', *Daily Mirror*, 20/3/91; 'Vatman goes robbin': Norm makes us all pay up', *Daily Star*, 20/3/91).

The response from the broadsheets was more mixed. The *Daily Telegraph* judged that the 'massive first aid to the poll tax' would 'provide a fair wind for an early election' ('Prudent for Britain, but bold enough to win', Editorial, 20/3/91), whereas *The Times* was more incredulous about the generosity of the subsidy, describing it as 'the nearest any British Government has come to handing out fivers on the street corner' ('Recession Unrelieved', Editorial, 20/3/91). The *Guardian* saw it as just a stop gap measure to deal with a policy that 'continues malevolently to distort domestic policies' (Editorial, 20/3/91: 22) and claimed it would ultimately disadvantage the poor ('The other side of the wheeze', Editorial, 21/3/91).

The national media had barely time to digest the Chancellor's surprise, before they faced the official announcement of the abolition of the Community Charge. Although the Secretary of State was deliberately evasive about its replacement, this public signing of the policy's death warrant sparked an orgy of comment about its failure, and the replacement in prospect. The relief of the pro-Conservative taboids was palpable. The *Sun* urged 'Don't weep for that tax' (Editorial, 22/3/91) and the *Daily Express* welcomed the tax's repeal because it significantly improved the chances of the Government's re-election ('End of a taxing Tory nightmare', Editorial, 22/3/91). The *Daily Mail* was similarly enthused but warned the Government against introducing a 'son of poll tax', and – conveniently forgetting its earlier vilification of Labour's 'roof tax' – urged a return to a property based tax linked to capital values ('The tax that turned traitor', Editorial, 22/3/91: 6). The non-Conservative tabloids were more centrally concerned with the Charge's replacement. The *Daily Star* cautioned the Government that there was 'no room for a botch up' (Editorial, 22/3/91: 8), and *Today* observed that 'the hard part of [Heseltine's] task lies ahead' ('Last rites for the poll tax', Editorial, 22/3/91: 6). The *Daily Mirror* was fiercely scornful of the Minister's deliberate imprecision and concluded that 'like the undead' the poll tax would continue 'taking its toll on people and haunting the Tory Party' ('Taking the Michael', Editorial, 22/3/91: 2).

The broadsheets shared the tabloid's unanimous support for the repeal of the Community Charge, but displayed a greater indulgence of Heseltine's reluctance to be too specific about its replacement. The *Independent* detected 'a refreshingly open-minded approach to the difficult task of relating local taxation to the structure and functions of local government' ('A nettle grasped', Editorial, 22/3/91: 20). The *Daily Telegraph* congratulated the Government on dealing with a 'great political embarrassment ... with political skill, almost panache' ('Release in sight from a lot of local difficulty', Editorial, 22/3/91: 22). *The Times* declared Heseltine's speech 'a political masterpiece' and, revealing a spectacular amnesia about its own endorsement of the policy during its legislative phase, chided Tory MPs and Cabinet ministers for not having been more resolute in their opposition to the tax during its early stages ('Towards the light', Editorial, 22/3/91: 17). The *Guardian*, too, regarded the turncoats in the Conservative ranks with a palpable contempt, describing their brazen support for the repeal of a tax they had actively supported, as 'one more ripe episode in a deeply shameful episode ... Any ring of competence in this miserable farce is yet over the hills and far away' ('Dead and buried with much ignominy', Editorial, 22/3/91: 22).

As the Minister proceeded with consultations about the Community Charge's replacement, national media attention started to waver. And when the Environment Secretary finally announced the details of his Council Tax, on 23 April 1991, it was received with a virtually unanimous chorus of approval from the national press. The *Daily Mail* discerned 'much to commend' in the proposals ('Mr Heseltine Spells it out', 24/4/91: 6). The *Daily Express* claimed the Council Tax combined 'fairness, common-sense, and clarity' ('Happy ending to Tory poll tax nightmare', Editorial, 24/4/91: 8). The *Sun* welcomed the Council Tax, but questioned whether it would be better to finance local government through income tax ('Hail to this brave new tax', 24/4/91). The *Daily Star*'s news report of the Minister's statement was accompanied by a cartoon of the Environment Secretary as St George, slaying the poll tax dragon ('By George, he's done it', 24/4/91). The response of the broadsheet press, if less ecstatic was broadly encouraging. *The Times* judged the Council Tax to be 'sound in its essentials' ('Sound and sensible', 24/4/91: 22). The *Independent* pointed to the growing consensus between the two main parties on the matter of local finance, and castigated the Labour leadership as 'idiotic' for promising to repeal the new tax before they had fully examined it ('Need for a tax that will last', 24/4/91: 20). The *Telegraph* concluded that although the new tax 'is not a triumph for radical reform or Government spending ... It is an important pragmatic, political achievement' ('The local solution', Editorial, 24/4/91: 16).

Following the announcement of the Council Tax, and its largely favourable response by the Conservative Party and the mainstream media, local finance disappeared from the media's political map. Although, the information provided in Fig. 5.1 only covers the period up until September 1991, data from our sample of broadcast news coverage during the 1992 General Election confirms the issue's continued relegation in media agendas from September 1991 onwards. In an ironic parallel to the absence of local finance from the 1987 campaign, the issue barely intruded into the national broadcast agenda during this period (Deacon and Golding, 1992). Indeed, who could have projected at the height of the poll tax riots in 1990, that only two years later the tax and its replacement would be the main focus in only one news item on the main evening news bulletins on BBC1 and ITV during the whole of the campaign period?

This neglect is in many respects as remarkable as the media's disregard for the Community Charge prior to the legislative period for England and Wales. For in April 1991, many salient issues remained. The Council Tax still faced many hurdles before its implementation, and the poll tax would remain in place for a further two years. Yet the national media were only rarely troubled by the death-throes of the latter or the birth pangs of the former.

Local coverage of the Community Charge

> 'Choose your poll tax! The *News* today gives readers a unique opportunity to have a say in the setting of the Wirral's Community Charge.

> On the assurances of the two political parties involved that they will heed the result of our phone-in, you are invited to cast your vote on the special *News* Poll Tax Lines set up by us' (*Birkenhead News*, 28/2/90).

We now turn our attention to the reporting of this policy by the regional and local news media. In Chapter 3 we showed that the local media, particularly the local press, were specifically targeted by the Government in its attempts to sell the tax reform. By the same token, many opponents of the policy – particularly those operating at local level, or who were unable to get their views presented in the competitive environment of the national media – also focused considerable attention on the same channels. Given the perceived significance of the local media, it is important to examine whether their discourses about the Community Charge appreciably differed from those in the national media.

Most of this comparison is based on local press and television coverage during the most intensive period of media and public debate – between 1 March and 5 May 1990. However, as a precursor to this, we present the results of a qualitative survey of a very early response by the local media to the policy, and the Government's news management, which provides a telling insight into the general disposition of local media to the new tax.

We have described how in September 1987 two Government ministers – Michael Howard and Christopher Chope – embarked on a 'whistle stop' tour of regional news rooms and conference halls to whip up local support for the policy prior to the introduction of the legislation for England and Wales. Even the most cursory of readings of the local press in the areas visited shows the limited effectiveness of this agenda-building by visitation. Although the *Kent Messenger* reported the Minister's 'evangelical mission to explain and persuade' in some detail ('Howard's way: crusading MP spells out the rates revolution', 18/9/87: 4), it gave equal prominence to a detailed critique of the proposals by Maidstone Council's Chief Executive ('New system is still not fair', 18/9/87). In Bristol the main story was Michael Howard's refusal to meet councillors – '"Busy" tax supremo slammed' (*Bristol Evening Post*, 16/9/87) leading to 'Minister's poll tax snub for council leaders' (*Western Daily Press*, 17/9/87). In anticipation of the Minister's arrival, the *Bristol Evening Post* also ran a 'special report' on 'The poll tax nightmare' (16/9/87: 6). Similarly, although the *Nottingham Evening Post* prominently recorded one of the Minister's optimistic projections about the new system ('Notts firms' 16 per cent rate cut. That's what the poll tax will mean' – Michael Howard, 17/9/87), it did so against an earlier condemnation of the tax and the promotional exercise ('City MP in salesman jibe at poll tax trip minister', 16/9/87).

Perhaps preferable for the Minister was his total invisibility in Reading, where there was no report of the visit, merely a letter castigating the poll tax and the Ministers' attempt to 'beguile the gullible' from a Ratepayers' Association spokesperson (*Reading Chronicle*, 25/9/87). The *Yorkshire Post* ran a leader beginning, 'It demands a special strain of optimism to imagine that the Government will win converts with its plans to introduce a Community Charge in place of domestic rates' ('Hollow opposition', Editorial, 2/10/87), while across the Pennines the *Manchester Evening News* ran a more equivocal leader raising several of the problems raised by the poll tax and making ambiguous comments about its introduction in April 1990 ('Cabinet Listens', Editorial, 18/11/87).

Elsewhere the story was similar. The *Newcastle Evening Chronicle* ran a series of unflattering stories concentrating on the Government's defensiveness over the reforms – 'Minister meets rate criticism' (29/9/87) – and survey findings – 'Majority think poll tax unfair' (29/9/87). Similarly in Birmingham, the *Evening Mail* reported that the 'Minister denies poll tax chaos' (23/9/87), only marginally softened the next day into 'Poll tax fears rejected'. In Plymouth the rural lobby was at work. The *Western Morning News* reported 'Rural revolt feared over poll tax on farming staff' (12/9/87).

These examples reveal a profound and considerable scepticism in the local press about the policy, even during its early stages. Furthermore, this suspicion starkly contrasts with the indifference and complacency displayed by many equivalent sections of the national media during the same period. When we look more closely at local and regional media coverage during the policy's implementation in England and Wales, the evaluative distinctiveness of local coverage becomes even more apparent.

Local media and the introduction of the Community Charge

The first and most basic disparity between local and national news reporting during the tax's introductory period was in whose views and activities were most frequently reported. Far more attention was given in the local media to local politicians and authorities (see Table 5.4). Furthermore, although party politicians still predominated, local media accessed a greater diversity of news sources, with representatives from the voluntary sector, business sector, trades union movement, and the anti poll tax federations being consistently more prominent. Particularly significant, was the far greater presence of local government finance officers in local reporting, which as we discuss later, exerted a considerable influence over the generation of local news agendas.

Table 5.4. Political actors in local Community Charge coverage (1 March – 5 May 1990)

		Disposition	
	Presence in item Col. 1 %	Critical Col. 2 %	Supportive Col. 3 %
Party political actors			
Government	24	0.5	20
Other national Conservative politician	10	39	17
Local Conservative politician/authority	17	10	23
Other Conservative party actor	3	24	9
Labour shadow cabinet	10	74	–
Other Labour national politician	6	83	–
Local Labour politician/authority	20	58	–
Other Labour party actor	4	51	–
All other party political actors	10	55	–
Party political actor (party not stated)	17	22	0.5
Non party political actors			
Local government associations/pressure groups	2	77	2
General public	22	69	0.5
Anti poll tax groups	6	64	–
Other voluntary organizations	4	36	3
Local government professionals	9	13	–
Trades unions	6	74	–
Research Agencies	4	11	1
Business & business federations	8	46	–
Other actors (other professionals, journalists)	19	25	0.5
Total of Local TV and Press items	1674		

Notes: Figures relate to news and feature poll tax items only (focused and related).
Column 1: percentages = proportion of items which featured at least one actor in category.
Columns 2 & 3: percentage = disposition displayed of each actor/frequency of appearance.
Percentages are separate and do not add up to 100.

There were also clear thematic differences between national and local news agendas, and across local media sectors (see Table 5.5). First, whereas national media relegated attention to local administration of the new policy behind central government decision-making (with the exception of the tabloids), the local and regional media paid far more attention to local government administration. They also attended to a greater diversity of issues concerning local administration, such as the workings of the rebate system, data protection matters and enforcement procedures.

Table 5.5. Themes in national Community Charge coverage (1 March – 5 May 1990)

		Local Press %	Local TV %
1.	Origins of policy		
	Iniquity of rating system and other	2	1
2.	Implementation of policy		
	governmental/parliamentary decision-making	10	9
	Local government administration	17	22
3.	Responses to the policy		
	Public responses	14	18
	Conservative Party responses	5	4
	Labour party responses	3	2
	Other actor responses	4	2
4.	Effects of policy		
	Inequities/anomolies of new system	8	9
	Electoral detriment of the Government	7	4
	Winners and Losers	6	6
	Negative impact on local services	5	7
	Other negative economic effects	3	3
	Culpability for high poll tax levels	3	3
	Inefficiency of new system	2	2
	Equity of new system	2	2
	Other effects	6	3
5.	Other themes		
	Explanations about aspects of the reforms	2	1
	Alternatives to the reforms	2	1
	Total themes coded	3022	689

Figures relate to news, feature and editorial items (poll tax focused and related). Up to four themes could be coded for each item. Percentages = frequency of appearance/aggregate of themes coded. All figures are rounded. $X^2 = 53.23$; df = 16; $P < 0.01$.

Local media also paid attention to a broader range of effects. There was more coverage of the inequitable and anomalous impact of the policy (for example, in eroding the link between 'ability to pay' and local taxation levels), actual redistributional implications ('winners and losers') and the detrimental effect on local service provision. Conversely, the impact of the tax on the electoral fortunes of the Conservative Party didn't command the same prominence.

There were also statistically significant differences between local media sectors in their reporting, with local television paying more attention to local government implementation and less to the electoral implications of the change. The variation in local media coverage probably reflected the different geographic range of these media sectors. Local television in Britain operates on a regional basis and therefore extends over many local authority areas, whose activities they routinely report. The local press, by comparison, tend to cover far more limited areas, and are therefore directly involved with a more limited range of councils. Therefore, in reporting charge levels alone, regional television would have a far greater number to cover than their press counterparts. The reasons for the difference in emphasis on the impact of the tax on the electoral fortunes of the Government are less easy to trace (not least because they contradict the trend in national coverage).

In spite of these differences, all local media shared an equivalent interest in public opposition to the tax to that of the national media. Yet, here again, qualitative differences were apparent in the reporting of the riots and demonstrations. On occasion, local reporting deferred to the conspiracy theories that abounded in the national media. One remarkable example of this was the BBC's *South East* evening programme immediately after the Trafalgar Square riot (2/4/90). In a lengthy post-mortem about the causes of the riot, a pre-recorded studio interview was presented with a representative from an Anarchist group, who described the protesters as 'working class heroes'. Being mindful of the sensibilities of the programme's audience, as well as the political contentiousness of the group's views, the interviewer displayed an overt aggressiveness and prefaced the item with the explicit disclaimer:

> '[Class War] are dedicated to the downfall of Parliamentary democracy and attacking the police, as well as advocating non-payment of the poll tax. Earlier today, I talked to their spokesperson, Andy Murphy. *Many of you may find his views repugnant, but they do give an insight into why Saturday's march turned to violence.* I put to him first the allegation that

> Class War is blamed for spearheading the violence' (*BBC South-east*, 2/4/90, our emphasis).

Despite examples such as this, local coverage more frequently emphasized the political significance of the demonstrations, and expressed concern that the violence would obscure the essential political issues at the heart of the poll tax debate. After the first skirmishes, the *Northern Echo* editorialized 'What is the poll tax about? Anybody looking at the events of the last week could be forgiven for thinking it was about rent-a-mob thuggery versus law and order, or militant subversion versus democracy. It is none of these things. It is about the imposition of an inequitable tax which the vast majority of people do not want' (Editorial, 12/3/90: 8). Similarly, the *Bradford Telegraph and Argus* warned 'The poll tax is a bad and unfair tax ... It would be a disaster if the violence of a few hundred rent-a-mob demonstrators across the country were to obscure that' (Editorial, 9/3/90: 10), as did the *Oxford Mail* ('Violent Protest', Editorial, 8/3/90). Immediately after the Trafalgar Square Riot, the Tyne Tees evening programme gave greatest prominence to a local Anti Poll Tax Federation spokesperson in explaining the course of the days events (2/4/90), and a *Yorkshire Post* editorial castigated the Home Secretary as 'patronising and arrogant' for drawing simplistic parallels between non-payment and violent disorder (3/4/90: 10).

However, if the relative weighting of local news concerns differed from the national news agenda – and suggests an even more critical evaluative stance than that of the national media – local and regional reporting did not noticeably expand the parameters of national discourse about the policy. Indeed, if media comment about the Community Charge was often intensive and highly critical, there were many important issues that concerned participants in the broader policy debate which only rarely surfaced in media reporting. It is towards these significant absences in coverage of the Community Charge that our discussion now turns.

Hidden poll tax agendas

When considering the influence of the media in framing political debate, what *is not* said is as significant as what is said. The first major absence in media reporting of the Community Charge related to the tax's relative prominence compared with other important financial reforms enacted by the 1987 and 1988 local finance Acts. Although the poll tax was just one component in a general restructuring of local government finance, it dominated coverage of these financial reforms. Only 10 per cent of focused local finance items in the national press between 1986 and 1991 concentrated on either business rates, central grants or safety nets. Similarly, during the most intensive phase of the media debate, the Uniform Business Rate was mentioned anywhere in only 5 per cent of local finance related coverage in the national media, and the new grants and transitional arrangements in a mere 11 per cent. This pattern was replicated in local coverage, with the UBR mentioned in only 5 per cent of items, and the grant system and safety nets in 9 per cent. Any assessment of the media's performance in informing public debate by providing a comprehensive overview of this policy innovation, needs to take this glaring, structural distortion into account.

Beyond this basic imbalance – where less than a quarter of the revenue base of local government commanded over 90 per cent of media coverage – many important constitutional and democratic questions were also neglected. For example, debates about the privacy implications of the new taxation arrangements, the deleterious impact the registration process might have on the electoral rolls and the franchise, and the constitutional impact of the tax on local/central government relations, only rarely surfaced in the news agenda (see Table 5.6). Furthermore, our longitudinal analysis of press coverage shows these issues became more marginalized in the media agenda as the policy proceeded.

Table 5.6. Absent issues in poll tax coverage

	National press (1/1986–9/1991)	All national media (1/3/90 – 5/5/90)	All local media (1/3/90 – 5/5/90)
	Col. 1 %	Col. 2 %	Col. 3 %
Privacy issues	1	0.4	0.5
Disenfranchisement	0.6	0.3	0.2
Local/central government relations	0.3	0.7	1.3
Number of items	3165	2604	2417

Column1 = proportion of poll tax focused items with these issues as main theme. Columns 2 & 3 = proportion of poll tax focused and related items with these issues as a main or subsidiary theme. Figures for Column 1 relate to news, feature and editorial items. Figures for columns 2 & 3 relate to news, feature, editorial items and readers letters.

When these issues did appear in mainstream media, their appearance largely depended upon three factors. Either the issues touched on pet concerns of particular media commentators,* or they could be tagged on to a more prominent issue in the mainstream news agenda. For example, the impact of the tax on the franchise briefly surfaced before the 1992 General Election, following claims that the tax would seriously undermine Labour's chances in many key marginals ('The Lost Vote of Martin Thow', *World in Action*, 23/3/92).

Summary and conclusions

In this chapter we have traced and compared local and national media discourses about the Community Charge and its related reforms. This analysis has identified several important features to that coverage.

First, media attention to the policy fluctuated dramatically, and neglected many key periods in the policy cycle. Prior to the introduction to Parliament of the legislation for England and Wales, national media attention was minimal, and the issue was almost completely neglected before the 1987 General Election. After the legislative phase, attention wavered again, only to dramatically re-emerge in early 1990, as the first bills were set in England and Wales. Over the following year, there were two further intense periods of media debate – during the Conservative leadership contest and the announcement of the tax's repeal – and then the issue disappeared almost completely from the national news agenda, despite the fact that the tax still had a two year period to run, and the many technical and procedural questions that remained about its replacement.

Second, local and national media coverage of the policy demonstrated a consistent parochialism, being either blind or indifferent to the lessons of the, much vaunted, Scottish 'experiment'. The passage of the Scottish Legislation in early 1987 went unremarked, as did the tax's introduction a year before its arrival in Britain.

Third, media evaluations of the feasibility and probity of the policy changed throughout the policy's cycle and across different media. At the outset,

* For example, the *Sunday Times*' early localist critique of the poll tax was significantly influenced by one of its most pre-eminent columnists, Simon Jenkins, who had for many years argued against any further extension of Whitehall control of local government.

national press opinions were mixed, with several Conservative orientated papers broadly endorsing the Government's plans. However, as the prospect of the tax's introduction in England and Wales approached, these evaluations became almost unanimously negative, and by the time the tax was introduced this opposition was widespread and entrenched. Interestingly, the local media appear to have been amongst the most critical of the Government's plans, both during the early stages and at the moment of introduction.

Fourth, the framework of local coverage, despite its independent posture, was still contained by the structure of national debate. That is to say, it was *evaluatively* autonomous but *interpretatively* dependent. Many alternative agendas about the Community Charge which have preoccupied campaigners concerned about the poll tax went virtually unreported, as did the very important associated financial reforms. If the Government's ideological offensive foundered under media scrutiny, as it manifestly did, it did so on its own terms. Further, our longitudinal analysis of national press coverage suggests that the interpretative features of media agendas both shifted during different stages of the policy cycle, and became increasingly constricted. For example, from the legislative period onwards, concerns about the civil liberties implications of the new tax were usurped by concern with public and parliamentary disputes and decision-making.

In the remaining chapters of this book we explore more directly the origins of media discourses on this subject, to explain why the coverage displayed the features identified in this chapter. We begin this task by examining the views and news gathering activities of those journalists who reported the tax and its implications.

Chapter 6

Journalists and the Poll Tax

In preceding chapters we have shown how centrally the media featured in the campaign strategies of the main protaganists in the poll tax debate, and how different media reported the issue. No doubt, to the perceptive reader, parallels are already evident between the two discussions. However, to fully understand the origins of media discourses on the Community Charge, we must also address the views and activities of the key intermediaries in the news production process – the journalists and editors who commissioned and authored these accounts. For news is far more than the sum of opinions and information received by news organizations. News professionals necessarily exercise value judgements in selecting and filtering the information they receive and in directing their news gathering. As such they are active participants in the encoding process, who have a 'licensed autonomy' (Curran, 1990) and a 'discretionary power' (Semetko *et al.*, 1991) to reframe and reinterpret the information they process and the occurrences they witness.

In this chapter we focus on three main themes: the different structural relationship of news organizations to political arenas; journalists' estimations of source credibility; and their awareness of their audience and public sensibilities more generally. Unless otherwise stated, all quotations in this chapter are based on interviews with the authors.*

News organizations and news sources

Herbert Gans has likened the relationship between journalists and their sources to 'a dance, for sources seek access to journalists, and journalists seek access to sources. Although it takes two to tango, either sources or journalists can lead, but more often than not, sources do the leading'

* See the appendix on methods for more details about these interviews.

(Gans, 1979: 116). Our research suggests this metaphor requires further elaboration. For, although the dance steps may be well defined and broadly rehearsed, not all journalists pursue (or are pursued by) the same partners, and not all news organizations can afford (or want) to enter the same ballroom.

The journalist interviews corroborated the content analysis findings: that different types of news organizations and journalists produced their accounts of the poll tax in very distinct political environments. The most fundamental difference was between national and local media. Colin Seymour-Ure (1987) suggests there exists a hierarchy of 'political leadership arenas' in terms of national news media coverage. At its apex are the Government and the parliamentary opposition, who are guaranteed media attention and coverage, and near its base are regional leaders and authorities, whose media presence is more uncertain and intermittent. Although presented as a 'notional ranking', this typology neatly captures the legislature orientated nature of national reporting of the Community Charge.

However, this ranking needs to be completely inverted to describe the principal leadership arenas for the local media. Local government towers over the newsbeats of local journalism, rather than being confined to the peripheries. Similarly, local voluntary agencies, pressure groups and constituency MPs have a far greater news value, whereas national political arenas have a relegated salience. In interviews, local news professionals repeatedly stressed how their news selection was driven by the test of local applicability:*

> 'I would not be happy to run something that was blatantly national and in no way impinged upon the lives of people around here. Even if it was an issue which was national and would have an impact, I would want to say "Well what's the special impact around here?" And that test is always applied' (Local radio news editor).

> 'The only time we would go to national figures, would be if they happened to be here, visiting, or if they also happened to be local people' (Political editor, regional TV).

* This principle has long applied in the local media. For example, research undertaken by one of the authors in 1970 into the local press identified the carrying of local information as one of the defining functions of local papers (Golding, 1970).

The distinctive structural orientation of the local and national media in their news gathering reveals their different audience, prestige and advertising goals (Tunstall, 1971). In Britain, the local and national media are to some extent parallel systems: addressing and informing the same audiences but in different ways. Just as the credibility and revenue base of all national media is tied up in their ability to articulate and address national concerns, so local media depend upon local specificity to ensure their distinctiveness from national media, and thereby secure a share of the advertising and circulation market.

However, in acknowledging the distinctive orientation of the national and local media, it is also important to recognize there was a degree of exchange between media sectors on this issue. News organizations always keep a weather eye on other media when reporting events,* and this practice was clearly evident in the reporting of the Community Charge. Inevitably, news rooms paid greatest attention to the output of their closest competitors, but editorial surveillance also extended to other forms of news media. However, whereas the national media only consistently surveyed national outlets, local media perused both immediate and national media sources. In this way local media were far more conscious of national media agendas than vice versa, where the national media relied on an idiosyncratic and uneven feedback provided by 'stringers' and local news agencies.

Another linking mechanism was the information distributed to local and national newsrooms via on-line news agencies. In reporting the poll tax, journalists from all media identified the Press Association (PA) as being a particularly important source of information in their reporting of the poll tax – both for editorial copy and as a lead for further news gathering. Indeed, for many local newspapers with no parliamentary or London staff, the Press Association was the sole source of immediate information about the legislature:

> '[Chris] Moncreiff 's [political editor of the Press Association] views on it – his interpretation and authoritative views – would be carried in stacks and stacks of evening papers, almost as holy writ, although not under his by-line' (News editor, regional newspaper).

* A MORI survey of newspaper editors found that 86 per cent cited 'articles in other newspapers' as one of the 'most useful sources of information' to their work as editors, compared with only 22 per cent who cited news releases (*Guardian*, 7/1/91).

Most news organizations had also invested in on-line networking, which pooled information from both internal and external sources. For example, all regional BBC newsrooms were networked to a computerized message switching system which gave editors and journalists access into all the external on-line information that the BBC received centrally. Through key word searches, news editors could swiftly monitor all the current agency information on a chosen topic. Regional BBC news editors also regularly received information and guidance from the organization's own Parliamentary Research Unit:

> 'They've got everything on file in one form or another, a lot of it computerized. Now we can't call it up directly, which is probably just as well, because the complexity of that is so great that we might call up the wrong things ... If we can't get them on the phone, we get them within ten or fifteen minutes on a fax machine' (BBC regional TV political editor).

By recognizing, on the one hand, the habitual and essential distinctiveness of local newsgathering and presentation from national reporting and, on the other, the linking mechanisms that bound the media sectors, we can explain why local media coverage was *evaluatively* distinct from national coverage, but *interpretatively* dependent. The daily exposure of local news professionals to the national news agenda inevitably influenced the kinds of issues they addressed. However, in the process of 'localizing' the issue, these journalists approached a different range of sources with their own particular views and opinions about the tax. These provided the foundations to the local media's distinctive evaluation of the policy.

Specialist correspondents and news sources

The journalist interviews also exposed how the reporting of different types of journalists was framed by distinctive political environments. This was most apparent in the reporting of specialist correspondents in the national media.

By assigning a specialist correspondent to either a subject area or a physical location, a news organization is not so much casting a news net (Tuchman, 1978), as nailing it to the quay. The investment in a specialist post both reveals a news organization's perception of the salience of a subject area (Golding and Elliott, 1978), and ensures its continuing news value – as the prestige correspondents file 'expert' (and expensive) accounts, that, by dint of their authorship, command editorial priority (Tunstall, *op. cit.*). The reporting of the Community Charge at national level was dominated by two types of specialist newsgatherers: local government correspondents and political specialists (such as political correspondents, chief political correspondents and political editors).

Local government correspondents

> 'I'm always conscious that every time local government comes to the fore, how little we really know about it and the way it works. And that we tend to have to start again from square one. Now that will be addressed ... because in two weeks time we will be appointing a local government correspondent. Knee-jerking when our people appear lobbing bricks through windows is not actually covering local government. It's covering news stories in the time-honoured fashion' (BBC regional TV news editor).

Although several newspapers had had designated local government correspondents for many years, their increasing proliferation in the national media during the late 1980s, was closely linked to the political furore over the Community Charge. For example, before 1988, local government issues were covered nationally at the BBC by their environment correspondents (mirroring the remit of the Department of the Environment). However, as local government and environmental issues separately, and coincidentally, rose up the political agenda, it was decided that the post should be split. Furthermore, as these were the days before the advent of bimedia at the BBC (where radio and TV news gathering have been merged), separate local government correspondent posts were established for both television and radio.

By 1991, under a national BBC initiative entitled 'the enhancement of regional broadcasting', local government correspondents were also being established in regional BBC newsrooms. The preponderance of bids for local specialists under this scheme reflected both the continued newsworthiness of local government, and a recognition that the poll tax debate had exposed deficiencies in their news gathering. As one regional news editor admitted:

> 'There was a certain feeling at a network level that the poll tax story sort of crept up on them. And I think that, in part, the arrival of the local government correspondent can be attributed to that sense that the BBC hadn't got its ear quite so closely to the ground as it might have ... It's also a recognition that local government finance is perceived as being, continuing to be, an important and complex story.'

The emergence of the local government specialist during this period was also evident in the national broadsheet press. Although several newspapers had had designated local government correspondents well before the advent of the Community Charge, the political furore over its implementation saw greater emphasis placed on the post. For example, one local government specialist working for a national broadsheet noted that before his appointment in 1989 there had been 'a very erratic level of coverage' of local government, due to the varying status of the local government correspondent. The previous correspondent had been employed on 'a part time specialist basis and for a short period. And then before that there was a period when we had nobody at all covering local government'.

Of course, not all news media had, or sought to acquire, specialist local government correspondents during this period. For example, both Channel 4 and ITV news had no such correspondents during the most intensive stages of the political debate, in early 1990. In this instance their absence reflected the historical (and increasing) financial pressures on independent television news and current affairs and their continued commitment to generalist news gathering, in spite of the Birtian revolution at the BBC, which saw journalistic specialism as playing a vital role in rectifying an endemic 'bias against understanding' in television news (McNair, 1994).

If the partial proliferation and investment in local government specialists during the implementation of the tax reflected a perception in many news organizations of the need for greater 'in-house' expertise in this area, all the specialist correspondents interviewed had acquired their expertise 'on the job', rather than through previous experience in local government matters. For example, one of the most influential local government specialists at the height of the political debate had been a political correspondent prior to the 1987 General Election, and his appointment to the post was directly motivated by his judgement that the poll tax 'was going to become a huge issue ... One of the reasons I took the job was that I knew ... it was going to be probably the best domestic story of this parliament, and it's turned out to be that'. This pattern is consistent with previous research on specialist correspondents (Tunstall, *op. cit.*; Morrison and Tumber, 1985; Negrine, 1993; Seymour-Ure, 1977).

Not surprisingly, to generate specialized knowledge, these correspondents developed specialized newsbeats. As local government correspondents in the national media were excluded from the parliamentary lobby, their governmental contacts mainly focused on its executive branches at the Department of the Environment. Beyond Whitehall, their main regular sources included politicians and officers of the national local authority associations, local authority research units, a small number of local government academics, specialist pressure groups and national voluntary organizations. Interestingly, despite their designation, their direct contact with local authorities was infrequent, and tended to be facilitated via the national offices of the various local authority associations. Certainly, whilst their newsbeat was far broader than those of the political specialists at Westminster, it still centred around the capital.

As a result of their distinctive information network, these local specialists both anticipated the likely salience of the poll tax issue earlier than other reporters, and sustained their interest in the issue for far longer. Furthermore, they revealed a broader perception of the issues surrounding the implementation of the Community Charge, and were more sensitive to its attendant technicalities. As one specialist explained:

> 'Its very difficult. Transitional relief I'll try to explain as a system whereby the Government protected people who were going from a very low rates bill or a comparatively low rates bill to a very high household poll tax. But SSAs! I mean, transitional relief was easier than SSAs. SSAs – people just glaze over at the very mention of them and you cannot get editors interested in them. I mean, even now, I was on the phone talking about "this is the great unwritten story about the poll tax system" ... The fact is that the Government, civil servants living in Whitehall, make up a formula about what they think councils need to spend, and in most cases it relates to nothing near their view of what they need to spend ... Rebates as well are quite difficult to put across on television, because, you know, rebates in principal sound simple enough, but when you actually look at how they work, it can get very complex.'

These journalists also had a greater awareness of the historical context to the introduction of the new tax, more readily linking it to earlier attempted and actual reforms of the local financial system:

> 'Six months ago I actually met the man who wrote the 1981 Green Paper ... And it had two interesting appendices. One was an appendix on why the poll tax wouldn't work alone ... and the second one was an appendix on financing the education service centrally which, both of which became absolutely key in debates later on. So I mean, so I had quite a large background in local government and perhaps was unusual in terms of thinking "oh this is an important issue" as opposed to simply on the basis of "how is this going to affect my readers?" full stop. "Well we don't know so what's the point in writing about it at the moment?" ' (Local government correspondent).

Political specialists: 'The big issues, local government wise'

> 'Good Lord! I don't really get involved in local government, particularly. I mean, not terribly much. I do the big issues, local government wise ... My function around here is to report what the government of the day does, what the opposition say, and that sort of thing' (Political editor, national newspaper).

If the increase of local government correspondents in the 1980s reflected contemporaneous domestic political developments, the lengthy history of specialist political correspondent posts reveals the perennial fascination of the British mass media with the legislature. Due to Britain's highly centralized political system, political correspondents are first and foremost *parliamentary* correspondents. (This principle generally applies even where local media have their own specialist designated political correspondent, or where a political correspondent is 'pooled' amongst a collective group on local newspapers.)

The first political correspondents were gallery reporters, who observed and recorded parliamentary debates and governmental decision-making. However, over time, interest increased in generating a 'behind the scenes' understanding of parliamentary processes and decision-making that could only be provided by journalists having more direct and informal access to politicians (Tunstall, 1970; 1971). Nowadays, the most prestigious political correspondents are the lobby correspondents, who are:

> '... specialists in the public face of central government power, assessors of reputations, students of party dynamics, critics of ministerial performance in Parliament, Cabinet and the wider arenas' (Henessey and Walker, 1987: 112).

Membership of the Lobby is highly restricted, and these select correspondents receive daily briefings from senior governmental and parliamentary sources, have privileged access to senior Government figures as well as physical access to the parliamentary lobby. Although not all political specialists are members of the Lobby, our discussion focuses mainly on the experiences of lobby correspondents in reporting the Community Charge, because of their élite status among political specialists.

Lobby correspondents' reporting of the Community Charge was informed by a very different range of sources from those used by local government correspondents. Their privileged but cloistered existence meant they were principally dependent on governmental and party political sources in reporting the tax, and had only occasional contact with other external news sources, such as the local authority associations. The narrowness of their poll tax newsbeat was not exceptional, but rather indicative of the traditional parochialism of the parliamentary specialists (Tunstall, 1970). When their contacts were broadened, it was generally because a non-parliamentary political source had brought their argument to Parliament, often with the support of an MP:

> '[The Anti Poll Tax Federation] had good solid links with Dave Nellist and a couple of Merseyside MPs and Scot MPs, so they got the opportunity of getting in ... People like [Steve] Nally and Tommy Sheridan came in and gave press conferences in the House to us, to the likes of us' (Political correspondent).

One particularly important element in their reporting was their opportunity to draw on covert, off the record briefings to inform their political analyses. Not surprisingly, other specialists were very envious of the privileged access lobby correspondents had to the legislature, recognizing that it provided a unique insight into the evolving political debate:

> 'There are differences between my position and the more privileged position of a lobby correspondent or a political correspondent, who is actually in the lobby, has access to the parties at closer hand, who can get off the record stuff. I miss that. I mean, I feel I ought to have that in a sense, because I'm missing out. I have to go off the back of something coming from the lobby, rather than getting it myself. But that's just the way the system works' (Local government correspondent).

As explained in Chapter 3, the lobby briefings were only rarely used to ease the introduction of the tax; and when they were it was mainly to smear back bench critics. However, during the policy's introductory and evaluative periods, these briefings assumed a crucial role, by allowing ministers to 'road test' various reform options for their broader political acceptability.

The main significance of the 'behind the scenes' access of lobby correspondents *prior* to the tax's introduction in England and Wales was in sensitising news organizations to the extent of dissent within Conservative ranks. Many back bench Conservative MPs only 'went public' with their criticisms once the political crisis had escalated out of the Government's control. However, they had been privately communicating their concerns to these journalists for a considerably longer period. Even more crucially, it was the lobby correspondents who were privy to the deep reservations of several cabinet ministers about the fairness and feasibility of the tax, that quickly became the received wisdom in the national media.

This narrow but privileged news gathering had a direct effect on their reporting of the tax. Firstly, they experienced greater difficulties in dealing with the more arcane aspects of local finance. Indeed, several of the most prominent parliamentary figures involved in the debate were highly critical of how misinformed several senior political correspondents were about some of its most crucial aspects:

> 'Local government finance is a minefield. It's such a technical area that many people shy away ... I understand that. But the media obviously take that view as well. We've had great difficulties with people like [National TV Political Correspondent] who simply cannot understand anything to do with local government finance ... Because if you've got to spend an hour every time explaining the most minute point to a journalist, you actually lose the ability to respond quickly, to get across

> a wider message, and that has been a genuine problem' (Opposition local government spokesperson, interview with authors).

> 'One could never persuade them to explain the problems of the uncollectability, for example. They didn't think that was important. Unfairness? They could get a hold of that' (Conservative MP, interview with authors).

Second, because of this disregard for the technicalities of the topic, political correspondents saw the issue as far less problematic and complex to report than the local government specialists. As one political editor put it:

> 'The thing about Mrs Thatcher, she did explain things, extremely succinctly. She could actually say the poll tax is about making sure that everyone who can pays towards the services that they use. That was how she would sell it. Which is a fairly simple concept. And Labour's concept, the opposition's concept was very much it is unfair and is unworkable. So once you've got those twin sort of concepts it's actually quite straightforward.'

Of all the journalists, political correspondents were most fixated with the *process* rather than the *substance* of the (party) political debate about local finance. One implication of this, was that their attention to the issue was far more transient than the local government specialists. They discovered the issue far later in its legislative timetable, and became bored with it far sooner, once the Conservative leadership issue had been resolved, and the Tory rebellions assuaged.

Finally, the perceptions and newsgathering activities of these élite correspondents exerted a powerful influence over the general orientation of their news organizations towards the issue. The fact that all national media had specialist political correspondents, even if they had few other designations, reveals the higher status of this specialist field compared with others (Tunstall, 1970). And whereas several local government correspondents complained about the dissonance between their interest in the tax and the general news agenda of their organizations – particularly during early and later stages of the policy cycle – political correspondents experienced no equivalent frustrations. Indeed, to a large extent, it was their reading of the political salience of the issue that determined the broader newsroom agenda. In other words, the political specialists set the interpretative framework within which local government correspondents had to work.

Reporting implications

It is important to consider whether the manifest differences between specialists in their newsgathering on this issue had any impact on their reporting. As Negrine notes, one of the most neglected aspects in a dearth of research into journalistic specialization is 'the relationship between the designation and the end product' (1993: 3).

Table 6.1. Actors featured in specialist correspondent authorized items in national TV & radio news (1 March – 5 May 1990)

	Political specialists	Local government specialists
	%	%
Parliamentary/government actors	93	71
Councillors	22	63
Local government officers	1	4
Local government associations/pressure groups	1	19
Opinion pollsters and other research	14	10
Business and business federations	1	4
Anti poll tax groups	3	4
Other voluntary sector groups	1	2
Unions	3	2
General public	22	23
Other (e.g. other professionals, journalists)	15	23
Number of items	(153)	(48)

Figures relate to news and feature items [poll tax related and focused]. Percentages = the percentage of items authored which feature at least one actor under each category. The percentages are separate and do not add up to 100.

Our study revealed clear differences in how specialist correspondents reported the poll tax, particularly in television news reporting. Reflecting the distinctive news gathering of both specialisms, news stories by political specialists reported a narrower range of political views than local government correspondents, mainly focusing on parliamentary actors (see Table 6.1). By doing so, they also emphasized different themes in their reporting (see Table 6.2). Whereas local government correspondents spent more time reporting aspects of central government decision-making and local implementation of the reforms, political correspondents were more interested in recording party political responses to the policy. Furthermore, although both types of correspondents revealed a similar degree of interest in the effects of the policy, for the political specialists these were almost exclusively construed in electoral terms, whereas local government correspondents presented them in broader terms (e.g. 'winners and losers' and service provision).

Table 6.2. Themes in specialist correspondent coverage on TV and radio news (1 March – 5 May 1990)

Themes related to:	Political specialists	Local government specialists
%	%	%
Origins	6	6
Government/parliament decision-making	11	16
Local government implementation	4	13
Responses	31	13
Effects	45	47
Alternatives to tax/explanations	2	6
Number of themes coded	361	141

Figures relate to news and feature items in polltax items [related and focused]. Up to four themes could be coded for each item. Percentages = frequency of appearance/aggregate of themes coded (all figures are rounded).

Perceptions of news source credibility

If journalist contact with news sources differed locally and nationally, and between particular types of correspondents, how did journalists generally view the performance and credibility of the main protaganists in the political debate? As Tuchman (1978) observes, the perceived credibility of a news source is a crucial factor in their inclusion and treatment in news. This section is divided into two, and begins by looking at journalistic perceptions of the credibility of key 'advocates' in the debate. It then identifies who journalists elected as the 'arbiters' of this policy debate.

Advocates

As we outlined in Chapter 1, 'advocates' are those news sources who are recognized by the news media as having an overt interest in a political process and outcome. As a controversial policy with far reaching ramifications, the Community Charge excited a diverse range of opinions from a considerable variety of political sources. However, our content analysis has shown that the main protaganists in media coverage were the two main political parties (whether nationally or locally). In this section we open this point up a little further, by looking at how journalists assessed the performance of these key advocates in the political debate, and what factors were seen to have increased or undermined their salience or credibility. Because of the strong links between 'maverick' Labour activists and external campaign groups, we also compare journalistic perceptions of the credibility and significance of the anti poll tax movement.

Government sources

When asked to assess the Conservative Party's performance in promoting the poll tax, journalists almost exclusively referred to *governmental* actions, rather than those of Conservative Central Office. This mirrored the preferred promotional strategy of the Conservative leadership, who only latently utilized their party political resources, when the issue had become politically unavoidable.

On a practical level, journalists and editors were deeply unimpressed with what they perceived as the ineptitude of the Government's publicity work. In part this reflected a longstanding cynicism about the efficiency of the Government's information services, which the complexities and controversies over the Community Charge only served to highlight. Particularly frustrating for the journalists was their inability to gain direct access to civil servants in their information seeking. As one local government correspondent complained:

> 'Throughout the entire period I actually felt I knew a lot more about what was going on in the Department of the Environment than the press office did. I know that sounds boastful, but I mean it was the fact for most of the time ... The press office were only as good as the time that the local government finance division [at the DoE] were prepared to answer queries from the press office ... I think their patience especially, basically went – dried up – and the relationship between the DoE press office and local government officials was gradually disintegrating.'

Local journalists were particularly critical of the information dissemination from the regional government offices. On the one hand, this was because they failed to release information with sufficient speed, and on the other because they were unable to provide access to senior politicians 'on the stump' in their area:

> '[Information] comes a day late from regional office. Why do they bother censoring it? If it is important we've had it faxed directly from the Department concerned. The regional office get this great wodge of paper in and send it out again the next day, a day late, so it's been in all the nationals that morning, or it's been on the *Today* programme that morning. I'm not about to carry something the following morning that's gone everywhere. Complete waste of time. And they're also no good at getting access to ministers. Theoretically you actually go to them and say "please, you know, so and so's up here tomorrow, can we have an interview with him?" You know you can do that but nobody pays you too much notice. It's better to deal with the Department directly' (Local radio news editor).

However, there were also specific elements of the Government's promotion of the tax that created a deep and abidingly negative impression in the media. Initially this related to the jarring contrast between the pretensions and slickness of the DoE public relations campaigns and the unreconstructed profile of the sponsoring minister:

> 'Nick Ridley famously had no concept of presentational skills whatsoever ... So I mean you had the two sides to it. On the one hand, you have this immense marketing operation ... who were trying to sell the Community Charge. On the other hand, you had a Secretary of State who had absolutely, was, you know, *nil point* on the question of marketing, and didn't care about it at all' (Local government correspondent).

Beyond this, the political furore over the Government's national publicity offensive in May 1989 offered an important early indication of the political difficulties the tax would encounter. On one level, this was because of its farcical and shambolic aspects:

> 'When they were distributing the poll tax leaflets ... I was told, perhaps off the record, that they were seriously thinking of sending John Gummer up to a monastery dressed as a monk to make the point that, of

> course, monks are exempt from the poll tax. But they never got around to that' (Local government correspondent).

> 'I suppose the peak of it was when they produced the "You and the Community Charge" leaflets, with the happy smiling toy-town folks on – it was yellow, wasn't it? And they had one black smiling dustman ... I mean it got absurd at some press conferences, where if you asked a question which contained the word "poll tax", you were then delivered a 10 minute lecture on "how dare you use words like poll tax?" Which was, you just kind of felt, this is time wasting' (Political correspondent).

On another level, because of the swift intervention of several opponents of the tax, journalists were very sensitive about the apparent misappropriation of public funds:

> 'I think that people really did feel that they were using public money to promote Conservative policy. And if there was one single issue which triggered it I would now ... identify that as it. And that was their first mistake I think. I think it could have been handled much more intelligently. Curiously, probably by making better use of the local media – as it removes you, it takes you a step away, so that you're not seen as doing a public promotion of a particular party political policy. That was the first thing they did wrong, wasn't it? Well I think it was a non starter after that. I mean it's like actually having the first eight batsmen knocked out in the first two overs and you're stuffed thereafter' (Local radio news editor).

However, despite the widespread scorn of the Government's public relations efforts, journalists were highly antagonistic to any suggestion that the main cause of the policy's difficulties lay in presentational miscalculations:

> 'There was that famous time when at a conference, when [Margaret Thatcher] said ... "the Minister has failed to get the message across". I think Michael Howard was sitting beside her at the time. Now that is just sheer, downright patronising' (Political correspondent).

In general, journalists saw these promotional difficulties as symptomatic of the political troubles the Government faced. This was most fundamentally revealed to the journalists by the way the policy in practice appeared consistently to confound Government predictions. As a tax intended to expose the disparity between Labour profligacy and Conservative parsimony in local government, the fact that several Conservative authorities set poll tax levels well in excess of £400 merely confirmed a growing scepticism in the media that had begun with the repeated revisions upwards of Government projections of likely Community Charge levels:

> 'The original plan was for £150, which again is about a rates bill isn't it? 300 quid for a couple, you can just about cover that, people could afford that ... And it stepped up and each stage it became £200, £250, then, you know, you thought "Jesus, this is big trouble" ... By the time they had 450 quid, or whatever it was, for Windsor, it was too late, there was no going back' (Political correspondent).

Furthermore, having been told that charge levels should be the sole barometer of the efficiency of a local authority (and being largely uninterested in the broader fiscal context in which charge levels were set) journalists paid little attention to Government rationalizations that high charge levels in Conservative areas were caused by Labour or Liberal Democrat profligacy at county council level, or were a temporary consequence of the safety net arrangements. For many journalists, the high poll tax levels in many Conservative areas drove an empirical stake into the heart of the Government's rhetoric.

Another major factor that seriously compromised the Government's credibility, was its inability to command support from its own party. At local level, the Government's 'top down' promotional strategy meant that the infrequently received Governmental endorsements were drowned out for local journalists by the constant criticisms from the Conservative grass roots. At national level, the haemorrhaging of internal support – first from the left of the Party, and latterly from the right and the senior echelons of the Government – served in a similar way, to portray the Prime Minister in an isolated position, and as being less interested in rational policy making than in ideological zealotry:

> 'It was politics of the crassest level. And it was absolutely, you know, it was ideology driven ... There's a Government Minister, just outside of cabinet. Been with the Department of the Environment. And he said to

> me, you didn't even raise the subject when she was there. Because he said you'd just get your head blown off. He said it got to the stage where you didn't even raise the question' (Political correspondent).

For many journalists the vehemence and extent of Conservative Party dissent on the tax was one of the most consistently newsworthy aspects of the whole debate. And this perceived significance not only affected how journalists viewed the Government's proclamations on the Community Charge, but also those of their political opponents.

The Labour Party

The juxtaposition of party opinions is one of the key strategies used by journalists to construct their impartiality and objectivity. Therefore, it was inevitable that Labour politicians would be perceived as one of the most prominent sources of dissenting comment on the tax and its effects. However, as discussed in Chapter 4, the poll tax also split the Labour Party over how it should be best opposed. Therefore, when describing journalist's appraisals of Labour's credibility, it is important to maintain a distinction between official and maverick Labour sources.

At the time of the interviews (late 1991 to early 1992), official Labour sources were generally seen as having far more credibility on local government matters than the Conservative leadership. Here again, we have a measure of the extent of the Thatcher government's political failure over the poll tax, for such a situation would have been difficult to foreseen back in the mid-1980s where Conservative attacks on the 'loony left' in local government were being widely amplified by local and national media.

If the political rehabilitation of Labour's reputation in this area was largely linked to the Government's political difficulties, it was also aided by an acknowledgement that the Party had played its hand quite efficiently. For example, several national journalists specifically commended the organization and effectiveness of Labour's local government team in Parliament in raising key issues:

> 'Probably the most vociferous campaign against [the Community Charge] has come from David Blunkett and his office, who have bombarded everyone with an almost daily press release on the iniquities of the poll tax. They've been very good ... Blunkett has a good research

team. The Liberal Democrats have been, frankly, not that active, at least not to my knowledge. And I'd be getting more stuff from Labour than I have from them' (Local government correspondent).

'In political parties, Labour's local government operation I always found fairly impressive' (Political correspondent).

In the local media, too, Labour activism was seen as having had a powerful influence on the terms of political debate about the issue:

'The Labour party were actually much cannier in their PR because they had a very simple message and they stuck to that utterly, simple message, and kept on banging on about it *ad nauseum*. Which is that it's an unfair tax. And if you were to identify one Tory message I'd be hard put to say "this was the message". The Labour party, I could tell you that was the message, no question. And I think that if you go out on the street and ask anybody what was their message ... most people in the street would identify that as the single, very clever, one line. Punch! Punch! Punch! So it goes in' (Local radio news editor).

However, journalists also shared the view that Labour hadn't had a difficult hand to play – particularly when their criticisms were supported by critics from within the Government's own party. Furthermore, although journalists perceived Labour Party views as an important component in the reporting of the political debate, in isolation they were seen as being far less newsworthy than Conservative criticisms:

'[The Community Charge] became inextricably linked with the politics of the future leadership – the post-Thatcher leadership of the Conservative Party. So that was an ingredient which complicated it and took it away from being just a local government issue ... It was no longer just a question of Labour banging their heads against another brick wall, which sort of didn't get anywhere, however much they may have won the argument' (Political correspondent).

'I think [Labour] conducted it well, but I think the things that defeated it was the kind of enemy within. The lack of support from within her own party, and doubts among ministers which finally killed it. I mean the Opposition can do as much as they like, but I think they waged a

> successful, I would say a broadly successful campaign coupled with the doubts within [Margaret Thatcher's] own party' (Political editor).

As we discuss in the next chapter, the subordinate news value of Labour to Conservative dissent had a profound effect on the conduct and intensity of media coverage.

Although the media were broadly receptive to *official* Labour Party campaigning, they were highly antagonistic towards those in the Party who supported more radical methods. Maverick sources in the Labour Party who advocated non-payment, were both seen as far less credible and attracted outright hostility from many national and local journalists. As one tabloid political editor asserted:

> 'Very few people down here have got time for MPs who refuse to obey the law which they as a body created'.

Their credibility in the eyes of the national media was further compromised by their close links with the All British Anti Poll Tax Federation (APTF), which many journalists viewed with considerable suspicion and antagonism.

Anti poll tax organizations

We previously noted that whereas the national media readily subscribed to the view that anti poll tax groups were stalking horses for the extreme left, such conspiracy theories were less evident in local reporting. From our interviews it appeared that the roots of this disparity lay in the different contact each media sector had with the movement.

The anti poll tax movement as a whole was an informal and devolved campaign, in which local groups and unions had a considerable degree of autonomy. As we have seen, attempts to unify groups under one national federation generated controversy within the movement itself. Although the Militant-dominated APTF assumed the national leadership mantle in late 1989, their authority to speak on behalf of the movement as a whole was often questioned by Federation members, who shared broader concerns about the hidden agenda to the activism of the Federation's committee (Burns, 1992).

Despite their questionable status as the national forum for the anti poll tax movement, the Militant-dominated APTF were the only regular point of contact national journalists had with the broader campaign. Although the stridency and forcefulness of comments by the Federation's two main spokespersons often made for good news copy, all the national journalists we interviewed were highly sceptical about both their political mandate and influence. This was accenuated by the context in which the most influential national correspondents met the Federation spokespersons, at news conferences held within the Houses of Parliament. These brought into sharper relief what correspondents perceived as the inappropriateness and presumption of the APTF 'leaders':

> 'My view of the Anti Poll Tax Federation was kind of moulded somewhat by sitting here at Westminster ... Where the Anti Poll Tax Federation generally meant press conferences chaired by Dave Nellist, with Tommy Sheridan or other members of Militant, in a small committee room upstairs, claiming to speak on behalf of seven million, eight million, nine million non payers, anti poll tax campaigners' (Political correspondent).

The parliamentary setting of these news conferences both served to decontextualize and accenuate the jarring nature of the Federation's rhetoric of street politics and community activism. As another political correspondent commented:

> 'I personally was terribly antipathetic towards their position. So I found it very difficult to swallow ... My feelings about them was that they were political charlatans. They weren't in there entirely because they wanted to see the back of the poll tax, they were in there to sort of ferment things ... [Tommy] Sheridan was, I thought, was quite impressive. But [Steve] Nally, I thought, yeah, I wouldn't trust him as far as I could throw me granny (I'll now find out he's your brother or something).'

The antipathy of national journalists towards the APTF was also framed by a deep disapproval of the non payment tactic. As one political editor observed:

> 'I went to the odd news conference they threw down here, but once it was very patently plain and obvious that they intended to break the law, I think that a lot of people lost interest in it ... And of course it

> means that people who don't pay, can't pay, won't pay – or whatever the slogan was – put a burden on other people who sort of obeyed the law and paid up. So, a lot of people down here – most people – had very little time for the Anti Poll Tax Federation because they made it plainly obvious that they intended to break the law. Simple as that.'

Although local journalists similarly disapproved of non-payment, they had more regular and direct contact with local anti poll tax groups, and were far less sceptical about their representative status. This was mainly because they witnessed the groups' community based activism first hand, and in its 'natural' context – i.e. public meetings and rallies – rather than decontextualized in small parliamentary meeting rooms. In these situations they found the 'rentamob' stereotypes less easy to apply. Furthermore, they were more regularly approached by the groups themselves. As one local radio journalist commented:

> 'Perhaps if you were sitting in Broadcasting House in London and you saw a poll tax protestor, that would appear to be something threatening and something alien from outside. In Bradford we could see that there were a lot of people who were suffering very real hardship, who literally couldn't pay under the proposals as they were initially put forward ... First of all [the local anti poll tax groups] were co-operative. And secondly, I think it is true to say that it was a genuinely mass movement in this area. You always get the professional protestors ... However, the thing that has been different about the poll tax, in my view, is that we've gone along to these protest meetings, and yes you've had Militant sitting in the corner with their newspapers, but you've also had a lot of what I would say are ordinary people – working class in Bradford who have come forward and taken part in the protest. Which has been great from our point of view, because we've been able to get some good audio we've people who say: "I've never been on a picket line in my life, but" or "I've never broke the law in my life, I'm now 65, but". And we have noticed that within the Anti Poll Tax Federation there has been a wide spread of people who I would describe as non-politically active, getting involved in it.'

However, the local media shared with the national media a perception that the salience of the anti poll tax groups was essentially transient – that they were beneficiaries of the political furore over the poll tax rather than instigators of it. And just as they were largely neglected prior to the poll tax demonstrations of March 1990, so their importance was seen to recede as the media tired of reporting public protests.

Arbiters: 'The guy that hadn't got a political axe to grind'

> 'Does anyone really understand the poll tax? We certainly don't – and we bet most other people are in the dark too. We went to Rita Hale, author of an encyclopaedia on the poll tax, to get a few answers' (Everything you wanted to know about poll tax – But didn't like to ask in case they got your address, *Sun*, 17/4/90: 9).

> 'There ought to be a way of making the needs assessment understandable to more than just two people in the country: one official in Whitehall, and the blessed Tony Travers of the London School of Economics' (Editorial, *Guardian*, 28/2/92: 20).

In our introductory discussion we identified a specific type of news source whose significant contributions to the framing of media discourse are lost in generalized discussions about the interaction between news gatherers and 'accredited', authoritative sources. These are the 'arbiters' in particular topic areas – professionals who are approached by journalists to evaluate assertions and interpretations made by advocates in a political debate.

The arbiters for local and national reporting of the Community Charge were, once again, very different. The principal arbiters for local journalists were local government finance officers, who, even in those areas where local media and council relations were strained, were trusted by journalists both to explain and to adjudicate on the performance of the new system:

> 'There was a wizzy guy, whose name totally escapes me. In Cambridge City Council. Who was actually an officer rather than a politician ... I can't remember his name for the life of me. But he was absolutely stunning at interpreting for us. He was the guy that used to come in, because he hadn't got a political axe to grind, and we actually wanted somebody who wasn't going to jump on any bandwagons, but was going to explain "this is what we collect the Community Charge for, this is what it pays for, this is why this council costs more than that council, etc. etc." And he came in and explained it to us. And because we had used him as an on-air consultant we also used him as an off-air

consultant, if ever we were baffled we would phone him up and say "help" ... He sort of came into the frame I suppose in the very, very early days. During the big political punch ups ... That's where we started doing a very public service, information journalism: you know, the "what it means to you" type stuff. And he just stayed with us all the way through. But because things are plainer now we've sort of tended not use him very much – which is probably why I've forgotten his name' (Local radio news editor).

'We never go to politicians for facts, for quite obvious reasons. We go to officials. And they are mandated to give that factual information. And that is always presented in "an expert says" type of way' (Local radio reporter).

All the local journalists we 'interviewed' had had some direct contact with these arbiters in their reporting of the tax.

The arbiters for national journalists tended to be a select group of academics and finance experts (most significantly Tony Travers from the London School of Economics and Rita Hale from the Chartered Institute for Public Finance and Accountancy), local authority associations, public research institutions, and business federations. The inclusion of local authority associations in this list might appear surprising, given the constituents they represent, and the manifest influence that party politics exert on their campaigning stance. Certainly, the issue of political control prevented the Local Government Information Unit from being seen as an arbiter. As one local government specialist explained:

'The problem we have with [the LGIU] is political balance, and they must know this. They are funded by Trade unions and Labour councils. That means they are in effect a Labour funded organization, which makes it difficult for us to use them as an independent research body.'

However, these concerns only tended to apply to local associations when journalists were dealing with their political membership or leadership. Just as local journalists drew a distinction between councillors and local government officers, so national journalists distinguished between the political leaders of the associations, and the professional experts in their employ.

In this way, the associations had a dual status – as both advocates and arbiters:

> 'You can use an officer from the AMA and not use the words "Labour-funded" because he's speaking as an officer. Similarly for the ADC ... If we were talking to politicians from the AMA and the ADC, we would certainly have to do that' (Local government correspondent).

Interestingly, this dual status was not conferred on civil servants at the Department of Environment, despite historical conventions of civil service neutrality. This was mainly because the succession of political rows about the Government's use of civil servants in promoting the tax, made national journalists highly sceptical about the objectivity of any information provided from these official sources. As one put it:

> 'The poll tax has been so highly political and so fraught with errors and problems, that you had to be suspicious all the way along that [civil servants] were giving you the best gloss, rather than the unvarnished truth' (Local government correspondent).

National journalist had less contact with arbiters than those working at local level. Instead, a two step information flow was evident, in which specialist national local government correspondents played a pivotal role. These correspondents, having far greater experience of the technical issues involved and more diverse and regular contact with sources of expertise, acted as both opinion leaders and as a residual source of in-house expertise for other journalists. This was particularly evident among many of the political correspondents in the lobby, who knew and cared little for the technicalities of local finance, but enjoyed enormously the political dramas that they sparked. During the later stages of the policy cycle, two ex-local government specialists joined the parliamentary press corps, and their knowledge and experience in local finance made them an important source of interpretation and evaluation of the complex issues being raised. One of these specialists became jokingly known as 'Professor Poll Tax' by his colleagues and competitors, and as he wryly observed:

> 'There were times [in the press gallery of the House of Commons] during the real crisis within the Tory party – when they were revamp-

> ing it every three months and bringing in new systems – where I was holding more popular briefings up here than the DoE were!'

Although journalists valued arbitrative sources as expert and impartial evaluators of the policy, many of these arbiters were actively engaged in the political debate. Furthermore, they were often highly critical of the new system, whether publicly or privately. For example, in early 1990, the Chartered Institute of Public Finance and Accountability (CIPFA) took the unusual step of writing to all MPs, attacking the unrealistic nature of the Government's £278 average poll tax target, which proved a devastating political intervention that 'added substantial weight to making the Government appear unreasonable' (Gibson, 1990: 239). At local level, although many of the local government finance officers acknowledged the dangers and impropriety of being seen to enter publicly into party political debate, they admitted they saw no reason to conceal the administrative difficulties and anomalies of the new system. In the words of one senior local finance officer:

> 'I have said off the record to a lot of these reporters that this is the daftest tax anybody ever thought of in their lives. But they know they can't print that' (Interview with authors).

Interestingly, the journalists saw no contradiction between the perceived 'impartiality' of arbiters and those occasions when they offered critical judgements about the new system. Rather, their expertise and professionalism added resonance to their evaluations, and their views became the hard truths against which all other claims were assessed.

Journalists and their imagined public: 'We're simply reflecting what people think'

Journalists are always mindful of their audience when deciding what issues should be reported. Indeed, their sense of professional integrity is bound up in the assumption that they are talking both to, and for, a broad public. However, as mass communicators, journalists are also isolated from the public and often have a high degree of uncertainty about the actual composition, interests and needs of their constituent audiences (McQuail, 1969; Anderson and Meyer, 1988; Elliott, 1972; Golding, 1974). To resolve this tension, journalists rely on professional judgements, established practice and idealistic or cynical images of their audience to guide their editorial decision-making.

These routine uncertainties about the audience, and the accompanying compensatory strategies, were clearly evident in journalists' reporting of the Community Charge. However, there was one public message that they received loud and clear, and from very early on in the policy's introduction. That was that the public hated the idea. The clarity and resonance of this message were deduced from four feed-back mechanisms: audience correspondence, opinion polls, public demonstrations and electoral outcomes.

Several journalists commented on the intensity and hostility of correspondence towards the poll tax. As one news editor observed:

> 'The feedback we were getting from our readers was that they just didn't want it. When it originally came in we had a huge mail bag about it. A lot of readers writing in saying they didn't want it, they couldn't understand why the Government was trying to replace the rates.'

However, journalists were also acutely conscious of the limitations of this channel of communication. Either because particular media had no forum for such correspondence ('We don't have a letters spot ... Although we're pleased to receive letters, there's no outlet for us to encourage it. Newspapers do that' [regional news editor]), or because of concerns about its representativeness:

> 'One of the things we're in danger of is pandering too much to minority groups. And its a big danger in that they're very "pestiferous" and they know how to manipulate the media and they do it quite successfully really. And we're ignoring the vast majority of the public' (News editor, local newspaper).

Opinion polls, however, were seen to provide a far more reliable guide to views of the majority, and confirmed a widespread and trenchant public hostility to the tax. Throughout the policy cycle the polls were used as a barometer of the Government's failure to win the political argument over the tax and its merits ('No! Big poll tax survey shock for Tories', *News on Sunday*, 4/10/87; 'Most voters believe poll tax less fair than rating system',

The Times, 11/1/88; ‘Public shift against poll tax’, *Sunday Telegraph*, 17/9/89).

However, it was only when this longstanding antipathy translated into public demonstrations, that many news professionals gained their first sense of the depths of public hostility towards the tax. Many journalists remembered the outbreak of public demonstrations in early 1990 as marking a watershed in their reporting:

> ‘It wasn’t something that happened in this region that actually made me perhaps think more seriously about [the poll tax] ... It was a meeting at Nottingham, at the Nottingham City Council where there was the most almighty bloody row and hoo-ha going on and, sort of, total chaos’ (Regional TV news editor).

> ‘If nothing had happened and everybody had accepted the poll tax, it wouldn’t have got much space and the poll tax would presumably still be there. It really only became an issue for the media and the Government when the opposition against became so patently obvious’ (Regional TV news editor).

When opinion poll data and gestures of public outrage translated into by-election defeats for the Government, the circle was complete (‘Tory defeat prompts poll tax re-think’, *The Times*, 24/3/90; ‘Ashdown tempers glory with realism – Poll Tax key to shock Ribble Valley result’, *Guardian*, 9/3/91). As one political correspondent put it

> ‘Let’s just accept the premise for a second, that [Margaret Thatcher] did go because of the poll tax ... It’s got to be one hell of a bad policy to have done that. It’s got to have been something that was going to turf Tory MPs out of what were regarded as safe seats ... That was, if you like, a barometer of how bad the policy was. Because if it was capable of doing that it must have been fucking awful. It really must.’

Collectively, these feedback mechanisms not only made journalists acutely sensitive to the depth of public antagonism towards the tax, but also very wary of being implicated as apologists for such an unpopular policy. As one BBC local radio editor acknowledged, the Community Charge had had ‘a very rough ride [in the media] ... And rightly so. I mean, if there’s something that people are feeling passionate about, I think we would be failing in our job if we weren't testing it, and asking the sorts of questions possibly that people ask in private'.

However, if the evidence of public antipathy exerted a powerful framing influence over reporting, journalists still remained uncertain about many important aspects of public knowledge and opinion. This confusion centred on the audience's sustained interest in the issue, and their ability to cope with the more complex aspects of the debate. In both instances, journalists relied on their own professional judgements about when the issue had become boring, and whether it would go over the heads of their audience. As one news editor put it:

> 'March is when the bills had gone out, demonstrations were starting, you know, the reality was coming home that the poll tax had arrived at last. But, given a month or so, *news editors and readers were getting a bit fed up with the poll tax* and so they were looking for something else to encourage the readers to buy the newspaper again. It's as simple as that I think ... *As a news editor I have to try and put myself in the shoes of the reader. And that's difficult, obviously, because I don't know really what the readers are thinking or saying.* But you just have to use your professional judgement. You know, at this stage readers are getting bored with the poll tax and, you know, we'll ease up on coverage of that. *You have to make your judgements I suppose and you assume that that's how the readers are feeling at the same time.* But you may be right, you may be wrong' (our emphasis).

The crucial point here is that, although public demonstrations played a crucial role in pushing the poll tax to the forefront of the media agenda in March 1990, they could not sustain media attention over the ensuing months. Once it became clear that the violence of the tax revolt hadn't significantly eroded support for the Labour Party, journalists and news editors rapidly tired of an issue they felt had nowhere else to go:

> 'When the riots started, people began to take notice a bit more ... The peaks really are determined by the novelty of the issue. I mean the first poll tax protester to be imprisoned was a story but the second, third, fourth, fifth and hundredth isn't unless someone suddenly sits up and say, says "Hang on a minute, there's been so many imprisoned we

> ought to do an article summarizing the position"' (Local government correspondent).

Underwriting these professional judgements were idealized or cynical constructions of their audience and their probable interests and competences. The influence of this 'canonical audience' (Anderson and Meyer, 1988) was very significant in determining which issues related to reform of local government received most attention, particularly in the more populist media. As a senior correspondent for a local radio station explained:

> 'We are not Radio 4. This station is aimed at a C2/D/E, tabloid reading, tabloid mentality, audience ... We don't have a great deal of time to go into the complexities of the more obtuse aspects of local government finance ... All the time, we try and personalize everything. It's always how much are *you* going to have to pay – not "ratepayers" or "chargepayers in Bradford" – it's "*you*". So it's always focusing down to the individual, and our perceived audience. That was a conscious editorial decision.'

One regional newsroom actually had a name for their protypical audience member, and constantly worried about how she might grapple with the information they provided:

> 'Our archetypal listener is called "Edna". We call her "Edna". And she is a 45-plus housewife, living on any large estate you can care to mention anywhere in Cambridgeshire ... Standardized Spending Assessment, I think, that caused us more problems than anything. Trying to explain that in "Edna speak" – again it comes down to "Edna Speak" – how do you explain to Edna, that the Government says that we should only spend X when the County Council are saying we should spend X + Y?' (Local news editor).

Within this remit the media's explanatory work concentrated on the pragmatics rather than the principles of local finance: on what people had to pay, rather than how underlying components affected poll tax levels. Even when news media ran explanatory pieces about the broader fiscal context of poll tax levels, they were sceptical about whether their audience were really interested:

> 'I would hate to know what the readership of that sort of explanation was. I think a lot of people just skipped it. All they were bothered about was the bloody "Where?", "How much?"' (News editor, regional newspaper).

However, despite these examples of how professional judgements and assumptions about audience interests and competences shaped what got reported many journalists were highly resistant to any suggestion that they may have framed the terms of reference of political debate:

> 'We're simply, you know, transporting the news: reporting it, reflecting it, reflecting what people think and trying to convey the issues' (Editor, regional news programme).

Summary and conclusions

Several key points emerge from our analysis of journalists' and their news gathering on the Community Charge.

First, different journalist and news organizations' reporting of the tax emerged from distinct environments. Whereas the national media were locked into the passage of events and dramas viewed from the legislature, local media focused on the direct experience of the local state. As we see later, these distinct orientations were crucial in creating the evaluative differences noted between local and national coverage. However, the local news agenda was influenced at an interpretative level by the national media, whether through daily exposure to national coverage or on-line news agency information.

Second, specialist correspondents in the national media interacted differently with news sources in reporting the tax and had different perspectives on it. Political correspondents focused their news gathering around Parliament, had only a transient interest in the issue, and largely disregarded the more technical aspects of the debate. By comparison, local government correspondents engaged in more diverse and specialized news gathering on the issue, had a more thorough grasp of its detail and gave more consistent attention to it. This had a clear impact on how these correspondents reported the policy.

Third, in comparing the performance of 'advocates', news organizations assigned the greatest news value to the views of critics within the Conservative Party. Although journalists were highly critical of the perceived incompetence of Government's campaign work, this was seen as largely symptomatic of the political problems created by the divisions within its own ranks. In the national media, it was the political correspondents who first picked up on the seriousness of the divisions within the Conservative Party, and who – during the latter stages of the policy – were made privy to the serious reservations of several senior Government ministers. This unreported knowledge was widely circulated and influenced journalists' evaluations of these ministers' public proclamations.

Fourth, local and national media sectors used different 'arbiters' to adjudicate over the complexities of the debate. The main influence of these sources was at an evaluative rather than interpretative level. Locally, the main arbiters were the local government finance officers responsible for administering the tax, who were routinely accessed by a wide range of local reporters. Nationally, the principal arbiters were academics, public research institutes, and local authority associations, and contact was mainly conducted via specialist local government correspondents. In this respect, these reporters were the principal mechanism by which national news organizations became sensitized to the often extremely critical judgements delivered publicly or privately by these sources.

Fifth, public opinion exerted a considerable influence over how journalists and editors reported the issue. News professionals recognized that the public disliked the tax from very early in the policy cycle, and the consistency of this antipathy both sustained and legitimized their own scepticism about the policy. In March 1990, the outbreak of public demonstrations was a crucial element in driving the issue to the forefront of the news agenda. However, although clearly aware of public antipathy, news professionals were also uncertain about many other aspects of public opinion and knowledge, and relied heavily on their own judgements about what their audiences find interesting and would understand. These assumptions were crucial in determining which issues were reported and which were neglected, and in legitimating a reduction in media attention to the issue during later stages of the policy cycle. In this respect journalists actively constructed, rather than reflected, public concerns.

Chapter 7

The Politics of Political Communication: The Determinants and Impact of Poll Tax News

In this final substantive chapter of the book we address two important remaining tasks. The first is to draw together the threads of the content analysis and journalist and news source interviews specifically to explain the factors that contributed to the construction of media discourses on the Community Charge. The second is to explore whether these discourses had any impact on the formation of public opinion. It is widely assumed that the poll tax failed because it never secured public support. Yet commentators have been generally incurious about exploring how its credibility was so emphatically eroded. In this chapter we present evidence that suggests the media, whilst being influenced by public antipathy, also exerted a considerable influence in shaping public opinion – both in providing information about the tax and drawing public attention towards some features of it, and away from others.

The origins of poll tax news

The media reporting of the Community Charge begs a range of questions. Why were several important aspects of the broader political debate ignored by the media? What were the reasons for the disparities in local and national reporting? How can we explain the broad consensus of media derision that had established itself by 1990? Why did certain media evaluations of the policy shift over time? And why was the tax neglected during its formative stages? In this section we address these questions under three broad discussions that explore the reasons behind the shifting intensity of media coverage, its interpretative limitations and evaluative hostility.

The shifting intensity of national media coverage

> 'What about the issues which are around but which the parties do not push and television does not spot? And the classic example of that seems to me, in '87, the poll tax ... Looking back on it, it's quite clear now that we should have dug harder and been able to find the poll tax, because it was around there if we had looked at it and looked for it hard enough' (Michael Brunson, Political Editor, ITN, quoted in *Democracy in Danger*, Channel 4, 18/3/92).

> 'The Poll Tax? That's old hat!' (Regional TV news editor observed at a morning editorial meeting, May 1990).

We have seen that the intensity of national media coverage of the Community Charge often bore little relation to the policy timetable itself. Indeed, many important periods in the implementation and abolition of the policy passed with only a modicum of media coverage. If these results suggest that in this instance the watchdog of democracy was both disturbingly myopic and easily distracted, we need to consider the reasons for this initial inattention and subsequent disinterest.

The fluctuation in national media coverage was the product of two interrelated factors. The first was the prominence, or otherwise, of key news sources in public discussion about the policy, and their public disposition towards it. The second was the news professionals' perceptions of the intrinsic news-worthiness of the issue.

It is clear that national media coverage was not fundamentally driven by the policy cycle, but rather by political events – or, to be more precise, the parliamentary process. If an issue is marginalized by the main political parties, it is highly unlikely to attract consistent attention in the media. Therefore, because the Government and the main political opposition avoided the issue before the 1987 General Election – for reasons discussed earlier – it is not surprising that the tax only started to attract attention after the electoral die had been cast.

Furthermore, because the media were never primarily interested in local finance policy *per se*, but rather in the political controversy the issue generated, the nature and composition of debate within the parliamentary arena had a direct bearing on the amount of attention the media gave to the issue. When inter-party duelling transformed into intra-party dissent, the issue gained a far greater news worthiness; when these divisions disappeared, media interest waned. During the earliest stages, party political debate was strictly divided along party lines: Conservative dissent hadn't mobilized, and many of the tax's later critics supported the policy. It was only with the legislative period for England and Wales, and the first Conservative rebellions, that the issue started to attract sufficient parliamentary status and party political 'spin' to gain sustained media attention. Once these party divisions gaped open, and coincided with open rebellion in 'little England' and the inner cities, in March 1990, the components were all in place to ensure an intensive, if transient, period of media concern.

However, just as the rise of the poll tax in the national media arena was directly influenced by transformations in the parliamentary arena, so its decline was underwritten by alterations in the configuration of party political debate. While public demonstrations were momentarily influential in attracting media coverage, their news value decreased as their novelty declined (although public demonstrations and non-payment campaigns continued into 1992). Journalists refocused their attention on the party political arena. However, the assuaging of Conservative dissent meant the issue lost its most reportable political 'spin', and reduced the controversy over the Council Tax to just one more inter-party dispute amongst many. As the wider cacophony increased in the lead up to the General Election, the poll tax became inaudible, despite the persistent efforts of the Labour Party to revive its spectre during the legislative passage of the Council Tax and the 1992 Election campaign.

However, in emphasizing the heavy reliance of the media on key political sources to identify the issue during the early stages of the policy's implementation, it is also important to appreciate that this dependency lessened during later stages of the cycle. Whereas in the early stages many journalists were ignorant about the policy and its likely effects and highly source-dependent, by the most intense phase of media coverage in 1990 they were more informed and sensitive to the issue, and consequently less reactive – often raising the issue in spite of the damage limitation strategies of the party news managers. In doing so, they amplified and influenced developments within the political arena. This increased awareness also meant that the professional judgements of the journalists and their editors exerted a far greater independent influence over deciding the relative prominence of the issue over subsequent periods. In this respect, the constrained parameters of news coverage also produced a repetitiveness that journalists and news editors soon found tedious, and accelerated the issue's decline in national coverage. As a news editor on a large regional newspaper put it four months after the repeal of the tax had been announced:

> 'There's a story today: "Britain's oldest poll tax prisoner was released from jail today". Oh that it should come to this! ... It's getting to the stage of a freak-show: he's the oldest so therefore that makes it unusual. I don't know whether we actually did, but I'm sure that every possible avenue has been explored ... "Poll tax" is now a narcoleptic word to use in a newspaper office. You say "poll tax" and most journalists start to nod off. It's a bit difficult to get excited about for me I'm afraid. I know it's a serious and abiding issue but, er ...'

Interpretations: absences in poll tax coverage

> 'For most people, poll tax bills weren't an invasion of privacy, they were an invasion of their bank balances. A severe invasion of their wealth' (Political correspondent).

We have noted how several issues that concerned poll tax campaigners went virtually unreported by the mainstream media, such as the constitutional implications of the new system, privacy issues, the impact of the tax on voter registration, and general information about the related restructuring of grant allocation and non domestic taxation. As we discuss later, these cumulative absences raise serious questions about the media's performance in informing public debate about the tax and its broader implications.

However, it is one thing to identify absences in media coverage and another to explain their exclusion. It is clear that the neglect of these issues reflected a combination of the professional and political values of news gatherers and processors, and the changing information strategies and capabilities of several key protagonists in the broader political debate.

Numerous studies have identified the crucial role that news values play in determining which events are most likely to be selected and reported as 'news' (Galtung and Ruge, 1969; Golding and Elliott, 1979; Ericson *et al.*, 1987; Chibnall, 1977). These values are a product of the pressures of the news production process and embody professional assumptions about the interests and needs of the mass audience. Essentially, the less complex and ambiguous an issue is, the more readily it can be personalized and dramatized, shown to have clear and immediate implications, and is consonant with previous news frameworks, the more likely it is to be reported. It is no coincidence that all the absences in coverage of the Community Charge contravened one or more of these criteria. Standardized Spending Assessments may have been of pivotal importance to poll tax levels – and thereby the system's political viability – but their complexity made them appear dry and arcane to many journalists (who, indeed, struggled to understand them). Evidence of the impact of the new tax on voter registration took some time to emerge, and when it was presented, proved difficult to isolate from the influence of other factors, such as the long term decline in voter registration and changes in the registration policy of electoral officers in certain areas (Butler and Kavanagh, 1992). The centralization of control of non-domestic rate revenue may have significantly eroded local government autonomy, but it lacked the personal drama that characterized previous clashes between the Thatcher Government and the demons of the municipal left.

By recognizing that news values systematically diverted journalists from the long term and technical aspects of the debate, we can also understand why many journalists viewed the poll tax as an easy issue to report. News values both sustained and legitimized a disregard for the more recondite aspects of the policy debate.

The exclusion of these issues from mainstream media discourses was also compounded by the political antagonism of many journalists towards some of the broader issues they raised. For example, there were few apologists for local government among the journalists we interviewed at either local or national level. As one parliamentary correspondent put it:

> 'You're not going to get any decent stories in [the paper] which say 'Poor old local government, it's had its power stripped'. People would say "well Hooray for that! That daft old bugger down the Town Hall!"'

Similarly, the impact of the new tax on voter registration and the prospect of increased intrusiveness by local government were subsumed by the political antagonism of journalists towards those advocating the non-payment strategy.* As one national journalist explained:

> 'You see the civil liberties issue became confused with the law breaking issue. There was a dilemma on deciding whether these were people whose civil liberties were being infringed or these were people who were breaking the law and should face the consequences?'.

The marginalization of these various issues from media discourses was further compounded by the changing information strategies of several of the main participants in the broader debate. For example, whereas the Labour Party and certain local authority associations frequently drew attention to the constitutional and privacy implications of the tax during the early stages of the policy debate, they mentioned these issues far less frequently during the latter stages. Away from the party political arena, the civil liberties pressure group, Liberty, who initially played a pivotal role in highlighting the privacy issues raised by the new system, latterly shifted its campaign work towards challenging judicial abuses in the prosecution of non-payees.

The reasons for these changes in the interpretative focus of news sources varied. In some cases, their shift reflected political considerations. For example, as the Labour Party came under attack over the issue of non-payment, its leadership became far more nervous about the disenfranchisement issue. Similarly, as local authorities saw their revenue dwindle due to persistently high non payment levels, they became less concerned with politicizing the electorate and more concerned about preserving their financial reserves.

On another level, these changes revealed how political sources became increasingly adept at recognizing which issues would play most effectively in the media arena, and cut their campaign cloth accordingly. During the early stages of the policy cycle the media appeared to have difficulty in locating the issue within pre-existing news frameworks. This had two effects. On the one level it made coverage highly intermittent, but it also meant that the media were more receptive to these alternative agendas

* For example, several local newspapers had no compunction about printing the names and addresses of local residents who had been served with liability orders for not paying the tax (*UK Press Gazette*, 24/9/90).

about the tax.* However, once the media were able to place the issue within the more familiar context of inter (and intra) party dispute, their interpretative focus constricted. In turn, several of the main news sources shifted their campaign agendas, in a way that both reflected and accelerated this political compression. In other words, a 'vocabulary of precedents' (Ericson *et al.*, 1987, 1989) quickly developed between journalists and news sources in the reporting of this issue, which exerted a powerful framing influence over subsequent coverage and information provision.

Finally, the changes revealed the limited 'carrying capacities' (Hilgartner and Bosk, 1988) of several key political sources, and their inability to campaign on more than one front. For example, once the civil liberty group, Liberty, became increasingly embroiled in the debate about the denials of defendants' legal rights, it had seriously to curtail its campaign work on the broader privacy implications of the tax. As a crucial information source on this area, its shift also accelerated the marginalization of the issue in media discourses.

Evaluations: the sources of media hostility

In many respects one of the most fascinating aspects to this debate is explaining why the British media – collectively not renowned for their rabid anti-Conservatism – were so critical of the Community Charge? And what does this suggest about the conditions and limitations of state agenda-building? It is important to emphasize that the Government's failure was at an *evaluative* rather than *interpretative* level, in that there was no fundamental challenge by the media to the ideological parameters of the Government's case for reforming local government finance. If the Government's ideological offensive foundered under media scrutiny, it did so on its own terms.

Another important qualification is that not all sections of the media were consistently hostile to the tax and its objectives. Although all of the journalists we interviewed claimed they had always recognized the tax to be fatally flawed, one has to wonder about the influence hindsight may have had in shaping such critical clarity. (All interviews were conducted after the abolition of the tax had been announced.) Whilst not denying there

* For example, civil liberties questions were among the most prominent themes in media coverage during the consultative period.

was often an early and considerable scepticism in many sectors of the media about the tax (particularly in the local media), our content analysis reveals that many influential sections of the media initially quite liked the idea, and only changed their stance during the tax's later crises. This leads one to question whether the journalistic consensus about the deficiencies of the system would have been so absolute, had the same questions been asked as the political debate was still active? At the very least, the content analysis suggests there was a *process* involved in the political delegitimization of the Community Charge. Somewhere, somehow, an argument was lost.

To explain the evaluative hostility of the media, we need to appreciate the distinctive roles played by advocates and arbiters in shaping media opinion. Firstly, the battle lines of advocacy in the debate were hugely unbalanced. The policy attracted a swathe of criticism from both private and public sectors, voluntary agencies and all the opposition parties. However, particularly significant were the major divisions within the Conservative Party ranks, which eventually extended to the most senior echelons of the Government. Not only were these internal wranglings intrinsically newsworthy, but the prevalence of Conservative dissent prevented the media from organizing their analysis along conventional party political lines. As one very influential broadcast journalist observed:

> 'By the end it was a bit like Apartheid ... You didn't have to balance the thing. You did at the beginning because everyone was divided on party lines, but by the end most Tories were condemning it as well and the Government was saying "well we're going to review it" ... So you didn't have to go through a farce of saying "but on the other hand they're saying everything's going smoothly".'

In conjunction with the imbalance in political advocacy, the arbiters of news coverage played a crucial part in securing the critical antipathy of the news media. None of the arbiters elected by journalists at local or national level corroborated the Government claims, and indeed many were openly critical of the new system.

The greater hostility of the local media towards the policy than their national counterparts, can also be explained with these factors in mind. If support for the Government's flagship was scant at a national level, it was almost completely absent locally. In this respect the Government's alienation of local government opinion in imposing the system, proved highly significant. Local authorities played a key role in informing and defining local media agendas on the poll tax, partly through the increasing, if variable, efficiency of their press, marketing and public relations departments, but also because of their traditional prominence in the routine newsbeats of the provincial media. This secured them a privileged access, and thereby an important definitional advantage.

Recognizing how the patterns of advocacy at both national and local levels altered as the policy process developed, also helps explain why certain sections of the national media initially supported the tax. Even during the back bench rebellions that marked the passage of the legislation for England and Wales, the Government could still depend upon a significant rump of opinion in the parliamentary party to support the principles of the policy. However, once the Conservative right crossed the the rubicon, and openly attacked the tax, the isolation of the Prime Minister was complete. The Thatcherite press could no longer construct the debate as part of a covert, left wing challenge to the Party leadership, and it is no coincidence that the last vestiges of media support evaporated at the same time as these high level defections.

Public perceptions and popular representation

> 'The public have not been persuaded that the [Community] Charge is fair' (Michael Heseltine, Secretary of State for the Environment, House of Commons, 21 March 1991).

We have seen how the main protaganists in the political debate over the poll tax presumed the media would play a key role in the battle for the hearts and minds of the British electorate. This presumption, in itself, constituted a very significant area of media influence, as the political process itself was contorted and distorted by the pursuit of editorial support. However, what evidence is there to support these political calculations about the public salience of the media? Although the primary research upon which this book is based contained no specific audience related component, the wealth of opinion poll data on public knowledge of and attitudes towards the Community Charge does provide an opportunity for comparisons that are at least suggestive about the relationship between media representations and public perceptions.

Public attitudes and media coverage

> 'The man in charge of the Community Charge register in Strathclyde said last week he was surprised to discover that there are 1,097 people in Strathclyde called "Donald Duck"' (*Today*, BBC Radio 4, 4 April 1989).

When tracing public attitudes in England and Wales towards the Community Charge over several years, there is little evidence of an independent media influence (See Table 7.1). Any initial public equivocation towards the policy rapidly translated into a confirmed and consistent hostility: from October 1987 onwards opposition to the tax never fell below 60 per cent, and by the time of its introduction consistently exceeded 70 per cent. Clearly, once the electorate began to understand the policy and its implications, the majority disliked it, and nothing shifted them from that opposition.

Table 7.1. Public Attitudes to the poll tax in England and Wales (1987–1990)

Fieldwork	Poll	Sample	For	Against	Don't know
11/6/87	MORI/*The Times*	1023	43	39	18
22–29/9/87	MORI/*Sunday Times*	1502	26	43	31
24–30/9/87	MORI/AMA/COSLA	1866	30	58	12
19/10/87	MORI/*Sunday Times*	1109	37	49	12
29–30/10/87	MORI/*Sunday Times*	1000	23	65	12
17–18/3/88	MORI/*Sunday Times*	1075	33	60	18
25–30/11/88	MORI/*Sunday Times*	817	28	61	11
16–17/3/89	MORI/*Sunday Times*	1098	23	69	8
22–23/11/89	MORI/*Sunday Times*	1068	25	68	7
10–12/2/90	NOP/*Independent*/BBC1	1577	16	73	11
19–24/4/90	MORI/*The Times*	1887	23	73	4

If the media did have an impact on public attitudes, it was most likely to have been in reinforcing public scepticism. Such an interpretation is consistent with the evidence from the journalist interviews, where the persistent antipathy of the public was widely cited by news professionals as a crucial contextual factor in shaping their own perceptions of the political viability of the policy. However, as a qualification to this general observation, it is interesting to note that the only recorded instance where public support for the policy exceeded public opposition was on the day of the 1987 General Election, which had been preceded by an almost complete absence of media coverage. A case, perhaps, of media influence by omission?

Further evidence of the resilience of public attitudes to media definitions emerges from polls conducted during the political furore over the poll tax demonstrations of March 1990. As we have seen, the Government successfully managed to shift media interpretations of the political significance of the demonstrations away from a framework that emphasized their negative implications for it, towards one fixated with conspiracy theories and the detrimental consequences of the riots for its political opponents.

Although the apparent success of this tactic sent shock waves through the Labour leadership – forcing them into ever more strident denunciations of those advocating non payment – it is clear that the public was very resistent to this diversion. Popular support for Labour increased to record levels and was sustained through March and April 1990, despite the media hysteria over the violence of the Trafalgar Square riot, and the Home Secretary's attempt to link the civil disobedience of non payment with the criminal act of 'breaking policemen's heads'. Indeed, an ICM poll conducted a week after the riot, found that two-thirds of respondents rejected the Home Secretary's assertion that Labour were to blame for the violence, more than a third directly blamed the Government for the violence, and over half said they didn't think the Labour leadership should take action against Party members refusing to pay the tax. A significant minority also said they thought the violence was understandable because of the unfairness of the tax (*Sunday Correspondent*, 8/4/90).

Here again, the consistency of public opinion exerted a considerable refractive influence on media evaluations. Once it became clear that the controversy over the demonstrations was not easing the electoral pressure on the Government, journalistic interest in the 'problems for Labour' issue disappeared and attention redirected on to the Government's travails.

However, if public attitudes appear to have been largely independent of, and resilient to, media evaluations (and indeed may have played a crucial role in shaping them) it doesn't necessarily follow that the media had only limited influence over public perceptions of the tax. Indeed, by restricting our search for media influence to attitudinal data, we are probably – to quote a familiar phrase – looking in the wrong place. Indeed, when we examine the extent of public knowledge of the tax, and its varying public salience, a more dramatic picture emerges.

The media and information acquisition

Throughout the policy cycle, research consistently highlighted the primary importance of the mass media as an information source about the tax. In 1988, a survey in Leeds found that 87 per cent of respondents cited 'television and radio' as their main source of information about the policy, and 71 per cent, 'newspapers'. (By comparison, Government information was cited by only 13 per cent and council information by 8 per cent.) Furthermore, local media featured very prominently in the respondents' media consumption (Campbell *et al.*, 1988). Later research confirmed this pattern – although by that stage other information sources had gained in importance. For example, a study into the effectiveness of the Welsh Office's public information campaign on the Community Charge (National Consumer Council, 1989) found television to be the main information source (40 per cent), followed by Welsh Office information (39 per cent); and local authority information (18 per cent). Similarly, a MORI survey (1989), commissioned by Leicester City Council, found that 51 per cent of respondents in the Leicester area, identified television as their most important source, followed by the local press (38 per cent) and a generic category of 'leaflets' (37 per cent).

The salience of the media as an information source is further confirmed when we examine the extent of public knowledge about this complex policy issue. The Leeds survey found that although 99 per cent of respondents had heard of the poll tax, there was evident confusion among a significant minority of respondents about its linkage with the right to vote and the existence and operation of the Uniform Business Rate (Campbell *et al.*, *op. cit.*). A survey of small business people in England and Wales, in December 1989, found that 76 per cent hadn't heard of the Uniform Business Rate; 87 per cent had no idea what 'UBR' meant; 95 per cent didn't know how it would affect their business; and 92 per cent didn't know what they could do about it (NFSE, 1990). In June and July 1990, a survey by the Policy Studies Institute into public attitudes to local government found that only 15 per cent of respondents knew that revenue from the Community Charge accounted for only around a quarter of local authority revenue (Bloch and John, 1991).

What is significant about these findings is how closely these areas of public confusion coincided with the absences noted in media coverage. Clearly, although the media may have had a central role in informing the public of this hugely significant policy innovation, as the new era of local accountability dawned, they were conspicuously unsuccessful in increasing public understanding of important basic principles and mechanisms of local democracy and finance.

News priorities and public priorities

If the media may have compounded public ignorance about many important aspects of the policy, they also appear to have played a crucial role in drawing public attention towards and away from the issue. Figure 7.1 compares aggregated opinion poll data on the changing public perceptions of the salience of the issue in England and Wales* with national press coverage, between April 1988 and September 1991, and highlights a dramatic correlation between the two.† Just as the poll tax dropped down the media agenda after its legislative passage, so it receded from public attention. However, as the prospect of its introduction in England and Wales approached, public concern increased, slowly at first, and then dramatically in March 1990. However, once introduced, public attention to the issue faded in a manner and at a pace almost identical to that in the media, only to be revitalized in November 1990 and March 1991, coinciding exactly with the two final bursts of coverage. After the Government's

* 'Public salience' is measured here by a question in monthly public opinion surveys conducted by MORI in England and Wales designed to assess which issues were considered to be 'most important' or 'other important'. The pattern revealed here is supported by similar data collected by NOP over the same period. In response to the question 'What are the most important issues which are influencing the way you intend to vote?', 22 per cent cited the poll tax in January 1990, rising to 50 per cent in March 1990, and falling to 47 per cent in May 1990. In January 1991, 37 per cent cited the poll tax, rising to 58 per cent in March 1991, and then swiftly falling to 19 per cent in August 1991. It is important to appreciate that these figures relate to England and Wales only. Public perceptions in Scotland revealed a different pattern, reflecting the policy's earlier implementation, and the greater intensity of media coverage during the policy's early stages.

† Correlating public opinion and media content in this manner can be problematic. One of the most serious criticisms is that in doing so one is not comparing like with like (Van Liere and Dunlap, 1980). For example, comparisons of environmental news with the salience of environmental issues in the public agendas are seriously compromised by the broad and diverse range of issues that are included within such an imprecise category. However, this is not a problem in this instance. From April 1988, MORI assigned a specific category to measure public attention to the 'poll tax' and the specificity of this category clearly permits a close comparison with the content analysis data.

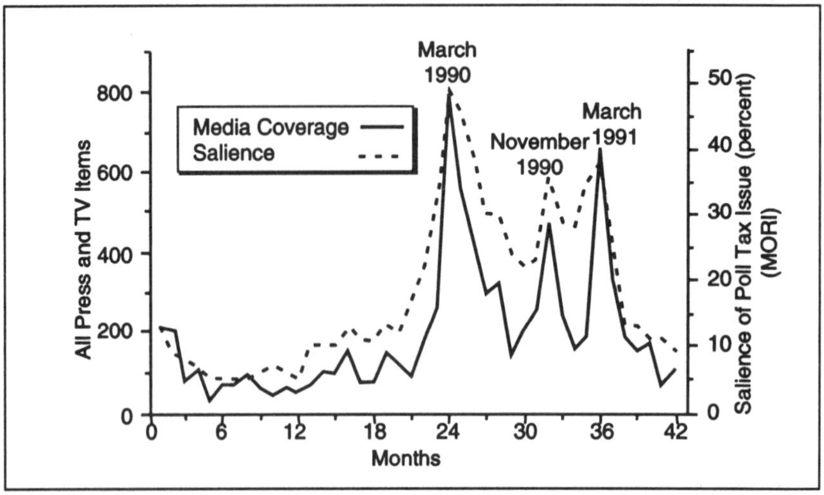

Fig. 7.1. Comparison of national media coverage and public salience of poll tax April 1988 – September 1991.

Council Tax announcement the issue was quickly relegated in the public agenda, and by the 1992 General Election had almost completely disappeared from public attention.

Is it possible that the relationship between public attention and media representation is spurious? The most obvious alternative explanation – that public concern was solely driven by the material impact of the policy on people's spending – cannot account for the timing in the shifts in public attention. The public in England and Wales were most concerned about the Community Charge before they had paid a penny, but as the first payments were made, and the controversial process of enforcement began, the salience of the issue receded in public importance. It then briefly re-emerged in November 1990 – halfway through the financial year of local authorities, and eight months after the tax had been introduced. Clearly, some factor other than the continued financial burden of the Community Charge conspired to push it back on to the public agenda at this juncture. The final, rapid and complete relegation of the issue from May 1991 onwards is also difficult to account for materially, when one considers that the tax still had two years to run, and many who had successfully avoided the tax during its first year were remorselessly tracked down over this period by local authorities desperate for revenue and increasingly unsympathetic to non-payers.

If, as seems clear, media coverage and public opinion were closely related, a further question presents itself: which factors exterted the greater influence over the other? One obvious explanation is that the media were largely mirroring shifts in public opinion, rather than creating them. However, there are two main problems with this argument. First, had public concerns been the driving force behind media attention, there should have been a clear lag between the public opinion and media data. This is because the opinion poll data was collected at the end of each month, whereas the media data quantifies the cumulative coverage for each month. The almost identical convergence of the two patterns confirms that news priorities shifted *before* any equivalent change in public concerns had been empirically established. Second, the journalist interviews demonstrated how isolated news professionals were from the public they addressed, and how their editorial decisions were driven by assumptions about public interests and capabilities. Rather than meticuously consulting public concerns, journalists trusted their own judgements about what their audience would find relevant. Even when public actions forced the issue to the forefront of the media agenda, as was the case with the widespread demonstrations of March 1990, this influence was largely transient, as journalists quickly tired of these performative gestures, and looked for other issues to sustain their attention.

This suggests the media were of primary significance in setting the public agenda. However, in arguing this we recognize the dangers of proposing a crude transmission model of media influence (Elliott, 1972; Hansen, 1991) – where it is assumed that powerful news sources shape media agendas, which in turn determine public agendas, in a linear and non reciprocated manner. Throughout this book we have identified several examples of where policy debates, public perceptions and media representations interacted dynamically in the formation of political discourses on the poll tax. However, we would emphasize that the interaction and feedback between these various arenas is structurally imbalanced, with certain arenas 'over-accessing' others. And whereas the public are constantly exposed to media messages in the formation of their political opinions, the public are largely an abstracted presence for journalists, whose opinions and needs they can only imperfectly know.

Summary and conclusions

In this chapter we have explored the formative political dynamics that shaped media reporting of the introduction and abolition of the Community Charge, and the impact that media representations may have had on public perceptions of the tax.

Three crucial points emerged regarding the construction of media agendas on the poll tax. First, the shifting intensity of media attention to the issue throughout the policy cycle reflected, on the one hand, the activity and public disposition of key political sources on the issue and, on the other, professional judgements by journalists as to the news value of the issue. Because the media were more interested in the political battles the poll tax sparked, rather than the substantive issues it raised, their interest in the issue was heavily dependent on the currency of the issue in key political arenas. The political and electoral implications of this should not be underestimated. This was a major, controversial reform that, due to the negligence of the media, was smuggled in under the noses of the electorate, and then prematurely whisked away from view. Furthermore, the fact that the most complete periods of silence coincided with two national elections, was no accident.

Second, the limited interpretative parameters of media coverage were partly due to the application of news values and journalists' political prejudices to this complex area. However, they also reflected the changing information strategies of key news sources, who altered their tactics and campaign agendas as the policy cycle unfolded.

Third, the widespread hostility towards the tax across all media sectors by 1990 was created by the imbalance in the patterns of advocacy and the critical interventions made publicly and privately by arbiters. Particularly significant was the prevalence of Conservative Party dissent, which prevented the media from constructing the issue as a party political conflict. The greater hostility evident in local coverage reflected the structural orientation of the local media to the local state and their lengthier exposure to a greater unanimity of critical opinion.

Concerning the relationship between the media and public opinion, the data highlights both the dependence and independence of public perceptions on media representations. The media's influence does not seem to have operated at an evaluative level, but rather at an interpretative level.

The public never liked the idea of the Community Charge and, indeed, their resilient antagonism fed the media's own scepticism about the advisability of the policy change. However, the public relied heavily on the media for information about the new tax, and displayed political blindspots that corresponded very closely to the noted absences in media content. On another level, public perceptions of the salience of the issue closely tracked the ebb and flow of media coverage rather than the policy timetable itself. Collectively, these findings provide clear, *prima facie* support to the classic agenda-setting proposition: that the media may not tell us what to think, but they are very influential in telling us what to think about (Cohen, 1963), and strongly confirms the presumption of the main protaganists in the debate, that the media would be the principal political arena in which the public battle for the poll tax would be fought.

Chapter 8

Rethinking Political Communication

In this book we have charted the dramatic failure of one of the most forcefully promoted and far-reaching British domestic policy initiatives of modern times, and identified the pivotal role of the media in the conduct of that political debate – both in informing public opinion and in shaping the political strategies of the most influential protagonists. It is not our intention here to repeat the substantive conclusions of this study, but rather to consider their broader implications. From the outset we have contended that the failure of the poll tax is more than just of intrinsic interest, but rather presents an opportunity to explore broader issues pertinent to the study of political communication. So what are these wider lessons?

Policy failures are communication failures

The first lesson is the importance of communication factors in explaining policy outcomes, which tend to be only paid lip service in many policy analyses. In this regard, we depart from John Gibson's assertion that 'the importance of presentation, relative to the *real effect* of the flat rate [poll] tax must not be exaggerated' (1990: 241, our emphasis). Indeed, we propose that it is only possible to explain several crucial aspects to the introduction of the Community Charge by attending to the 'presentation' and broader political construction of the policy. This is demonstrated by the opinion poll evidence which shows that public concern with the issue corresponded only weakly with the material impact of the policy, and by the many specific occasions where the emphasis of parliamentary, media and public debate had a direct impact on the form and structure of the policy, with profound material consequences. For example, the Government's decision to revise the self financing safety net arrangements had nothing to do with the 'real' effects of the tax (implementation was seven months hence) but rather its inability to convince its own supporters and a hostile mass media that such arrangements weren't effectively subsidising Labour councils at Conservative councils' expense. Conversely, Conservative Central Office's successful redefinition of the Party's disastrous 1990 local election results as a vindication of the principle of the tax, not only temporarily stymied Conservative dissent, media comment and public attention, but also – as Gibson himself concedes – directly influenced the outcome of the ministerial review then underway, ensuring 'that the flat rate principle of the poll tax was retained' (*ibid.*: 244).

At root, our analysis challenges the widely held received wisdom, particularly among journalists, that the poll tax could never have been sold because it was a 'bad' policy with too many negative implications for too many people. Whilst we wouldn't deny that the material inconsistencies and regressiveness of the policy played an important part in its abolition, we would challenge whether they provide a sufficient explanation for its defeat. Rather we suggest that the material difficulties and political failures of the tax fed into and off each other. Certainly, if the political failure of the tax was just caused by its intrinsic regressiveness and inefficiency, one would have expected the same Government to have experienced far more serious political crises as a consequence of many of their preceding policies. For example, before the 1980s it was unthinkable that a government could preside over unemployment levels well above three million – outside of a depression – and sustain any electoral credibility, but this was precisely the dubious achievement of the Thatcher administration. Yet there was no equivalent media or public outrage about the wastefulness and inefficiency of this situation, or the regressiveness of a broad economic strategy that handed generous tax concessions to the affluent professional classes, whilst dramatically cutting back benefit entitlements for low income groups. The truth is you can fool quite a lot of the people for much of the time, and our case study simply demonstrates the limits to the powers of state delusion.

To understand the political failure of the Community Charge, you need to understand the process by which its credibility was eroded, and the particular conditions that compromised the Government's management and control of that political debate. One of the central objectives of this book has been to explain what it was about the poll tax that led the media to seize on its unfairness and material failings, rather than gloss over them.

Looking beyond elections

The second broad conclusion to be drawn from this case study is the converse need for those interested in the role of the media in the political process to attend more closely to the complexities of that process. To do so properly, there is a need to loosen the stranglehold that election studies still exert on the imagination of political communication research. Although elections are obviously significant moments in the political calendar, their freneticism makes them unusual, atypical political periods, which have more to do with the form rather than substance of policy making. As a result of this, election studies cannot properly explore significant nuances in the political process that have important implications for the construction of public discourses on political issues. For example, we have shown how tensions and dissent within political parties significantly influenced the ability of their leadership to control the terms of media discourse – yet it is precisely these complex intra party affiliations of the media that are lost in the rough and tumble of a national election, where concerns about inter party affiliations are inevitably at their most prominent (Billig *et al.*, 1992; Linton, 1992; Harrop and Scammel, 1992; Miller, 1990). Similarly, a national election campaign temporarily obscures important local and regional differences and negates the important political contributions of non party political institutions. To investigate these important matters we need to extend the temporal scope and focus of our enquiry beyond election campaigns and attend more closely to the 'natural history' of issues in the public domain.

Rethinking primary definition

The third lesson to be drawn from this case study involves reassessing some of the central assumptions in the influential model of primary definition (Hall *et al.*, 1978). In promoting the poll tax, the Government would seem to have had all the advantages and qualities of a 'primary definer'. It had authority, unique access to both information and journalists, and control over timing. The policy was ideologically driven, part of the Conservative mission to inject a consumer philosophy into public services whilst curbing the perceived excesses of municipal socialism. In the event, the fate of the poll tax illustrates how the ideological advantages of primary definition can be eroded by political vulnerability, so that an 'accredited' source becomes largely 'discredited' – consistently on the defensive and increasingly unable to control the direction of public and media debate. This underlines the importance of addressing both evaluative and interpretative dimensions of policy presentation and media coverage when considering the influence of authoritative sources over a particular debate. Successfully defining the terms of a policy debate during its generative stages may be an important victory, but there is no guarantee that those interpretative parameters will remain constant throughout the policy cycle, or that its evaluative aspects will not erode ideological credibility from within. Therefore, not only does primary definition have to be won, it must also be sustained interpretatively and evaluatively through a series of battles, in which its political vulnerability may progressively increase.

The research also provides another essential qualification to the primary definition model, regarding the relative importance of tensions within the power structure for the construction of media discourses. In this study we have shown that media scepticism about the Community Charge did not emerge independently. Rather, the seeds of dissent were sown and nurtured by other élite sources – from within the Conservative Party, local government, the voluntary sector, public and private sectors and the academic community – which the media subsequently reported. However, in applying their own professional and political values to the reporting of the tax, the media exerted a highly significant influence on the debate: in amplifying particular issues and ignoring others; in pressurizing certain political sources on occasions and allowing others to escape with the scantest scrutiny. Despite this influential role, the ultimate dependency of the media's critical disposition on the broader configuration of élite debate, shows the danger of too readily assuming a congruence in the interests and aims of the 'ruling classes'. This study clearly corroborates the conclusions of other recent studies and commentaries which have shown how the relative openness of media discourses on particular issues is largely dependent upon the degree of coherence in the views of authoritative sources (Hallin, 1986; Schlesinger, 1990; Miller, 1993). However, it also identifies an important distinction in the relationship between journalists and élite sources. This is between 'advocates' and 'arbiters'. Although all news sources can be thought of as 'advocates' – who each have a preferred image or message they would like to convey in the media – some are selected by journalists to act as 'arbiters' on particular issues. The views and opinions of these arbiters – provided they are comprehensible to journalists and, crucially, can be broadly assimilated within their inferential framework –

are treated with greater deference than those of even the most senior 'advocates' and play a very important part in shaping media evaluations of the issues upon which they are invited to comment.

The poll tax was a curious excursion into the limits of radical statecraft. The power to create and distribute meaning still resides with centres of material and political power, both within the state and amongst the higher reaches of corporate and financial authority. But this power is exercised dynamically. It is fought over, challenged, and abused, both within and without. The citizen is both witness to and participant in that process. Our understanding of it is a contribution both to the study of political communication and to the enlightenment and insight which are the hallmarks of citizenship.

Appendix 1

Methods

The Content Analysis

Criteria for inclusion

A 'poll tax focused' item was defined as any news or feature story that had any aspect of the reforms to local finance enacted by the 1987 Abolition of Rates (Scotland etc.) Act and the 1988 Local Government Finance Act as its main theme. A 'poll tax related' item was any news or feature story that referred to these matters in a subsidiary context.

The sample frame

The quantitative analysis of media coverage of the Community Charge covered three sample periods. The first was a longitudinal sample of national press and television coverage between 1 January 1986 and 30 September 1991. The national press sample comprised all poll tax focused and related coverage in every edition of the *Guardian*, the *Sunday Times* and *The Times* for this period. Items were identified via a key-word search of the 'Profile' data base. The national television sample comprised all poll tax focused coverage from BBC1's *9pm News*, ITN's *News at Ten*, Channel Four's *7pm News* and BBC2's *Newsnight* for the same period. These were identified by analysing library records held by ITN and the BBC.

The second sample period covered the apex of media coverage of the poll tax debate, between 1 March and 5 May 1990, and provided a more detailed comparison of poll tax related coverage across an extended range of local and national media content. The national media sample during this period was expanded to include three radio news and current affairs programmes (BBC Radio Four's *6pm News* and *The World Tonight* and BBC Radio One's *News '90*) and three tabloid newspapers (the *Sun*, the *Daily Mirror* and the *Daily Mail*). The local media sample comprised all poll tax related coverage in all local newspapers and television covering six selected local authority regions.

The selection of local sample areas was determined by six criteria: (1) the political complexion of the Council (Labour/ Conservative); (2) the political orientation of the parliamentary constituency over-arching each authority (Conservative/Labour); (3) how marginal these parliamentary constituencies were (marginal/non-marginal); (4) the geographic locality of the local authority (north/south); (5) the type of area (urban/rural); and (6) the level of Community Charge levied in relation to Government recommendations (high/low). The areas selected for the sample were:

(1) Easington, County Durham (a northern, rural, Labour authority area in a non marginal Labour constituency with a 'low' Community Charge);

(2) Liverpool (a northern, urban, Labour authority area, covering several non-marginal Labour constituencies, with a 'high' Community Charge);

(3) Bradford (a northern, urban, Conservative authority area [nb: at the time of the analysis], covering several marginal Labour constituencies, with a 'low' Community Charge);

(4) Guildford, Surrey (a southern, rural, conservative authority area in a non marginal Conservative constituency, with a 'high' Community Charge);

(5) Oxford City (a southern, urban, Labour authority area in a marginal Conservative/Labour constituency, with a 'high' Community Charge);

(6) Huntingdonshire, Cambs (a southern, rural Conservative authority area in a non marginal Conservative constituency, with a 'low' Community Charge).

All daily and weekly newspapers in each area were examined (paid-for and free-sheets), along with the main, weekday BBC and ITV regional evening news programmes covering the six regions (BBC East, BBC South East, BBC North East, BBC North West, Anglia TV, Yorkshire TV, Granada TV, Central TV, Thames TV, London Weekend TV).

The final sample period covers the four week campaign period of the 1992 General Election (11 March to 9 April 1992), and assessed the prominence of poll tax focused coverage in the main national evening news programmes (BBC1's *9pm News*, *News at Ten* and *Newsnight*) and the main morning news and current affairs programme (BBC Radio Four's *Today* programme).

Interviews with journalists and news sources

The analysis of journalists and news sources is based on transcripts of 84 semi-structured interviews, which varied in length between 15 minutes and an hour. Local interviewees were selected qualitatively from the six sample areas. 35 national and local journalists were interviewed, including local government correspondents, political correspondents, political editors and general news editors. 15 interviews were conducted with national politicians, party political press officers, and representatives from the civil service, local authority associations, the academic sector and national pressure groups. 34 interviews were conducted with local news sources, including local politicians, local government finance officers and press officers, voluntary organizations and business leaders. Although repeatedly approached, no Government minister would agree to be interviewed for the research.

Appendix 2

References

Alexander, A. (1990): 'Lessons for the locals: poll tax troubles'. *Marxism Today*, 16–17 April.

Anderson, J.A. and Meyer, T.P. (1988): *Mediated Communication: A Social Action Perspective*. Newbury Park: Sage.

ALA (Association of London Authorities) (1988): *Black People, Ethnic Minorities and the Poll Tax*. London: ALA.

Audit Commission (1990): *The Administration of the Community Charge, Occasional Papers (13)*. London: Audit Commission, November.

Baker, K. (1993): *Turbulent Years*. London: Faber and Faber.

Barker, R. (1992): 'Legitimacy in the United Kingdom: Scotland and the poll tax'. *British Journal of Political Science* **22**, 521–533.

Bauman, Z. (1987): *Legislators and Interpreters*. Cambridge: Polity Press.

Berry, S. (1992): 'Party strategy and the media: the failure of Labour's 1992 election campaign'. *Parliamentary Affairs* **45**, 563–581.

Billig, M., Deacon, D., Golding, P. and Middleton, S. (1992): 'In the hands of the spin-doctors: Television, politics and the 1992 general election', in *It's Live But is it Real?* (eds. N. Miller and R. Allen). London: John Libbey.

Blair, P. (1989): Administering the Community Charge, Paper presented to the Institute of British Geographers' Annual Conference, Coventry Polytechnic, 4 January.

Bloch, A. and John, P. (1991): *'Attitudes to local government'*, Joseph Rowntree Foundation: Local and Central Government Relations Research Findings, 13 September.

Blunkett, D. and Jackson, K. (1987): *Democracy in Crisis: The Town Halls Respond*. London: Hogarth Press.

Boddy, M. and Fudge, C. (eds) (1984): *Local Socialism? Labour Councils and New Left Alternatives*. London: Macmillan.

Boyne, G.A. (1986): 'Rate reform and the future of local democracy'. *The Political Quarterly* **57**, 426–437.

Bramley, G. *et al.* (1988): How Far is the Poll Tax a 'Community Charge'? The Implications of Service User Evidence, Paper presented to the International Seminar on 'Local Government Finance in Theory and Current Applied Research', Ferrara, Italy, 16–17 September.

Broom, D. (1994): 'Taxing experiences'. *Search* **19**, Spring, 11–13.

Brown, C. (1984): *Black and White*. London: PSI/Gower.

Bruce, B. (1991): *How the Image Makers Shape Our Leaders*. London: Kegan Paul.

Burns, D. (1992): *Poll Tax Rebellion*. Scotland: AK Press.

Butler, D. and Kavanagh, D. (1992): *The British General Election of 1992*. London: Macmillan.

Campbell, M., Feather T., Karran, T. and Leach, B. (1988): *The Community Charge (Poll Tax). The Leeds View*. Leeds: Leeds Polytechnic Policy Research Unit.

CIPFA (Chartered Institute for Public Finance and Accountancy) (1987): *Women and the Community Charge*. London: CIPFA.

Chibnall, S. (1977): *Law and Order News*. London: Tavistock.

Cohen, B. (1963): *The Press and Foreign Policy*. Princeton: Princeton University Press.

Commission on Citizenship (1990): *Report: Encouraging Citizenship*. London: HMSO.

Committee of Public Accounts (1990): *Publicity Services for Government Departments, 19th Report.* London: HMSO.

Coxall, B. and Robins, L. (1989): *Contemporary British Politics: An Introduction*. London: Macmillan.

Curran, J. and Seaton, J. (1981): *Power Without Responsibility: The Press and Broadcasting in Britain.* London: Fontana Books.

Curran, J. (1990): 'Culturalist perspectives of news organisations: a reappraisal and a case study', in *Public Communication: The New imperatives – Future Directions of Media Research* (ed. M. Ferguson). London: Sage.

Dale, A. (1989): 'Implications of public relations in local government', *Local Government Review* **153** (28), 15 July, 548–549.

Dalton, R.J. (1988): *Citizen Politics in Western Democracies*. New Jersey: Chatham House.

Davis-Smith, J. (1988): 'Taxing the community', *Involve*, 1 September , 3.

De Bens, E., Kelly, M. and Bakke, M. (1992): 'Television content: Dallasification of culture?' in *Dynamics of Media Politics: Broadcast and Electronic Media in Western Europe* (eds. K. Siune and W. Truetzschler). London: Sage.

Deacon, D. and Golding, P. (1991): 'The voluntary sector in "the information society": a study in division and uncertainty'. *Voluntas: International Journal of Non-Profit Organisations* **2**(2), 67–88.

Deacon, D. and Golding, P. (1993): 'Barriers to centralism: local government, local media and the charge on the community'. *Local Government Studies* **19**(2), 176–189.

Deacon, D. and Golding, P. (1992): Media Coverage of the Abolition of the Community Charge, End of Project Report for ESRC Grant R000 23 3523, Department of Social Sciences, Loughborough University.

Deacon, D. and Golding, P. (1991): 'When Ideology Fails: The Flagship of Thatcherism and the British Local and National Media'. *European Journal of Communication* **6**(3), 291–314.

DoE (Department of the Environment) (1981): *Alternatives to Domestic Rates*. London: HMSO, Cmnd. 8449.

DoE (Department of the Environment) (1983): *Rates: Proposals for Rate Limitation and Reform of the Rating System.* London: HMSO, Cmnd. 9008.

DoE (Department of the Environment) (1986a): *Paying for Local Government*. London: HMSO, Cmnd. 9714.

DoE (Department of the Environment) (1986b): *Paying for Local Government: Summary of Responses to the Green Paper in England.* London: Department of the Environment.

Downing, J. (1986): 'Government secrecy and the media in the United States and Britain' in *Communicating Politics: Mass Communications and the Political Process* (eds. P. Golding, G. Murdock and P. Schlesinger). Leicester: Leicester University Press.

Dunleavy, P. (1989): 'The end of class politics?' in *Politics in Transition* (eds. A. Cochrane and J. Anderson). London: Sage.

Dunleavy, P. and Rhodes, R.A.W. (1988): 'Government Beyond Whitehall', in *Developments in British Politics (2)* (eds. H. Drucker *et al.*). London: Macmillan.

Easton, D. (1965): *A Systems Analysis of Political Life*. New York: Wiley.

Eco, U. (1979): *The Role of the Reader; Explorations in the Semiotics of Texts*. Bloomington and London: Indiana University Press.

Elliott, P. (1972): *The Making of a Television Series*. London: Constable.

Entezari, M. (1988): 'The Community Charge: its implications for the voluntary sector'. *Voluntary Voice* **22**, February, 10–11.

Ericson, R.V., Baranek, P.M. and Chan, J.B.L. (1987): *Visualising Deviance: A Study of News Organisations*. Milton Keynes: Open University Press.

Ericson, R.V., Baranek, P.M. and Chan, J.B.L. (1989): *Negotiating Control: A Study of News Sources.* Milton Keynes: Open University Press.

Esam, P. and Oppenheim, C. (1989): *A Charge on the Community: The Poll Tax Benefits and the Poor.* London: CPAG and LGIU.

Franklin, B. (1988): *Public Relations Activities in Local Government.* Croydon: Charles Knight.

Franklin, B. and Murphy, D. (1991): *What News? The Market, Politics, and the Local Press.* London: Routledge.

Galtung, J. and Ruge, M. (1969): 'The structure of foreign news', in *Media Sociology: A Reader* (ed. J. Tunstall). London: Constable.

Gandy, O. (1982): *Beyond Agenda Setting: Information Subsidies and Public Policy.* Norwood, New Jersey: Ablex Publishing.

Gans, H. (1979): *Deciding What's News.* New York: Vintage.

Gavin, N. (1992): 'Television News and the Economy: the Pre-Campaign Coverage'. *Parliamentary Affairs,* 45: 597–611.

Gibson, J. (1990): *The Politics and Economics of the Poll Tax: Mrs Thatcher's Downfall.* Cradley Heath: Emas.

Golding, P. (1970): The Concept of Gatekeeping in Mass Communication Research: A Critique and Illustrative Study, Dissertation, Essex: Department of Sociology, Essex University.

Golding, P. (1974): *The Mass Media.* London: Longman.

Golding, P. (1981): 'The missing dimensions – news media and the management of social change' in *Mass Media and Social Change* (eds. E. Katz and T. Szecsko). London: Sage.

Golding, P. (1989): The Limits to Leviathan: the Local Press and the Poll Tax, Paper for the panel on Local Politics and the Local Press, Political Studies Association Annual Conference, Warwick University, April.

Golding, P. (1990): 'Political communication and citizenship: the media and democracy in an inegalitarian social order' in *Public Communication: the New Imperatives* (ed. M. Ferguson). London: Sage.

Golding, P. (1993): Telling Stories: Sociology, the Media and the Blinkering of Democracy in the Information Age, Inaugural Lecture, Loughborough: Loughborough University.

Golding, P. (forthcoming): 'The mass media and the public sphere' in *Debating the Future of the Public Sphere* (eds. S. Edgell *et al.*). Aldershot: Avebury.

Golding, P. and Elliott, P. (1979): *Making the News.* London: Longman.

Golding, P. and Middleton, S. (1982): *Images of Welfare: Press and Public Attitudes to Poverty.* Oxford: Basil Blackwell.

Golding, P. and Murdock, G. (1991): 'Culture, Communications and Political Economy' in *Mass Media and Society* (eds. J. Curran and M. Gurevitch). London: Edward Arnold.

Goldsmiths' University Media Research Group (1987): Media Coverage of London Councils, Interim Report. London: Goldsmiths University.

Goldsmith, M. (1979): 'The changing system of English local government' in *Local Government in Britain and France* (eds. J. Lagroye and V. Wright). London: George Allen and Unwin.

Gyford, J. (1985): *The Politics of Local Socialism, Local Government Briefings (3).* London: Allen and Unwin.

Gyford, J., Leach, S. and Game, C. (1989): *A History of Local Government in the Twentieth Century.* London: Unwin Hyman.

Hall, S., Critcher, C., Jefferson, T. and Roberts, B. (1978): *Policing the Crisis.* London: Macmillan.

Hallin, D. (1986): *The Uncensored War: The Media and Vietnam.* Oxford: Oxford University Press.

Halloran, J., Elliott, P. and Murdock, G. (1970): *Demonstrations and Communication: A Case Study.* Harmondsworth: Penguin.

Hansen, A. (1991): 'The media and the social construction of the environment'. *Media, Culture and Society* **13**, 443–458.

Hansen, A. and Murdock, G. (1985): 'Constructing the crowd: populist discourse and press presentation', in *Popular Culture and Media Events, The Critical Communcation Review vol.3* (eds. V. Mosco and M. Wasko). New Jersey: Ablex.

Harrop, M. and Scammell, M. (1992): 'A tabloid war' in *The British General Election of 1992* (eds. D. Butler and D. Kavanagh). London: Macmillan.

Harris, R. (1990): *Good and Faithful Servant: The Unauthorized Biography of Bernard Ingham.* London: Faber and Faber.

Haslam, C. and Bryman, A. (1994): *Social Scientists Meet the Media*. London: Routledge.

Hefferman, R. and Marqusee, M. (1992): *Defeat from the Jaws of Victory: Inside Kinnock's Labour Party*. London: Verso.

Hennessey, P. and Walker, D. (1987): 'The lobby' in *The Media in British Politics* (eds. J. Seaton and B. Pimlott). Aldershot: Avebury.

Herman, E. (1986): 'Gatekeeper versus propaganda models: a critical American perspective' in *Communicating Politics: Mass Communication and the Political Process* (eds. P. Golding, G. Murdock and P. Schlesinger). Leicester: Leicester University Press.

Herman, E. and Chomsky, N. (1988): *Manufacturing Consent; the Political Economy of the Mass Media*. New York: Pantheon Books.

Hilgartner, S. and Bosk, C.L. (1988): 'The Rise and Fall of Social Problems: A Public Arenas Model' in *American Journal of Sociology* **94** (1), 53–78.

Hillyard, P. and Percy Smith, J. (1988): *The Coercive State*. London: Pinter.

Hoggett, P. and Burns, D. (1991/92): 'The revenge of the poor: The anti poll tax campaign in Britain'. *Critical Social Policy* **33**, Winter, 95–110.

Hurd, D. (1989): 'Freedom will flourish where citizens accept responsibilities', *Independent*, 13 September.

ILP (Independent Labour Party) (1988): *Axe The Poll Tax*. ILP Paper, 2.

Ingham, B. (1991): *Kill the Messenger*. London: Fontana.

Inglehart, R. (1977): *The Silent Revolution*. Princeton: Princeton University Press.

Jenkins, J. (1991): 'Taking Liberties'. *New Statesman & Society*, 31 May, 6.

Jenkins, J. (1992): 'Missing Millions'. *New Statesman & Society*, May, 13.

Keith-Lucas, B. and Richards, P.G. (1978): A History of Local Government in the Twentieth Century, The New Local Government Series, No. 17. London: Allen and Unwin.

Knight, G. and Curtis, B. (1987):'The publicity of state subjects' in *Political Communication Research* (ed. D. Paletz). New Jersey: Ablex.

Labour Party Young Socialists (1989): Fight the Poll Tax, London: Labour Party Young Socialists, Pamphlet No.1.

Lamb, L. (1989): *Sunrise*. London: Papermac.

Lavalette, M. and Mooney, G. (1989): 'The struggle against the poll tax in Scotland', *Critical Social Policy*, **26**, Autumn, 82–100.

Lavalette, M. and Mooney, G. (1990): 'Undermining the north-south divide? Fighting the poll tax in Scotland, England and Wales', *Critical Social Policy* **29**, Autumn, 100–119.

Lavalette, M. and Mooney, G.(1992/3): 'The poll tax struggle in Britain: a reply to Hoggettt and Burns, (CSP 33)'. *Critical Social Policy* **36**, Winter, 96–108.

Lawson, N. (1992): *View from Number Eleven: Memoirs of a Tory Radical*. London: Bantam.

Layfield Committee (1976): *Local Government Finance*. London: HMSO, Cmnd 6453.

Lee, M (1989): 'Poll tax safety nets: facts and fantasy'. *Low Pay Review* **38**: 8–9.

LGIU (Local Government Information Unit) (1989): *LGIU Guide to the Poll Tax*. London: LGIU.

Liberty (1989a): *Civil Liberty: Newsletter of NCCL* **5**(4), August. London: Liberty.

Liberty (1989b): *Privacy and the Poll Tax: Your Rights and the Law*. London: Liberty.

Liberty(1989c): *Privacy and the Poll Tax: A Guide to Good Practice for Local Government Officers*. London: Liberty/Association of London Authorities.

Liberty (1989d): *Privacy and the Poll Tax: A Guide to Good Practice for Councillors*. London: Liberty/Association of London Authorities.

Liberty (1991): Minutes of Annual General Meeting. London: Liberty.

Linton, M. (1992): 'Press-ganged at the polls', in *The Guardian Guide to the House of Commons* (ed. M. Linton). London: Fourth Estate.

Loughlin, M. (1990): 'Law ideologies and the political administrative system', in *Thatcher's Law* (eds. A. Gamble and C. Wells). Kent: Basil Blackwell.

Low Pay Unit (1987): *Low Pay Review* **29**, Spring.

McNair, B. (1994): *News and Journalism in the UK*. London: Routledge.

McQuail, D. (1969): 'Uncertainty about the audience and the organisation of mass communications', in *The Sociology of Mass Media Communicators* (ed.P. Halmos). *The Sociological Review Monograph* 13.

Mabbott, N. (1992): *Local Authority Funding for Voluntary Organisations*. London: NCVO.

MacGregor, S. (1988): The Poll Tax and the Enterprise Culture: The Implications of Recent Local Government Legislation for Democracy and the Welfare State. London: Centre for Local Economic Strategies.

MacGregor, S. (1991): 'Poverty, the poll tax and Thatcherite welfare policy part 1: how the poll tax axed Mrs Thatcher', *The Political Quarterly* **62** (4), 443–450.

Marsh, D. and Rhodes, R. (1989): *Implementing Thatcherism: A Policy Perspective*. Essex University: Essex Papers in Politics and Government, 62.

Mason, D. (1985): *Revising the Rating System*. London: Adam Smith Institute.

Miller, D. (1993): 'Official sources and 'primary definition': the case of Northern Ireland', *Media, Culture and Society* **15**(3), 384–400.

Miller, S. (1989): 'Thatcherism, citizenship, and the poll tax' in *Social Policy Review 1988–89* (eds. M. Brenton and C. Ungerson). London: Longman.

Miller, W., Clarke, H.D., Harrop, M., Leduc, L. and Whitely, P. (1990): *How Voters Change: the 1987 British General Election Campaign in Perspective*. Oxford: Oxford University Press.

MORI (1989): *Attitudes to Poll Tax in Leicester*. London: Mori.

Morrison, D. and Tumber, H. (1985): 'The foreign correspondent; date-line London'. *Media, Culture and Society* **7**, 445–470.

Murdock, G. (1984): 'Reporting the riots: images and impact' in *Scarman and After* (ed. J.Benyon). London: Pergamon Press.

NFSE (National Federation for the Self-Employed) (1990): *First Voice: Magazine for the Self Employed* **15**(2), February/March: 5.

Negrine, R. (1993): The Organisation of British Journalism and Specialist Correspondents: A Study of Newspaper Reporting, Leicester: Centre for Mass Communication Research, University of Leicester, No. MC93/1, November.

Norton, P. (1990): 'Choosing a new leader: Margaret Thatcher and the Parliamentary Conservative Party, 1989–1990', *Parliamentary Affairs* **43**(3), 249–259.

NCCL (National Council for Civil Liberties) (1987): The Privacy Implications of the Poll Tax. London: NCCL, Briefing Number 7, November.

NCVO (National Council for Voluntary Organisations) (1987): The Community Charge System: A Briefing for Voluntary Organisations. London: NCVO.

NCVO (National Council for Voluntary Organisations) (1990): Effectiveness and the Vountary Sector: Report of a Working Party Established by NCVO. London: NCVO.

Nimmo, D. and Combs, J.E. (1990): *Mediated Political Realities*, 2nd edn. New York: Longman.

Nixon, J. (1980): 'The importance of communication in the implementation of government policy at the local level'. *Policy and Politics* **8**, (2).

Oppenheim, C. (1987): *A Tax on all the People: the Poll Tax*. London: CPAG.

Peck, J. (1987): *Poll Tax: How it Will Affect You*. London: Communist Party of Great Britain.

Pimlott, B. (1988): 'The politics of the poll tax: a touch of spring in the air', *New Statesman*, 22 April: 9.

Population Trends (1991):'In Brief'. *Population Trends* **64**, 1–3.

Quirk, B. (1986): 'Paying for local government: beyond the financial issues', *Local Government Studies* **12**, September/October, 3–11.

Raban, J. (1989): *God, Man, and Mrs. Thatcher*. London: Chatto.

Richards, P.G. (1980): *The Reformed Local Government System*, 4th edn. London: Allen and Unwin.

Ridley, N. (1988): *The Local Right: Enabling Not Providing*. London: Centre for Policy Studies, Policy Study No. 92.

Royal Statistical Society (1990): *Official Statistics: Counting With Confidence*. London: Royal Statistical Society.

Saunders, P. (1981): *Social Theory and the Urban Question.* London: Hutchinson.

Saunders, P. (1982): 'Why study central-local relations?' *Local Government Studies* **8**, 55–66.

Schlesinger, P. (1990): 'Rethinking the sociology of journalism: source strategies and the limits of media centrism', in *Public Communication: The New Imperatives – Future Directions of Media Research* (ed. M. Ferguson). London: Sage.

Schlesinger, P. (1989): 'From Production to Propaganda', *Media, Culture and Society* **11**, 283–306.

Scottish Anti Poll Tax Federation (1989): *No Poll Tax Here. This Far and no Further. Don't Collect. Don't Pay.* Scotland: SAPTF pamphlet.

Semetko, H.A., Blumler, J., Gurevitch, M., Barkin, S. and Cleveland Wilhoit, G. (1991): *The Formation of Campaign Agendas: A Comparative Analysis of Party and Media Roles in Recent American and British Elections.* London: Lawrence Erlbaum.

Sewell, R. (1989): *Battle Against the Poll Tax.* London: Militant.

Seymour-Ure, C. (1977): 'Science and medicine and the press', in *Studies on the Press* (eds. O. Boyd-Barret, C. Seymour-Ure and J. Tunstall). London: HMSO.

Seymour-Ure, C. (1987): 'Leaders', in *The Media in British Politics* (eds. B. Pimlott and J. Seaton). Aldershot: Avebury.

Sigal, L. (1973): *Reporters and Officials.* Lexington, USA: DC Heath.

Sills, A., Taylor, G. and Golding, P. (1988): *The Politics of the Urban Crisis.* London: Hutchinson.

Silverstone, R. (1990): 'Television and everyday life: towards an anthropology of the television audience', in *Public Communication: The New Imperatives – Future Directions for Media Research* (ed. M. Ferguson). London: Sage.

Smellie, K.B. (1968): *A History of Local Government*, 4th edn. London: Allen and Unwin.

Smith, J. and Maclean, I. (1992): The UK Poll Tax and the Declining Electoral Roll: Unintended Consequences. Warwick Economic Research Papers. Warwick: Department of Economics, University of Warwick.

Solomos, J. (1986): 'Political language and violent protest: ideological and policy responses to the 1981 and 1985 riots', *Youth and Policy* **18**, 12–24.

Stoker, G. (1991): *The Politics of Local Government*, 2nd edn. London: Macmillan.

Straw, J (1993): The Decline of Press Reporting of Parliament, unpublished.

Thornton, P. (1989): *Decade of Decline: Civil Liberties in the Thatcher Years.* London: Liberty.

Topf, R. (1989): 'Political Change and Political Culture in Britain 1959–87', in *Contemporary Political Culture – Politics in a postmodern age* (ed. J.R.Gibbins). London: Sage

Tuchman, G. (1978): *Making News: A Study in the Construction of Reality.* New York: Free Press.

Tunstall, J. (1970): *The Westminster Lobby Correspondents: a Sociological Study of National Political Journalism.* London: Routledge & Kegan Paul.

Tunstall, J. (1971): *Journalists at Work.* London: Constable.

Van Liere, K.D. and Dunlap, R.E. (1980): 'The social bases of environmental concern: a review of hypotheses, explanations and empirical evidence', *Public Opinion Quarterly* **44**(2), 181–197.

Welsh Consumer Council (1989): *A Study into the Effectiveness of the Public information Campaign in Wales About the Community Charge.* Cardiff: Welsh Consumer Council/Cyngor Defnyddwyr Cymru.

Westley, B. and MacLean, M. (1957): 'A conceptual model for mass communication research' in *Journalism Quarterly* **34**, 31–38.

Willmore, C. (1988): 'The Community Charge: letting people know'. *Municipal Review and AMA News*, No. 690, August/September: 124–126.

Winetrobe, B. (1992): 'A tax by any other name: the poll tax and the Community Charge', *Parliamentary Affairs* **45**, 421–427.

Young, H. (1987): 'The furtive decision to go from bad to worse', *Guardian*, 23 July.

Appendix 3

Index